IBSEN IN CHINA 1908–1997

Related Titles Published by The Chinese University Press

The Other Shore: Plays by Gao Xingjian
Translated by Gilbert C. F. Fong (1999)

Soul of Chaos: Critical Perspectives on Gao Xingjian
Edited by Kwok-kan Tam (2001)

Sights of Contestation: Localism, Globalism and Cultural Production in Asia and the Pacific
Edited by Kwok-kan Tam, Wimal Dissanayake and Terry Siu-han Yip (2001)

Classical Chinese Literature: An Anthology of Translations Volume 1: From Antiquity to the Tang Dynasty
Edited by John Minford and Joseph S. M. Lau (2000)

Taipei People (Bilingual Edition)
Chinese text by Pai Hsien-yung
Translated by the Author and Patia Yasin
Edited by George Kao (2000)

Leaves of Prayer: The Life and Poetry of He Shuangqing, a Farmwife in Eighteenth-Century China
Elsie Choy (Second Edition, 2000)

The Discourse on Foxes and Ghosts: Ji Yun and Eighteenth-Century Literati Storytelling
Leo Tak-hung Chan (1998)

Memories of Peking: South Side Stories
Lin Hai-yin
Translated by Nancy C. Ing and Chi Pang-yuan (1992)

The Yellow Earth: A Film by Chen Kaige with a Complete Translation of the Filmscript
Bonnie S. McDougall (1991)

Ibsen in China 1908–1997

A Critical-Annotated Bibliography of Criticism, Translation and Performance

Kwok-kan Tam

The Chinese University Press

Ibsen in China 1908–1997: A Critical-Annotated Bibliography of Criticism, Translation and Performance
By Kwok-kan Tam

ISBN 962–201–907–2

THE CHINESE UNIVERSITY PRESS
The Chinese University of Hong Kong
SHA TIN, N.T., HONG KONG
Fax: +852 2603 6692
+852 2603 7355
E-mail: cup@cuhk.edu.hk
Web-site: www.chineseupress.com

Printed in Hong Kong

Front cover illustration: *A Doll's House* performed by Shanghai Theatre Academy, 1962. Final scene in which Nora triumphs in her confrontation with Helmer and decides to leave the house: "We must both be quite free. Here is your ring back. Give me mine." Courtesy of Liu Minghou, Shanghai Theatre Academy.

Contents

A Doll's House performed by Shanghai Theatre Academy, 1962. Scene of Nora practising Tarantella. Courtesy of Liu Minghou, Shanghai Theatre Academy.

A Doll's House performed by Shanghai Theatre Academy, 1962. Scene of confrontation between Nora and Helmer. Courtesy of Liu Minghou, Shanghai Theatre Academy.

A Doll's House performed by Hong Kong Movie and TV Theatrical Company, 1997. Scene in which Dr. Rank reveals to Nora his secret thoughts. Courtesy of Lo Wai Luk, Hong Kong Baptist University.

A Doll's House performed by Hong Kong Movie and TV Theatrical Company, 1997. Scene of confrontation between Nora and Helmer. Courtesy of Lo Wai Luk, Hong Kong Baptist University.

Preface

Ibsen has been considered by many literary historians as the most important source, besides Goethe, of Western influence in modern Chinese literary thinking. While Goethe is recognized for his impact on the romantic trend in modern Chinese literature, particularly in the 1930s, Ibsen remains influential in both the modern Chinese theatre and the Chinese women's movement throughout the twentieth century.

Most of Ibsen's major plays have been translated and staged in China, and scholars in the field of modern Chinese intellectual history fully acknowledge the contribution Ibsen made to the May 4th Movement that marked the beginning of modern Chinese culture. Apart from its value as a reference tool for the study of Western influence in modern Chinese theatre and the women's movement, this critical-annotated bibliography serves, more importantly, to chart an aspect of the path along which modern Chinese culture has developed.

Commenting on Ibsen's last play, *When We Dead Awaken*, Michael Meyer makes the point that Ibsen "was intending to break out into new and experimental fields." For me, the publication of this bibliography signifies not an "epilogue" of a phase of research, but a "prologue" to many more studies on Ibsen in new global contexts.

Reading Ibsen gives me much more than pleasure in research. Every time I read *When We Dead Awaken*, I cannot help but recall an incident about my earlier work on Ibsen. In 1985, I was urged by a university press in Norway to submit a book manuscript on the reception and influence of Ibsen in China. As the editor of the press said, he had to urge me because the *reviewer*, who was working on the same subject, was eager to see my manuscript. After I submitted the manuscript, the press told me that they decided not to publish my book because they were *informed* that I had given the same manuscript to an Asian studies institute in Scandinavia — an accusation that was absolutely groundless. Upon my inquiry, the editor apologized for having been *misinformed*. While he reassured me it was unlikely that my work would be "stolen," as there were not "that many crooks," he remarked that "publishers and authors alike" had no means to safeguard themselves from the infringement of copyrights. To my great surprise, a few months later, that same institute in Scandinavia announced in their catalogue the publication of a book on the same subject as that of my manuscript. This is how my earlier work on Ibsen was "received" in Norway. Since then, I have come to read, in a new light, what Ibsen says in *When We Dead Awaken*: "with the faces of beasts beneath their human masks."

This bibliography is the work of twenty years' research, for which I am indebted to many institutions and individuals. I must acknowledge the service that I have obtained from the National Library of China, the National Central Library in Taipei and the libraries at Peking University, The Chinese University of Hong Kong, the University of Hong Kong, Columbia University, Harvard University, Stanford University, Yale University, University of California, Berkeley, University of Chicago, University of Hawaii at Manoa, University of Michigan, and University of Illinois at Urbana-Champaign, as well as the archive at Shanghai Theatre Academy. A. Owen Aldridge and Jack Stillinger of the University of Illinois at Urbana-Champaign, William S. Tay of Hong Kong University of Science and Technology, and Chang Mei-shan, formerly of Peking University and currently in Hong Kong, are among many who have given me support and advice on the project. Liu Minghou of the Shanghai Theatre Academy and Lo Wai Luk of Hong Kong Baptist University kindly supplied photographs of their stage productions of *A Doll's House*. Timothy Weiss, my colleague at The Chinese University of Hong Kong, read the "Introduction" and gave me valuable suggestions. I should also thank Katy Ho for her assistance with Chinese word processing in the preparation of the manuscript.

This book would not have come to its present form without the help and technical advice of Olivia Wong, Project Editor at the Chinese University Press, whose professionalism makes the revision of my manuscript an enjoyable learning experience.

November 2000

Introduction

Ibsen in the Global Politics of Transcultural Reception*

Henrik Ibsen (1828–1906) has been revered as the father of modern drama because of his technical innovations that ushered in a new structure for modern dramatic experiments, but more importantly he is considered as a modern thinker, whose ideas of individualism, feminism and iconoclasm have produced far-reaching impacts all over the world. Of the various aspects of Ibsen's influence upon modern society and modern culture, Martin Esslin comments in his article, "Ibsen and Modern Drama," that Ibsen's first and most obvious impact was social and political, as Ibsen's drama is "a means to bring into the open the major social and political issues of the age" and has revolutionized the theatre, which was previously regarded as "a place of shallow amusement" (p. 71). As an influential intellectual figure, Ibsen is unsurpassed in many ways in that he is "the only playwright who, in his lifetime, became the centre of what almost amounted to a political party — the Ibsenites who in Germany, England, and elsewhere appear in the contemporary literature as a faction of weirdly dressed social and political reformers, advocates of socialism, women's rights, and a new sexual morality" (p. 71), all of which have been vividly shown in the Ibsen Club and in Shaw's *The Philanderer*.

Despite the fact that Ibsen's dramatic techniques and stage innovations have been gradually succeeded by the more avant-garde experiments since the 1950s, he is still revered as the father of modern drama in that many of the later techniques dramatists use today are developed from his open-ended dramatic structures, and that he is considered by English-speaking critics as the most important non-English-speaking playwright besides Chekhov and has become a classic in the theatre of the English-speaking world. Martin Esslin even ranks Ibsen next to Shakespeare, but above Chekhov, among

* Part of the material in this introduction has appeared in the article, "Decoding Literary History: Cultural Transformation and the Chinese Reception of Ibsen," *Tamkang Review*, 22.1–4 (Autumn 1991–Summer 1992), pp. 263–286.

the three most important playwrights in the English-speaking theatre. There is no exaggeration in Martin Esslin's saying that Ibsen is "one of the principal creators and well-springs of the whole modern movement in drama" (p. 71). Ibsen has become part of the modern culture, as can be evidenced in the fact that a special volume of *The Critical Heritage* is devoted to the study of him and that today Ibsen is never absent from the course catalogues of the English departments in major universities all over the world.

Before the critics discovered his technical innovations in drama, Ibsen, however, was treated in his own days more as a social reformer than as an artist. Since his middle plays — *The Pillars of Society*, *A Doll's House*, *Ghosts*, *An Enemy of the People* — were closely associated with the social movements of the nineteenth century, they were taken by critics in one way or another as reflections of his disputes with his enemies, and hence, for a long time, Ibsen's plays have been considered political documents. It is true that Ibsen became both popular and controversial in his life time mainly for the disputes he raised in his plays. However, as society changed and the political and social issues — such as women's rights, freedom of speech, syphilis, and water pollution — depicted in Ibsen's plays were no longer as acute as they previously were, Ibsen's social ideas and themes gradually lost their explosive appeal to the audience. Thus when Salvarsan was discovered as a remedy for syphilis, Bertolt Brecht joked in 1928 that Ibsen's play *Ghosts* would no longer have any significance, meaning that a problem play can only have an influence so long as the problem exists. Brecht's observation is correct insofar as Ibsen's social influence is concerned, but why did people begin to shift their interest in Ibsen's social themes to other aspects of his drama, despite the fact that the social themes were once so influential? Even more interesting is the question why there has been a revival of interest in Ibsen since the 1950s. The controversy over whether Ibsen's plays were political documents or works of art has become an important issue in the history of modern dramatic criticism.

The Politics of Transcultural Reception

For the literary historian, it has been a puzzle why there are such varied attitudes toward an author. Answers are different. Some critics attribute it to a change in taste, but what then is taste? Others explain the phenomenon from a sociological point of view and regard literature as a product of social change, which therefore has its flows and ebbs. Ibsen's fame has lasted longer in China and many Asian countries than in Europe. To the European critics, Ibsen belongs to the present and is mainly a dramatist, not a social critic. But in China, Ibsen is often considered a revolutionary figure and has been variously represented in Chinese politics in the past ninty years. Take *Peer Gynt* as an example. It seldom appears in today's Western theatre repertoire, but it was translated in 1981 and staged in Beijing in 1983 as a political allegory. How and why would an author enjoy a greater fame and longer lasting influence in another country than in his own? Is it purely a matter of the audience's changing response due to changes in taste effected by the progress of society? Or has it to do with the internal structure of the plays themselves? At least three things need to be considered in answering these questions: What are Ibsen's original ideas? What do his social plays tell the reader? And what are the cultural and social contexts that cause readers in different periods to respond differently to his plays? In other words, the answer has to be sought from the complex relations in the politics of the reception of Ibsen in China, as well as in the world.

The reception of an author, as Hans Robert Jauss puts it, can be treated as a matter of literary communication between the author, the text, and the audience, the relationship of which Roman Jakobson's structuralist communication model provides a useful point of reference in examining the controversies in the reception of Ibsen. For a communication event to take place effectively, all the six elements, "addresser," "addressee," "context," "message," "contact" and "code," which are interrelated, have to be present. In terms of drama as a form of literary communication, the playwright is the addresser, with the reader or audience as the addressee.[1] Contemporary theories of reception show that there is no communication between the addresser and the addressee without the mediation of the text. Furthermore, the addressee is not a passive element in the process of literary communication. The limitation of Jakobson's model in the study literary reception can be seen in its assumption that the addresser and the addressee come in direct contact. In actual fact, they may not even be of the same historical period and therefore not share the same context and code. Jakobson's model can be appropriated as follows to show the relation between literary production and consumption:

Context		Context		Context
Author (Production)	——	Message (Text)	——	(Reception/Consumption)
Code		Contact Code		Reader Code

The author has his/her own context and code in his/her production of a text, but the reader may approach the text with his/her own context and code. Here the problem of varied interpretation in literary reception is concerned mainly with the two elements, context and code, as they are external to the text and are dependent on the reader and his/her actual historical and social situation. At this point, it will be useful to bring in two concepts in interpretation theory: "meaning" and "interpretation." Defined by E. D. Hirsch in his *Validity in Interpretation* as whatever the writer may have intended, meaning is concerned with the level of communication between the author and the reader, while significance, referring to whatever a text may mean to a reader, is the central task of interpretation. Interpretation is the interaction between the reader and the text, but communication is that between the author, the text, and the reader. The text can be seen either from the author's end or from the reader's. A text may have a significance created by the reader's code, but it may not have a meaning beyond the author's intention. Both textual production and reception are active processes, in the sense that the reader is also an author, since in each reading he/she has to reconstruct the text, according to his/her own code and context, which may or may not be the same as the author's original intention, and will thus produce his/her own version of the text.

For the literary historian, what is important, perhaps, is not so much the validity of different interpretations of Ibsen, but the reason why there would be diversified, and sometimes even contradictory, interpretations of the same author. Besides the reader's code and context that constitute a large part of the external cause for such changes of attitude, the structure of Ibsen's plays is accountable for the internal cause of variety in interpretation, for it is the interaction between the reader and the text that produces such a variety. As an assembly of signs, Ibsen's plays have different "significances" in different signification systems. Yet, as signs the plays have their own thematic and linguistic structures, which are exposed to the reader or the audience in different ways and in different situations. Thus, when Ibsen's plays are treated as works of art and considered in the light of their structures, the element that comes foremost to be considered is the use of language.

Although it is hard to differentiate the literary use of language from its scientific use, or more restrictedly in Tzvetan Todorov's terms, "literary and scientific discourses," it is still useful to distinguish the different uses of language and their corresponding different functions.[2] The literary use of language allows a higher degree of indeterminacy, which in turn provides more freedom of interpretation. Even though the distinction between scientific and literary uses of language may not be as significant as some critics suggest, it is still useful to note that some texts have more elements of indeterminacy than others in their structure.[3] To complicate the issue, this high degree of indeterminacy plays an important role in effecting different translations of Ibsen across cultures of the East and the West.

Ibsen's social plays are equally successful as drama and as social criticism because the moral themes are presented in such a highly skillful way that the situations described seem as real as actual happenings to the readers. Ibsen's illusionistic techniques are an effective means that makes the readers identify the dramatic context of the plays with actual situations in their lives and, hence, arrive at the moralistic conclusion that Ibsen's social plays have real life events as sources or identify them with their own experience in daily life. Expressed more concretely, it is the external realistic elements, such as the use of familiar dialogue in everyday language, illusionistic setting, and the incorporation of socio-moral issues that make the situations in the plays seem real even though the stories are made up by the playwright without any necessary correspondence between them and the real world. Traditional approaches in literary criticism, with an emphasis on *explication de texte*, grant validity only to readings that are able to bring together the minds of the author and the reader so that the reader's code and context meet those of the author's. Since no isomorphic correspondence between the author's conception and the reader's reception can be discovered in the text, the method of explication tends to go a long way round to reach the author's mind by routing through the external reference of the text as well as through the author's biography.

It is in this way that nineteenth-century critics tended to think of Ibsen's plays as stage reproductions of actual experiences in life. In the reception of Ibsen in both the East and the West, there have been different emphases, each of which employs the use of a different interpretive strategy. When the critics take the moral issues in Ibsen's plays as reflective of his attitude, they are taking a historico-biographical approach and are more concerned with what Ibsen the person is than with what his plays are. However, when the critics are more concerned with how what is presented in the plays than with what social problems the plays actually represent, the emphasis is placed on the formal aspects of the plays. In fact, the two kinds of interpretation, Marxist-socialist on the one hand and aesthetic-formalist on the other, are the result of not only a difference in reception strategies, but also a difference in politics.

In regarding Ibsen as a dramatist or as a social critic, the difference lies in the critics' choice of strategy whether or not there is the belief of correspondence between a dramatist's works and social reality. In terms of Jakobson's model of communication functions, a dramatist's works may or may not have a referential function, which points directly to external reality, whereas in a social critic's works, there must be a referential function aiming at exposing the evils in society, otherwise there is no point of criticism. Whether or not Ibsen intended his middle plays, *The Pillars of Society*, *A Doll's House*, *Ghosts*, *An Enemy of the People*, for social criticism, they were for a long time placed in such a social context and decoded in a political way, thus making them important documents in feminism and social reform. In this way, Ibsen's middle plays were taken as representative of his political views and personal inclinations. Seldom did the critics of the nineteenth century pay serious attention to Ibsen's early and late plays, which have been categorized as Romantic and Symbolist, respectively. His influence upon the modern dramatic form was not immediately recognizable, partly due to the critics' preoccupation with the social context of Ibsen's plays and partly due to the lack of time distance necessary for an understanding of the dramatist's significance in literary history. In this period of Ibsen studies, critics tended to seek messages from Ibsen the author via an explication of his plays.

As Karl Robert Mandelkow, a theorist of reception studies, has observed, in a particular historical period only a certain aspect of the works is regarded as representative of the author's views and art. This particular aspect will become the standard for the author's reception as a whole. The fluctuating reception of Ibsen in different historical periods is in effect a result of the readers' changing emphasis on the different structural elements in his works, as well as on the different kinds of plays Ibsen wrote. The history of reception of literary works can thus be objectified into a process of interaction between the reader's expectations and the works' structural elements. A review of the reception of Ibsen in the global-historical scene will illuminate the issues involved in the processes affecting the critics' responses. The historical reception of Ibsen in various parts of the world follows a course that can be represented in the following chart.

Nineteenth-century people came to know Ibsen mainly through his involvement in debates on moral and social issues. Ibsen's middle plays were

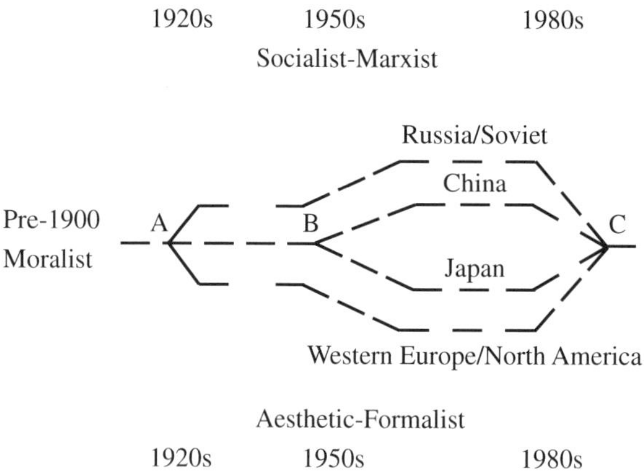

Key: A — Split between the socialist-Marxist paradigm in Russia/Soviet and the aesthetic-formalist in Western Europe/North America in the 1920s

B — Split between the Chinese and Japanese orientations along the lines of the socialist-Marxist paradigm and the aesthetic-formalist in the 1950s

C — Merging of the two orientations and beginning of the cultural-literary paradigm in the 1990s

generally labelled as "social problem plays." Such a labelling does not necessarily reflect Ibsen's "intended message." When by the end of the nineteenth century such social issues as women's rights and corruption in government became passé in Norway and many other European countries, Ibsen's middle plays lost their political significance because of the absence of the social context, in which his readers used to put them. The referential function of Ibsen's plays as previously interpreted still existed, but the readers did not feel that they were attacked. In terms of the above modified model, the readers' context of interpretation is not the same as the author's. As a result, Ibsen's battle with his countrymen came to an end, and he was finally able to return to Norway after a long period of self-exile. In Jakobson's terms, such a situation shows the referential function of Ibsen's plays still existed, but the emotive and conative functions were suppressed in the reader's reception.

Ibsen and the Political Discourse

By the latter half of the 1920s, there was a general decline of interest in Ibsen in Western Europe and North America. As in Norway some thirty years earlier, the zest for Ibsen cooled because of the change in social context, which was needed for the functioning of the moralist code in order to arouse the interest of the readers. The referential function of Ibsen's middle plays was lost in a new context. With the passing of the social movements, the public was not as interested in Ibsen the political reformer as it had been in the past. Thus change occurred not just in context but also in the politics of reception.

Despite the decline of political zeal in Ibsen in Northern Europe toward the end of the nineteenth century, Ibsen's social influence began to spread more widely in England, the United States, and the rest of Europe as a result of the rising social movements there. William Archer, the English authority on Ibsen, employed a moralist code in his reading of Ibsen, thus making him the centre of the feminist movement in England. From the late nineteenth century to the 1920s, Ibsen was generally regarded as a moralist writer whose plays were discussions of social morals and reflections of social reality. The critics, like Edmund Gosse, William Archer, James Huneker, and Bernard Shaw, all treated Ibsen as a social reformer and propagated for him such ideas as iconoclasm, feminism, and individualism. Ibsen's plays were treated as true-to-life portrayals of and protests against male chauvinism, corruption in government, false morality, and hypocritical conventions. Thus much critical effort was made on hunting the social sources of Ibsen's plays. It was the nineteenth-century mimetic mode of thinking, which assumes in the necessary correspondence between literature and social reality, that made the critics spend most of their energy finding out which social events were represented in literature. Even some of today's critics, as J. L. Styan remarks, fail to note *A Doll's House*'s "extraordinary technical achievement, because its explosive subject matter is still so obsessive that no room seems left for objective appraisal"(p. 20).

Ideological Split and the Shift of Critical Paradigm

From the 1920s onward, there began to be a split in ideology as well as in critical methodology between the Western camp (Western Europe and North America), on the one hand, and Russia/Soviet, on the other. In fact, the split was not quite that neat, dividing the reception of Ibsen into two geographical and political camps. In both the United States and West Germany, there were groups of socialists advocating a politicized interpretation of Ibsen, whereas in Russia/Soviet there were also non-Marxist Ibsen critics. The dichotomy of Western Europe/North America versus Russia/Soviet is used for the sake of convenience in discussion. It actually represents two views in the reception of Ibsen: one is to aestheticize Ibsen, and the other to politicize him. In Western Europe and North America, not only had the sociopolitical context for the interpretation of Ibsen changed, but the code had also switched from that of the moralist to aesthetic-formalist. The social movements of the late nineteenth century no longer existed in the early twentieth century as people's morals and attitudes changed. The social protests of the past century simply lost the objects of their attacks. Since Ibsen was still treated as a playwright of social protest, his plays lost their sensational appeal to the audience.

Only after a decade or so when the aesthetic-formalist code, arising as a result of the emergence of New Criticism, allowed the critic to approach Ibsen's plays in isolation from their historical and social contexts did Ibsen begin to appear to the audience in a new light. There is truth in the claim that Ibsen's dramatic art began to appeal to the drama critics only after the controversies and social movements in which Ibsen and his supporters were involved were over, but there is more truth in acknowledging the fact that it was because of the shift of critical paradigm that the critics were able to discover Ibsen's achievements in dramaturgy. Suffice it to name a few of the books published in the 1940s that reevaluated Ibsen from an aesthetic-formalist code: M. C. Bradbrook's *Ibsen the Norwegian: A Revaluation* (1946), Brian Westerdale Downs's *Ibsen: The Intellectual Background* (1946), John Richard Northam's *Ibsen's Dramatic Method* (1946) and *A Study of Six Plays by Ibsen* (1950), and P. F. D. Tennant's *Ibsen's Dramatic Technique* (1948), all of which read Ibsen in the light of New Criticism. It is also the distance of time that allowed the critics to have a more complete and balanced view of Ibsen. The failure of Ibsen's contemporaries to employ an aesthetic-formalist code and distinguish fiction from fact, as P. F. D. Tennant pointed out in 1948, was due to Ibsen's "skills" in making his plays "centre around the burning moral or social problems of the day" (p. 15). So far as their social function is concerned, the social and moral themes are indeed the source of power in Ibsen's social plays, while therein also lies their weakness, which the perspective of time reveals to be socio-historically limited. When considered as a dramatist and artist, but not as a moralist, Ibsen's social ideas do not stand the test of time as well as the characters who enunciate them and the dramatic effect of his technique, which is as fresh as ever. It is not Ibsen's social ideas, but his dramatic form that constitutes "his greatest contribution to the theatre" (pp. 15–16). Put in another way, it was the change of critical mode, that is, the code, that enabled the critics to discover the artistic qualities of Ibsen's plays.

The shift of attention from "the burning moral or social problems" to "skill" is the greatest achievement and breakthrough of modern literary criticism. In the theory of Russian Formalism, this is the change in modern critical mode from the study of a literary work to the study of its literariness. Historically, this is, as Hans Robert Jauss says, the shift of paradigm in literary criticism from the historicist to the aesthetic. This change of emphasis is due also to the discovery of Ibsen's historical importance in the development of modern drama. This is a discovery made possible only by the distance of time. The shift of critical focus in Ibsen studies is a reflection of the general trend to place emphasis on an author's works rather than on the author himself as a historical figure.

In the Soviet Union, as well as in some Eastern European countries after the Second World War, not only did the context for a sociopolitical interpretation of Ibsen change, but the code also shifted from that of the moralist to the Marxist, represented by the views of such socialist-Marxist critics as Georg Plekhanov, Konstantin Derzhavin, and Klara Zetkin, who all tended to read Ibsen with a political code, placing him in the historical context of class struggle in nineteenth-century Europe. The new social reality in the socialist countries, with the Soviet as a typical example, presented a new context for the reception of Ibsen. The Nora and Stockmann themes were reinterpreted as themes of class struggle, and dramatic conflicts were taken as a reflection of social contradictions. The issue is not whether this interpretation is far-fetched, but that the new context and code gave Ibsen's plays new social significance. In fact, the use of a socialist-Marxist code to interpret Ibsen's plays can be traced back to the early 1910s when Emma Goldman, an American anarchist-feminist critic, tried to decode Ibsen's middle plays as social protest in her essay, "The Modern Drama: A Powerful Dissemination of Radical Thought." The social movements in Western Europe and North America before the First World War presented a social condition that gave rise to the popularity of the socialist-anarchist code in interpreting literary writings. In other words, it is the co-functioning of both the new code and new context that allowed Ibsen to be continually well received in different societies and in different periods.

Ibsen in China: Literature as Social Discourse

The social conditions in the Far East since the 1900s provided a context for the referential function in Ibsen's middle plays to emerge and effect in both China and Japan a great impact upon the feminist movements. It was around the end of the nineteenth century that Ibsen was first introduced to Japan, mainly via England and Germany; hence, the initial Japanese reception of Ibsen was influenced by William Archer's moralist views. If translation can be used as an index to determine the reception of an author in a foreign country, then the formal introduction of Ibsen to China occured around the beginning of the twentieth century. While the first Japanese translation of *An Enemy of the People* appeared in 1893, the first Chinese translation of *A Doll's House* did not appear until 1918. China started late but was more fortunate in being able to compare the different views of other countries in the reception of Ibsen. Since Ibsen's works were introduced to China much later than they were in Japan and in the countries in Western Europe and North America, it was natural that the reception process was affected by all the various approaches to Ibsen available over the world, particularly first by the Japanese views of Ibsen and later by those of Western Europe and North America. China's nation-wide reception of Ibsen occurred around the end of the 1910s and was necessarily affected by the coexistence of the moralist and socialist-Marxist codes in European interpretations of Ibsen.

Martin Esslin's observation that "Ibsen's first and most obvious impact was social and political" can as well refer to the situation in China. From the beginning, the modern Chinese theatre was a social and political theatre. Although there were no distinctively formed Ibsenite groups in China, there were dramatists, such as Hong Shen and Tian Han, who openly professed themselves "Chinese Ibsens." Ibsen's influence in China is manifested in two aspects: sociopolitical and artistic (both literary and theatrical). In different periods, there have been different emphases on these two aspects, which in turn reflect more of the readers' critical orientation than Ibsen's own message. The two major trends, namely, "the social-realistic" and the "personal-romantic," that had contributed greatly to the development of modern Chinese literature in the 1920s and 1930s can in one sense be attributed respectively to the influence of Ibsen and Goethe. However, different from Goethe who was mainly received as a romantic writer, Ibsen was regarded by the Chinese critics and dramatists both as a social-realist and as a romantic playwright. The difference in the reception of Ibsen in China had actually become a nation-wide debate in the 1920s and 1930s, which reflected not only the multiplicity and complexity in Ibsen's drama, but also the historical junctures at which modern Chinese literature developed in different directions. The history of the reception of Ibsen in China can be divided roughly into four major periods: 1908–1927, 1928–1948, 1949–1976, and 1977–present. These four phases correspond to the historical divisions in the world reception of Ibsen charted above. In the first period, Chinese interpretations of Ibsen were closely associated with social movements and were greatly influenced by the moralist code then prevalent in Europe, particularly in the views of William Archer, Bernard Shaw, Emma Goldman, and Janko Lavrin. Ibsen's social influence was first seen in the advocacy of individualism and iconoclasm in the writings of Lu Xun and Hu Shi. The social movements in China gave the interpretation of Ibsen's plays a new political context by which the critics conveyed their messages to Chinese readers. Ibsen was hailed as a champion of individualism, uncompromising moralist, and advocate of feminism. The iconoclastic elements derived from Ibsen's plays were most valued in this period as a means of resistance against the traditional moral system deeply rooted in China's Confucian collectivism. In fact, one of the major reasons for introducing Ibsen to China was that the messages derived from his plays constituted a powerful attack on the conventional moral institutions in China.

In an age of political turmoil and ethical chaos, people needed moral messages more than art. With a highly stylized form of acting and historically remote themes, traditional Chinese drama, typified by the Peking opera, were too detached from contemporary life to arouse the interest of the newly awakened intelligentsia. It was thus for such political and social reasons that Ibsen was hailed as a figure of hope and new values. Political needs were the major cause for introducing Ibsen. When Lu Xun introduced *An Enemy of the People* to China in 1908, Ibsen's iconoclasm was given a much higher value than any other of his social ideas. Lu Xun thought that iconoclasm was the only prescription that could cure the spiritual illness of China. Next came Hu Shi's account of Ibsenism, in which social criticism was treated as Ibsen's realistic attitude toward life and toward works of art. Hence, *When We Dead Awaken* was taken by Hu Shi as a play most representative of Ibsen's attitude and was considered as a powerful remedy for China's social diseases. Both Lu Xun and Hu Shi put Ibsen's plays in the context of Chinese society and interpreted them accordingly, for at that time China was in much the same social condition as Norway was in the latter half of the nineteenth century.

In the process of introducing Ibsen to China, Chinese dramatists were more attracted to his explosive themes than to his dramatic subtlety. Almost all the social problem plays in the early 1920s were modelled after Ibsen's middle plays, without considering the appropriateness of such an approach to the theatre. The influence became so powerful that even well established Chinese dramatists could not resist the temptation to imitate Ibsen, which at that time was considered by some critics as an act of contempt equivalent to plagiarism. The problem play became a new fashion and orthodoxy, and the social effects of a play were considered by many critics of primary importance to its achievements. A dramatist, by expectation, was at the same time a social educator.

The second period in the reception of Ibsen was accompanied by the gradual maturity of modern Chinese drama and literary criticism. From 1928 to 1948, Ibsen attracted the attention of more and more serious Chinese dramatists and critics, such as Xiong Foxi and Chen Zhice, both of whom were trained in Western Europe and North America and therefore put more emphasis on Ibsen's dramatic innovations than on his social themes. As in Western Europe and North America where critics began to lose enthusiasm in politics, Chinese dramatists gradually shifted their interest to the artistry in Ibsen's drama in the late 1920s when the zeal for social reform in China was in low tide. Unlike a political event, a literary work has "no unavoidable consequences subsisting on their own that no succeeding generation can ever escape" (Jauss, p. 22). A literary work may have influence in later periods only if there are readers who come after it and once again respond to it. In the case of China, it was the change in context that led to a low tide in the reception of Ibsen. Ibsen's plays lost their appeal to Chinese readers simply because in a new context they did not produce the effects they had in the past.

Reflecting the influence of the West and at the same time the split in critical paradigm between Western Europe and the Soviet, there was in China also a controversy over whether Ibsen was a social reformer or an artist, and whether his popularity was due to his political themes or to his art. Some critics took the middle way and affirmed that it was a mixture of both. Although in the late 1920s and early 1930s some Chinese critics called for a reconsideration of Ibsen from the perspective of art, still the general tendency was to moralize him, which, however, was supported by the practical view that Ibsen's drama was useful for social reform in China. The debate over the nature of Ibsen's drama not only signified a Chinese reconsideration of the general nature of drama, but also provided an opportunity for modern Chinese drama to develop in a more balanced way. Unfortunately, before the debate yielded any fruitful results, the war between China and Japan broke out and destroyed the hope of developing Chinese drama along a normal artistic path. Political considerations and the nationalist responsibility of saving China from disgrace and sufferings again became the first concern of serious, patriotic writers. The moral-political tradition, which had a long history in Chinese literature, was revived to the dismay of the writers and critics who favoured aesthetic considerations in literary works more than their social effects.

Ibsen in Wartime China: Literature and the Nationalist Discourse

As a matter of fact, the call for a "Drama of National Defence" in the latter half of the 1930s during the Sino-Japanese War had its origin in the concept that the theatre must serve a social purpose, a notion that was deeply rooted in both the traditional and modern Chinese theatre and was in turn derived from the social themes of Ibsen's middle plays. Facing the question of life and death, most Chinese dramatists chose national struggle as subject-matter, directly or indirectly, to encourage the resistance against Japan. Tian Han's *Abixiniya muqin* (Abyssinian mother), Yu Ling's *Jinghao* (Warning signal), Zhao Shuli's *Dadao hanjian* (Knock down traitors), Ma Yanxiang's *Shenghuo zhi dao* (The way to live), Bai Wei's *Chong chu Yiulingta* (Fight out of ghost pagoda), Zhang Min's *Guxiang* (Hometown), Song Zhidi's *Luohen* (The branded scar), Yang Hansheng's *Qianye* (The night before last), and Xia Yan's *Sai Jinhua*, *Ziyou hun* (The soul of freedom), and *Shanghai wuyan xia* (Under the eaves of Shanghai) are good examples of this kind of drama. There were other dramatists who devoted themselves to reflecting social conditions of the time and achieved much success in the art of drama. In this respect, Cao Yu deserves admiration. His well-known trilogy, *Leiyu* (Thunderstorm), *Richu* (Sunrise), and *Yuanye* (Wilderness), become milestones in the history of modern Chinese theatre. The social problem plays, such as Hong Shen's trilogy, *Wugui qiao* (Wugui Bridge), *Daomi xiang* (Fragrant rice), and *Heilong Tan* (The Black Dragon Lake), and Ouyang Yuqian's *Tongzhu de sanjia ren* (Three families in the same house), are also modelled after Ibsen in theme as well as in technique.

The Chinese interest in Ibsen revived during the war years because of the need for a new dramatic form that could arouse the reader's emotional response. In a new context of oppression and invasion, the theme of *A Doll's*

House already interpreted as "exploitation of women" was redefined as "exploitation of Chinese women under foreign invasion," as can be exemplified in such Chinese adaptation of the play as *Nüxing de jiefang* (Female emancipation, 1940). Almost all the Chinese stage productions of *A Doll's House* in the years from 1937 to 1945 were adaptations to serve as a nationalist discourse for the patriotic cause.

Ibsenism and Socialism

The year 1949 marked a drastic change in the cultural life of the Chinese when the Communist revolution succeeded on the mainland. The third period in the reception of Ibsen in China started in 1949 and ended around 1976. In these years, Chinese interpretations followed closely the footsteps of the Soviet bloc. Friedrich Engels's analysis of Ibsen's plays in terms of "class struggle" and the redefinition of the "Ibsenian concept of majority," which were considered necessarily reactionary with reference to "the bourgeois class in the nineteenth-century semi-feudal Norwegian society." These were the two doctrines every Marxist had to follow in studying Ibsen.

Although social and political events similar to those depicted in Ibsen's social plays did not exist in China in these thirty years, Ibsen was still revered in terms of his historic importance as a critic of the bourgeois social system and thus was taken as politically useful to the new socialist system. To put it another way, Ibsen was still interpreted in a nineteenth-century context to serve an indirect political function in contemporary China. Take Xiao Qian's two contradictory interpretations of *Peer Gynt* as an example. In 1949 the play was interpreted by Xiao Qian as an indictment of bourgeois individualism, but in 1979 it was given a new meaning, attacking the "ultra-leftists" in China for the lack of individuality and for being no less opportunistic than Peer Gynt. In 1949 Xiao Qian thought that individualism was a bad thing, but in 1979 he considered it a good thing. He thought individualism was what the Chinese lacked during the Cultural Revolution when so many people followed the "Gang of Four" without any sense of individual judgement.

In the thirty years after 1949, Ibsen was interpreted in a way to serve another purpose besides being treated as a supporter of socialism. The well-made dramatic conflicts in Ibsen's plays were taken as reflections of class struggle in capitalist society. Hence, for the Chinese Marxists every reading of Ibsen's social plays was a lesson on the evils of capitalism. For Chinese dramatists, Ibsen's plays, redefined in the light of socialist realism, were excellent examples to learn how to reproduce class struggles as dramatic conflicts on the stage. Li Jianwu, a noted contemporary Chinese dramatist, was the major advocator of such a reading of Ibsen.

During these thirty years, the Soviet socialist realistic code was adopted in China for the reinterpretation of Ibsen. It was this change of code that accorded Ibsen such an important place in contemporary Chinese politics. Jauss's observation of the social function of literary works in historical periods other than their own may serve as a footnote to the contemporary Chinese reception of Ibsen: "The new literary work is received and judged against the background of other works of art as well as against the background of everyday experience of life" (pp. 41–42). Hence, there was the attempt to indigenize Ibsen to serve local politics in China.

Social Change and the Interpretive Context

Anachronistic and insinuative interpretation failed to survive the test of time. The new social and political reality in China after 1976 allows Ibsen readers to see that there are alternatives to the vulgarized political doctrines in the interpretation of literature. There was in effect little literary criticism in the first thirty years of the People's Republic. Government intervention in the interpretation of an author allowed little freedom beyond politics. Yet a political commentator can never replace a literary critic, whose duty is to point out the aesthetic qualities of a work of art. The discovery of the pitfalls of using literary works to insinuate political events in China has led to the recognition of literature as an entity with relative autonomy. The new political and social environment in China since 1977 has given rise to the influx of the once-condemned "Western bourgeois literary criticism" into socialist China. Chinese critics thus have an opportunity to come into contact with contemporary Western orientation in literary studies, resulting in the gradual adoption of the aesthetic-formalist code.

The four periods in the Chinese reception of Ibsen fall into a pattern of fluctuation between the Western political camps, signifying two diametrically opposed ideologies as well as modes of literary criticism: the multidimensional system of thought in Western Europe and North America versus the single-dimensional one in the Soviet bloc. The history of Ibsen interpretation in China shows that the reception of an author in a culture other than his own involves a complex interplay of the author's own ideology, the recipient country's culture, and the influence of other countries' interpretations of the author. Transcultural studies have demonstrated that in reading a text from a culture other than its own, a reader is prone to bring different systems of background knowledge into the interpretation process.

China and Japan: Two Approaches

It is interesting and, perhaps, illuminating to note the difference in the Chinese and Japanese reception of Ibsen. Besides reflecting the split between the Euro-American and Russian/Soviet interpretations of Ibsen, this difference has its social and historical sources, too, in the different internal developments of China and Japan. Two important historical events have helped shape the history of modern China: the 1911 Republican Revolution which brought China into large-scale contact with the West, and the 1949 Socialist Revolution, which withdrew China from its contact with the West. Both events had far-reaching social effects upon the reception of Ibsen. The large-scale introduction of Ibsen occurred only in 1918, seven years after the 1911 Revolution, which led to a temporary hope for democracy in China, and one year after the October Revolution in Russia.

For its instrumental value in ideological reform, Ibsenism was held up as a banner of new morality in China. However, before Ibsenism could take a foothold in China, it had to fight a battle on two fronts: both with the conservative Chinese tradition and ironically with the radical Chinese advocates of Ibsenism. The failure of the 1911 Revolution to democratize China gave rise to the experiment with Socialism. The Marxist-historicist interpretation of Ibsen, accompanied by the Chinese pursuit of a utopian ideology to revitalize the country, was in general welcomed by intellectuals. The debate over the nature of Ibsenism and Ibsen's drama in the late 1920s and early 1930s, though being a temporary conscious effort of reflection over the intellectual crisis, evidenced the fact that the American and Western European influence in China was receding in the face of growing Russian impact. The rise of the Marxist-Maoist ideology as the only orthodox system of thought and interpretive code in China after 1949 immediately followed the Russian politicization of Ibsen. Since literature does not exist in a void, both its production and consumption are in some degree determined by social and political conditions. No example can better show this relationship than the government control in China of the publishing industry up to the late 1970s, which not only helped shape the interest of the reading public but also restricted the circulation of Ibsen's plays and thus his influence.

In Japan, the first translation of an Ibsen play took place in 1893, twenty-five years after the Meiji Reform, which gradually democratized Japan and guaranteed more and more Western European and North American influence. The twenty-five years after the Meiji Reform prepared Japan to receive and respond to Ibsen, and other Western authors, more readily than China did. Hence, Ibsen would not appear so much as a shock to the Japanese as to the Chinese. When the Japanese Bluestocking Society was founded in 1911, there were already established in Japan a number of women's colleges (Sato, pp. 73–74).

Although at the beginning of this century Japan was far behind in the emancipation of women and in social reform in comparison to the social reality in Western Europe and North America, it soon caught up with the development in the West. The development toward a capitalist economy in Japan prior to the outbreak of the 1917 Russian Revolution was an important factor that safeguarded Japan from Russian influence, though leftist ideas also had strong influence in Japan. The rise of Japan as an Oriental power not only antagonized her relation with China but even more sharply first with czarist Russia and then the Soviet Union. Hence, at the beginning Japan was resisting Russian influence in both politics and cultural life. When Ibsen was introduced to Japan, the path came from Europe through England, Germany, and France, but not through Russia.

In the case of China, Ibsen came from the major countries that had power and influence in China. Thus in the 1920s and 1930s when there was a split in the reception of Ibsen in the West, China and Japan took different paths leading them farther and farther apart. Today the Japanese reception of Ibsen generally corresponds to that of the West. The transition from using a moralist code to using an aesthetic-formalist one in the interpretation of Ibsen's message took place not only in the West but also in Japan. Yet, with China moving closer and closer to the West since the 1980s, Chinese critics are more inclined to the adoption of an aesthetic-formalist code in literary criticism. It is a sign of change from the critics' preoccupation with politics to that with literature as art. Like in the West, Ibsen is becoming a subject more of artistic than political concern in today's China.

The (Dis-)Continuity of History

The four periods of changes in the Chinese reception of Ibsen can be viewed both as a continuous and discontinuous process. The first three periods are of course interrelated as they may be put under the general interpretive category of the "historicist-positivist," whereas the last period, influenced by the West, is under the "aesthetic-formalist" and is manifested as a reaction to the former category. Some historians, such as Michel Foucault, believe that the displacement of epistemes in history is often due to external causes and they look at history as a discontinuous process. Hans Robert Jauss distinguishes three paradigms in the history of literary studies: the classical-humanist, historicist-positivist, and aesthetic-formalist. To him, each of the paradigms is a reaction to the previous one. Unlike Foucault, he sees history as a continuous process of actions and reactions.

For the Marxists, however, literature does not claim a history of its own. It is a continuous process not in itself as a superstructure but in relation to the infrastructure. As Georg Lukács thinks, literary history is a surface structure built on a large, but more basic, structure of history, society, and politics, which form an intricate, complex continuity. Thus viewed, modern Chinese drama seems to be a break from traditional Chinese drama, for it is a form imported from the West. The cause of the rise of modern Chinese drama lies, however, in its social function, which traditional Chinese drama cannot serve. The social needs of China have given rise to the popularity of this foreign form, which was later indigenized. As Ulrich Weisstein claims, the emergence of a new genre is often due to inspiration of "foreign models in protest against prevailing artistic theories and practices" (p. 34). The history of modern Chinese drama is discontinuous when viewed in isolation, but continuous when viewed in relation to social history and as a reaction against traditional drama. So is the history of the reception of Ibsen in China.

After all, Ibsen belongs to the past as well as to the present century, for his influence in literature, theatre, and society can still be felt today. No matter how contradictorily Ibsen has been represented in China over the past ninty years, he has made a threefold contribution to Chinese society and culture: the growing Chinese awareness of the importance of individuality as well as the spirit of iconoclasm, the need for women's emancipation, and the development of a modern theatre in China. Ibsen has now become a classic not only in the English-speaking theatre, but also in today's Chinese theatre.

Notes

1. The context refers to the social and historical background wherein the communication event takes place. The message is what the author Ibsen wants to tell in his plays. In this study, the plays are mainly Ibsen's middle plays, or social

problem plays. The contact is the physical channel through which the addresser communicates with the addressee. Hence, it may be the play as a text for reading or as a performance on the stage. The difference in the physical contact between reading and watching a performance will definitely affect the addressee's experience of the play. The element of contact in the Chinese reception of Ibsen is rather stable since the most widely read and staged texts are those translated by Pan Jiaxun.

The code is the socio-cultural and literary framework by which the addressee interprets the play. Codes are, as Roger Fowler defines them, "systems of literary knowledge possessed by the reader, inscribed in the literary community to which he belongs, and realized in the experience of the language of the texts" (97). Communication exists not only in the message but in the entire system; any change in the six elements will cause corresponding changes in the effects of communication. Basing on the structuralist model of communication, Jakobson projects six functions of language:

Referential
Poetic
Emotive ———————— Conative
Phatic
Metalingual

Jakobson points out that a verbal communication may entail more than one of these functions, but there must be a predominant one. Thus in poetry the poetic function of language dominates the other functions of the text. In scientific texts, for example, the referential function dominates. This is what I. A. Richard calls the practical use of language and what Tzvetan Todorov calls scientific discourse.

The emotive function is that which expresses the character state of the speaker; the conative function refers to language directed at the addressee, such as imperative sentences. Phatic function is the special use of language to check or prolong the working of the communication channels, such as the question: "Do you hear me?" The metalingual function of language refers to the purpose of the communication event which aims at checking whether or not the addresser and the addressee share the same code. All these different functions of language, which are beyond the considerations of grammar, have been in recent years studied by more and more philosophers, linguists, and political scientists under the name of discourse analysis.

2. In science it is improper to say that something is hot or cold; it has to be expressed in exact temperature. Thirty-five degrees Celsius is hot, but so is forty. Hence, in science the word "hot" is less exact than temperature in degrees. For a poet, however, it is non-figurative to express the idea of "hot" in degrees or in

plain words. A poet has to choose between words like "burning" and "fire," or other ways to express the idea in figurative language. For these two simple different functions of language use, the decoding methods are different. To decode the "heat" of forty degrees Celsius, the scientist just has to compare it to human body temperature in the same temperature scale. The decoding process is objectifiable and can be understood in universal terms. On the other hand, there is no way to know exactly how hot "burning" is, for the idea of "burning" as an expression of heat is culture-specific. To an Alaskan and a Mexican, "burning" may have totally different meanings.

3. It should be noted that there are always determinable elements in a text, otherwise it would be impossible for readers to respond in similar ways or to share common elements in their interpretations of the same text.

Works Cited

Esslin, Martin. "Ibsen and Modern Drama." In *Ibsen and the Theatre*. Edited by Errol Durbach, pp. 71–82. New York: New York University Press, 1980.

Fowler, Roger. *Literature as Social Discourse: The Practice of Linguistic Criticism*. Bloomington: Indiana University Press, 1981.

Jauss, Hans Robert. *Toward an Aesthetic of Reception*. Translated by Timothy Bahti. Minneapolis: University of Minnesota Press, 1982.

Sato, Toshihiko. "Ibsen and Emancipation of Women in Japan." *Orient/West*, 9.5 (September–October 1964), pp. 73–74.

Styan, J. L. *Modern Drama in Theory and Practice*, vol. 1. Cambridge: Cambridge University Press, 1983.

Tennant, P. F. D. *Ibsen's Dramatic Technique*. Cambridge: Bowes & Bowes, 1948.

Weisstein, Ulrich. *Comparative Literature and Literary Theory: Survey and Introduction*. Translated by William Riggan. Bloomington: Indiana University Press, 1973.

1

Ibsen and the Literary Revolution 1908–1919

1.01

Cao Juren 曹聚仁. "Jinian Ouyang Yuqian" 紀念歐陽予倩 (In memory of Ouyang Yuqian). In *Renshi xinyu* 人事新語 (New words on people and events), pp. 339–369. Hong Kong: Yiqun chubanshe 益群出版社, 1963.

In this essay, Cao Juren reviews the career of the famous Chinese dramatist Ouyang Yuqian in relation to his contribution to the Chinese theatre and the development of modern Chinese drama. Ouyang Yuqian was one of the earliest Chinese dramatists who had adapted Ibsen's *A Doll's House* in their plays. Although the essay is not a study of Ibsen, much of the theatre history it deals with bears a relation to the influence of Ibsen on modern Chinese drama.

1.02

Chen Juntao 陳駿濤. "Zhongguo zaoqi huaju de lishi pingjia" 中國早期話劇的歷史評價 (A historical evaluation of early modern Chinese drama). *Wenyi luncong* 文藝論叢 (Studies on literature and art), 11 (1980), pp. 339–429.

In the historical context of modern Chinese drama that was first developed in the early 1900s and 1910s, Chen Juntao comments on the early modern Chinese dramatists and theatre directors, such as Chen Dabei and Wang Zhongxian, and reevaluates their achievements in relation to their indebtedness to Western drama and theatre. In the context of historical development, Ibsen's dramaturgy as well as the whole European movement of the social-realistic theatre can be regarded as a major source of inspiration that led to the development of modern Chinese drama and theatre in a new form, "the spoken drama."

1.03

Chen Shouzhu 陳瘦竹. "Wu Si Yundong he xiju geming" 五四運動和戲劇革命 (The May 4th Movement and theatre revolution). *Wenshizhe* 文史哲 (Literature, history and philosophy), 2 (1979), pp. 47–50.

This article studies the May 4th Movement that occurred in China in 1919 as a movement of cultural reevaluation that attempted to introduce to China the new ideas that could be found in the West. In this review study, the political and social functions of the modern Chinese theatre in introducing new Western modes of thought to China are given due consideration. And in so doing, the study provides the background for understanding how Ibsen's plays were received in China in the 1910s and 1920s.

1.04

Chien, Ying-ying (Jian Yingying 簡瑛瑛). "Feminism and China's 'Nora': Ibsen, Hu Shi & Lu Xun." *The Comparatist: Journal of the Southern Comparative Literature Association*, 19 (May 1995), pp. 97–113.

This is a study of how Ibsen was received in China in the 1910s and 1920s, especially by Hu Shi and Lu Xun. Much of the information given in this essay can also be found in the research done by Elizabeth Eide and Kwok-kan Tam.

The essay is a further development of the feminist argument presented in the Chinese article: Jian Yingying 簡瑛瑛. "Panni nüxing de juejiao: Cong *Kuilei jiating* dao 'Shafei nüshi de riji'" 叛逆女性的絕叫：從《傀儡家庭》到〈莎菲女士的日記〉 (The cry of despair from rebellious women: From *A Doll's House* to "Miss Sophie's Diary"). *Zhongwai wenxue* 中外文學 (Chung-wai literary monthly), 18.10 (1990), pp. 51–74.

1.05

Danton, G. H. "Henrik Ibsen." *Tsing Hua Journal*, 4.5 (April 1919), pp. 107–133.

Originally presented as a speech delivered to students at Tsing Hua (Qinghua) University, the article differs from other similar writings in that it focuses on the artistic aspects of Ibsen's drama. Danton shows that Ibsen learned a great deal from French drama. Eugène Scribe was to a large extent the master from whom Ibsen learned the trick of playwriting. In contrast to all previous Chinese writings on Ibsen, Danton's article avoids going into the moral messages of Ibsen's plays and, hence, is able to treat him as a dramatist. Danton reads in *A Doll's House* much more than the fight for women's rights. Danton's argument is not meant to be a counter-statement against the over emphasis on Ibsen's social messages, but it allows the Chinese an opportunity to see something about Ibsen beyond the dogmatic views set forth in Hu Shi's essay, "Yibusheng zhuyi" (Ibsenism), published in 1918.

1.06

Ding Luonan 丁羅男. "Lun woguo zaoqi huaju de xingcheng" 論我國早

期話劇的形成 (On the formation of early modern Chinese drama). *Xiju yishu* 戲劇藝術 (Theatre arts), 3 (1981), pp. 114–125.

This is an essay based on the research Ding Luonan did as a student at the Shanghai Theatre Academy. The essay is a historical study on how Western drama was transmitted to China through Japan, and how the form of spoken drama was assimilated and became a powerful means of social reform. It provides a useful review of the background of how the various theatre groups and companies were formed in the 1910s.

1.07

———. *Zhongguo huaju xuexi waiguo xiju de lishi jingyan* 中國話劇學習外國戲劇的歷史經驗 (Historical lessons: The indebtedness of modern Chinese drama to foreign drama). Shanghai: Zhongguo xiju chubanshe 中國戲劇出版社, 1983.

The little book is a publication of Ding Luonan's M.A. thesis, which studies how modern Chinese drama was influenced by Western drama, particularly by Ibsen. The book analyses the major stages of Western influence in the history of modern Chinese drama. It provides a socio-historical perspective on literary and theatre influence, thus the Chinese reception of Ibsen and other Western playwrights is put in a context of social change in China.

1.08

Eide, Elisabeth. *China's Ibsen: From Ibsen to Ibsenism*. Scandinavian Institute of Asian Studies Monograph No. 55. London: Curzon Press, 1987.

This is a Ph.D. thesis that studies the influence of Ibsen in China up to 1937. Most of the materials given in this thesis can be found in Kwok-kan Tam's Ph.D. thesis, "Ibsen in China: Reception and Influence" (University of Illinois at Urbana-Champaign, 1984).

1.09

———. "Et kinesisk syn pa Ibsen. Hu Shi og Ibsens betydning for liberale strominger in Kina." *Edda*, 6 (1979), pp. 349–363.

This is a study of Ibsen's influence upon Hu Shi during the May 4th

Movement in China. It summarizes Hu Shi's ideas of Ibsenism as expressed in the essay, "Yibusheng zhuyi," published in *Xingqingnian* (New youth) in 1918.

1.10

———. "Hu Shi and Ibsen. Ibsen's influence in China 1917–1921 as seen through the eyes of a prominent Chinese intellectual." M.A. thesis, University of Oslo, 1973.

This is a Master's degree thesis that studies the influence of Ibsen upon Hu Shi during the May 4th Movement. It shows that Ibsen was considered by Hu Shi mainly as a social reformer.

1.11

———. "Ibsen in Kina. En bibliografi." In *Norge-Kina: Kompendium fra seminar varen og hosten 1972*, pp. 130–139. Oslo: East Asian Institute, University of Oslo, 1973.

This short bibliography lists some of the major Chinese works that deal with Ibsen's influence in China during the May 4th Movement, such as Hu Shi's essay on Ibsenism.

1.12

Fujian shifan daxue zhongwenxi 福建師範大學中文系, ed. *Lu Xun lun waiguo wenxue* 魯迅論外國文學 (Lu Xun on foreign literature). Beijing: Waiguo wenxue chubanshe 外國文學出版社, 1982.

A section of the book deals with Lu Xun's idea of the rebellious romantic spirit that he found in Ibsen and other Western writers, whom he called the Satanic poets, or *Mara* poets. It gives an overview of how Lu Xun was influenced by Ibsen's uncompromising idea of "All or Nothing."

1.13

Ge Yihong 葛一虹. "Guanyu waiguo xiju zai Zhongguo qingkuang de san feng xin" 關於外國戲劇在中國情況的三封信 (Three letters on foreign drama in China). *Xiju yanjiu* 戲劇研究 (Studies on drama), 12 (1982), pp. 65–67.

This is an open letter in reply to Elisabeth Eide's request for information about the reception of Ibsen in China. In this letter, the Chinese playwright and theatre historian Ge Yihong recounts the story of how Ibsen was introduced to China in the early 1910s and 1920s, and how Ibsen became so popular in China in 1934–35. Both years 1934 and 1935 have been referred to by theatre historians as "Year of Nora" in the history of modern Chinese theatre.

1.14

Ge Yunsheng 葛雲生 and Lu Jia 盧嘉. "Ouyang Yuqian zai Guangdong" 歐陽予倩在廣東 (Ouyang Yuqian in Guangdong). *Xiju yishu ziliao* 戲劇藝術資料 (Sources on dramatic arts), 6 (March 1982), pp. 56–86.

This is a study of the Chinese dramatist Ouyang Yuqian's theatre activities in Guangdong. The essay gives background information on the early modern Chinese theatre so that the influence of Ibsen can be seen in a broader perspective. In Ouyang Yuqian's early writings there are a number of plays in which there is strong evidence of the influence of Ibsen.

1.15

Goldman, Emma. "Jindai xiju lun" 近代戲劇論 (The modern drama: A powerful dissemination of radical thought). Translated by Zhen Ying 震瀛. *Xinqingnian* 新青年 (New youth), 6.2 (Feburary 1919), pp. 179–195.

In February 1919, three months before the May 4th student demonstration in China, there appeared in *Xinqingnian* (New youth) Zhen Ying's (pen-name of Yuan Zhenying 袁振英) Chinese translation of the American anarchist Emma Goldman's essay, in which modern drama is taken as a manifestation of social justice, "the strongest and most far reaching interpreter of our deep felt dissatisfaction." This essay was originally published as a chapter of the book *Anarchism and Other Essays* (2nd rev. ed. New York: Mother Earth Publishing Association, 1911). In illustrating the powerful effects of drama on revolutionary activities in Russia, France, and Germany, Emma Goldman takes numerous examples from the drama of Ibsen. In this essay by Emma Goldman, the history of modern Western drama is given a historical analysis in the Marxist-anarchist perspective as a means of social opposition. In this way, Ibsen is put in the context as an oppositional discourse. The Chinese translation of this essay gave the Chinese readers in the 1910s a socio-cultural view of the relation between modern Western drama and society.

1.16

Gong Shuduo 龔書鐸. "Xinhai geming yu xiju" 辛亥革命與戲劇 (The 1911 Revolution and the theatre). *Xiju yanjiu* 戲劇研究 (Studies on drama), 11 (1981), pp. 75–85.

This essay is a study of the relation between the theatre and the 1911 Revolution in China. In this essay the theatre reform in China is considered both as a result of the revolutionary needs in China and as a cause that contributed to the 1911 Revolution, which ended the rule of the Qing dynasty. The essay is useful for background information not only on theatre reform, but also on the introduction of Ibsen to China, as well as on other social issues, such as freedom for women and ideas of liberalism.

1.17

Hsiao Ch'ien (Xiao Qian 蕭乾). "Ibsen in China." In *The Dragon Beards Versus the Blueprints*, pp. 16–20. London: Pilot, 1944.

Prior to his critique of Ibsen's individualism in 1949, Xiao Qian published a book, *The Dragon Beards Versus the Blueprints*, in London in 1944 during his stay there as a correspondent for the *Dagongbao* 大公報. This book has a chapter on how Ibsen was received by the Chinese in the 1910s and 1920s. Contrary to his later attitude, in the book he hails Ibsen as a "daring doctor capable of prescribing the most desperate remedies" for China, which "was so hopelessly ill" in those days. The mixed feelings Xiao Qian, as well as other Chinese intellectuals, had towards Ibsen were a result of the complex transformation in the intellectual history of modern China. Ibsen then appeared to them as "the most violent iconoclast."

1.18

Hu Shi 胡適. *Hu Shi liuxue riji* 胡適留學日記 (Hu Shi's diary during his study abroad), 4 vols. Taipei: Shangwu yinshuguan 商務印書館, 1959.

In this book there is information on how Hu Shi was influenced by Ibsen after he had seen the performance of Ibsen's plays in the United States. There is detailed description of his response to *A Doll's House* and *Ghosts*, as well as his comments on the plays, which gives useful historical information on the background that led to his interest and incessant effort in promoting Ibsen in China in the 1910s and 1920s.

Hu Shi was educated in the United States. He received his doctorate in philosophy from Columbia University and was a follower of John Dewey's philosophy of pragmatism. Soon after his return to China, in June 1917, he was appointed professor of philosophy at Peking (Beijing) University, then an important centre for the dissemination of Western culture in China. In 1918, Hu Shi published his influential essay, "Yibusheng zhuyi" (Ibsenism), in *Xingqingnian* (New youth).

1.19

———. "Yibusheng zhuyi" 易卜生主義 (Ibsenism). *Xinqingnian* 新青年 (New youth), 4.6 (June 1918), pp. 489–507.

With the launching of the Literary Revolution in 1917 and the call for replacing traditional Chinese drama with modern Western drama in the mid-1910s, the social background necessary for the introduction of Ibsen in China was prepared in the late 1910s. The credit for this campaign went first to *Xinqingnian* (New youth), the leading intellectual journal at that time in China. In June 1918, with a special issue on Ibsen, the journal for the first time seriously and systematically presented Ibsen to the Chinese reader. In this essay, Hu considers Ibsen more as a social revolutionist than as a dramatist. To him, the basic idea of Ibsenism is a realistic attitude towards life. In this way, the plays are seen as an expression of Ibsen's indictment of social conventions and traditional morals. Putting aside Ibsen's artistic achievements as a dramatist, Hu Shi explores mainly his social philosophy. Moreover, Hu Shi believes that Ibsen's greatest contribution to modern thinking lies mainly in his ideas of individualism.

To Hu Shi, the most fascinating aspect of Ibsenism is the uncompromising courage and determination represented in Dr. Stockmann, the protagonist in *The Pillars of Society*. Hu Shi was eager to introduce this concept to the Chinese, for he thought that the majority rule was not a political principle suitable for adoption in China. In introducing Ibsen, Hu Shi's purpose was to provide a cure for the social ills in China, though it was, according to him, a prescription of no prescription, or in Bernard Shaw's words, "a formula of no formula" (*The Quintessence of Ibsenism*, p. 172. London: Constable and Company Ltd., 1913).

Hu Shi did not mention the sources from which he formulated the principles of Ibsenism, but obviously he was inspired by Bernard Shaw's book *The Quintessence of Ibsenism*. The historical significance of Hu Shi's essay lies more in its criticism of Chinese society than in its explication of Ibsen's ideas. Thus Ibsen became the mouthpiece of "Hu-Shi-ism" and for a long time since the publication of this essay, Hu Shi's interpretation not only went unquestioned, it actually became a definitive statement on Ibsen. In the initial period of Chinese reception of Ibsen, this essay was the most important in terms of its influence upon later critics. It was partly because of this essay that many later critics tended to treat Ibsen more as a social reformer than as a dramatist.

1.20

Huang, Tsokan. "Ibsen in Chinese Eyes: The Ibsen Issue in *Hsin Ch'ing-nien* (1918)." *Symposium*, 34 (1980), pp. 199–216.

This essay reviews how Ibsen was received by the Chinese in 1918, a year before the May 4th Movement broke out in China. It gives information on the significance of the Ibsen issue in *Xinqingnian* (*Hsin Ch'ing-nien*, New youth), a leading journal in Chinese intellectual debates in the 1910s.

1.21

Huneker, James Gibbons. "Yibusheng" 易卜生 (Ibsen). Translated by Pei Qingbiao 裴慶彪. *Tsing Hua Journal*, 5.1 (December 1919), pp. 19–26.

James Huneker's study of Ibsen was given in Pei Qingbiao's Chinese translation of the first two sections of the chapter "Henrik Ibsen" in his book *Iconoclasts: A Book of Dramatists* (New York: Charles Scribner's Sons, 1917, pp. 1–138). It provides an overall view on Ibsen's plays in terms of general themes and their social implication. Huneker cites Ferdinand Brunetiére, a nineteenth century French drama theorist, who says that "there can be no tragedy without a struggle; nor can there be genuine emotion for the spectator unless something other and greater than life is at stake." He suggests that what Brunetiére says may be used to describe specifically the dramatic and ethical content of Ibsen's plays: "Whatever else Ibsen's works may be, they are first soul dramas; the human soul is not only their shadowy protagonist, but it is the stake for which the characters breathlessly game throughout the vast halls of his poetic and historic plays and within those modern middle class apartments, where the atmosphere seems rarefied by the intensity of the struggle." What Huneker tries to point out is the nature of Ibsen's plays, which can be summed up as conflicts between the individual and society, between free will and environment, and between heredity and personal temperament. Huneker presents Ibsen more as a philosopher than as a dramatist.

1.22

Le Shui 樂水 (Hong Shen 洪深). "Jiaoqi" 嬌妻 (A lovely wife). *Xiaoshuo yuebao* 小說月報 (*Short Story Magazine*), 6.6 (June 1915), pp. 1–6.

Inspired by Lu Jingruo, one of the earliest Chinese critics and dramatists who introduced Ibsen to China, many Chinese intellectuals in the 1910s began to direct their attention to the social effects of Ibsen's drama. *Xiaoshuo yuebao* (*Short Story Magazine*) published in 1915 a synopsis of *A Doll's House* in the title of *Jiaoqi* (A lovely wife), which indicates the author's interpretation of the play. The author, Le Shui (pen-name of Hong Shen), praises Ibsen as a talented writer, who incorporates in his works "novel ideas saying what other people dare not express." The two-page long synopsis is written in dense classical Chinese. The story of the play would have been retold in a faithful way had Le Shui not presented the departure scene in a way much more dramatic than the original: "'My (Nora's) heart is not made of stone, and I am not going to change my mind. From now on, I no longer care about the world.' Then she leaves. No one knows where she goes." Instead of presenting Nora as an enlightened woman, Le Shui makes her an escapist who is entirely disillusioned.

As for the theme of the play, Le Shui thinks that at least two levels of implication can be discerned. First, women have their own way of mind, which is different from that of men. People should understand the difficulties they have and help them, but not demand them to have the viewpoint of men and blame them for not possessing a broader vision. Second, the relationship between husband and wife is difficult to maintain. Both husband and wife should tolerate each other, compromise for their common interest, and must not act contrary to it. Husbands, however, seldom take into consideration this common interest, and whenever they are frustrated, they act according to their natural leanings. Women are often shortsighted and shallow in knowledge.

1.23

Li Jianwu 李健吾, et al., eds. *Zhongguo xiandai wenxue dashiji* 中國現代文學大事記 (A chronology of major events in modern Chinese literature). Jilin: Jilin daxue shehui kexue xuebao bianjibu 吉林大學社會科學學報編輯部, 1981.

This is a useful reference tool that gives the dates of the important events in modern Chinese literature that have taken place since the early 1910s. The information on the publication of literary works and the activities of the literary organizations provides the context to see how Ibsen has been received. It also provides information on the publishing industry in China so that the reception of foreign authors, including Ibsen, can be seen in a sociological perspective.

1.24

Liu Xianbin 劉獻彬 . "*Xinqingnian* yu waiguo wenxue fanyi" 《新青年》與外國文學翻譯 (*New Youth* and the translation of foreign literature). *Fanyi tongxun* 翻譯通訊 (Bulletin of translation), 7 (1983), pp. 39–41.

The essay deals with the general historical period around the May 4th in the context of how Chinese translation of foreign literary works provided an impetus for the movement of cultural reform. The journal *Xinqingnian* (New youth) is recognized for its great contribution to the spread of Western thoughts in China.

1.25

Lu Jingruo 陸鏡若. "Yipusheng zhi ju" 伊蒲生之劇 (Ibsen's drama). *Paiyou zazhi* 俳優雜誌 (Actor's magazine) (1914). (Source: Ah Ying 阿英. "Yibusheng de zuopin zai Zhongguo" 易卜生的作品在中國 (Ibsen's works in China). *Wenyibao* 文藝報 (Literary gazette), 17 (1956). Reprint. In *Ah Ying wenji* 阿英文集 (Collected works of Ah Ying), vol. 1, art. 739. Beijing: Sanlian shudian 三聯書店, 1981.)

The first Chinese evaluation of Ibsen as a dramatist appeared in the actor Lu Jingruo's "Ibsen's drama," which was published in the inaugural issue of *Paiyou zazhi* (Actor's magazine) in celebration of the Shanghai Spring Willow Society's presentation of *A Doll's House* in 1914. Ibsen is considered by Lu as a "great writer," "a rival of Shakespeare," and "a significant fighter in drama reform." "The vitality expressed in his works is so forceful that it has become immortal," he wrote. Lu also gives a summary review of Ibsen's major middle and later plays, such as *A Doll's House*, *Ghosts*, *An Enemy of the People*, *The Wild Duck*, *Rosmersholm*, *The Lady from the Sea*, *Hedda Gabler*, *The Pillars of Society*, *Little Eyolf*, *John Gabriel Borkman*, and *When We Dead Awaken*. Unlike Lu Xun, Lu Jingruo presents Ibsen mainly as a dramatist.

1.26

Lu Xun 魯迅. "Moluoshi li shuo" 摩羅詩力說 (A discourse on the power of *Mara* poetry). *Henan* 河南, 2 & 3 (1908). Reprint. In *Lu Xun quanji* 魯迅全集 (Complete works of Lu Xun), vol. 1, pp. 63–115. Beijing: Renmin wenxue chubanshe 人民文學出版社, 1981.

The earliest reference to Ibsen in Chinese writing dates back to 1908 in Lu Xun's essay, "Moluoshi li shuo" (A discourse on the power of *Mara* poetry) that appeared in *Henan*, a radical journal published by Chinese students in Japan. The essay was written in 1907, the same year in which the Spring Willow Society experimented with the performance of Western-style drama and one year after the death of Ibsen, and was intended primarily to introduce the poetry of Byron and other Romantic poets. *Mara* is a Sanskrit term, referring to the god of destruction in Indian mythology, and was used by Lu Xun to refer categorically to the Byronic poets, who "have a rebellious spirit and are revolutionary in action, but are not welcome in the world" (*Lu Xun quanji,* art. 67). This is the first Chinese article that discusses in a comprehensive manner the literary pursuits of the Byronic poets. Lu Xun ranks Ibsen as one of these poets and compares the rebellious spirit exemplified in Ibsen's drama to Byron's Satanic tendency. Lu Xun has a particular liking for the play *An Enemy of the People*, in which Ibsen presents his ideas through the iconoclast, Dr. Stockmann, who in upholding truth against the prejudices of society is attacked by the people. Dr. Stockmann's being isolated by society, to Lu Xun, is an example of the follies of society. He values greatly Dr. Stockmann's motto: "The strongest man in the world is he who stands most alone." Lu Xun believes that Dr. Stockmann's persistence in upholding his own principle is the courage that the Chinese needed at the beginning of the twentieth century. Lu Xun's purpose was not just to introduce Byron or Ibsen, but also to call the Chinese attention to the need of an iconoclastic spirit and a determination to face injustice, even when alone. This is the spirit later expressed by Lu Xun's in his motto: "Hengmei lengdui qianfu zhi" (To face the accusations of a thousand men with indifference and cold eyebrows). According to Lu Xun, China became weak in the nineteenth century just because the Chinese had been too strong in the past and the people were complacent about their present life. He thinks that China needed more rebels like Ibsen to wake her people up from their dream.

1.27

———. "Wenhua pianzhi lun" 文化偏至論 (On cultural extremes). *Henan* 河南, 7 (August 1908). Reprint. In *Lu Xun quanji* 魯迅全集 (Complete works of Lu Xun), vol. 1, pp. 43–62. Beijing: Renmin wenxue chubanshe 人民文學出版社, 1981.

In 1908, Lu Xun again quoted Ibsen in another essay, "Wenhua pianzhi lun" (On cultural extremes). Dissatisfied with the traditional Chinese attitude that regarded Western culture as barbaric, Lu Xun shows the achievements of Western civilization by summarizing its development since the nineteenth century. He says that one of the greatest achievements of Western culture is the recognition of individuality. Lu Xun thinks that individualism and non-materialism were most needed in China. From admiring the iconoclastic courage of Dr. Stockmann to the recognition of Ibsen's ideas of individualism, Lu Xun takes a step further in his own understanding of Ibsen. In traditional China, the family system was emphasized at the expense of the individual. Thus individualism was never developed. To save China from the imminent cultural collapse, Lu Xun proposes Nietzsche's ideas of the superman and Ibsen's advocacy of individual and social integrity as a remedy. As is known, Ibsen was considered in the nineteenth century as an interpreter of Kierkegaard. In this essay, Lu Xun once again expresses his high opinion of *An Enemy of the People*. Lu Xun's knowledge of the play is probably based on the Japanese translations, which appeared in 1893 and 1901 (see Toshihiko Sato, "Henrik Ibsen in Japan," Ph.D. thesis, University of Washington (Seattle), 1966. pp. 57 and 174). To Lu Xun, Ibsen is more important as a social critic than as a dramatist.

1.28

Mao Dun 茅盾. "Waiguo xiju zai Zhongguo" 外國戲劇在中國 (Foreign drama in China). *Waiguo xiju* 外國戲劇 (Foreign theatre), 1 (1980).

Reprint. In *Zhongguo xiju nianjian* 中國戲劇年鑑 (Yearbook of Chinese theatre), 1981, p. 217. Beijing: Zhongguo xiju chubanshe 中國戲劇出版社, 1981.

This is a survey essay on the reception and performance of foreign drama in China since the May 4th Movement in 1919, which gives very useful information on the context of the reception of Ibsen. The publication of this essay had a political implication for the reinstatement of the open-door policy in China in the 1980s.

1.29

———. "Zhongguo jiuxi gailiang wojian" 中國舊戲改良我見 (My view on the reform of old Chinese drama). *Mao Dun wenyi zalunji* 茅盾文藝雜論集 (A collection of Mao Dun's literary essays and other writings), vol. 1, pp. 62–64. Shanghai: Shanghai wenyi chubanshe 上海文藝出版社, 1981.

This is an essay Mao Dun published in the 1920s, in which old Chinese drama is seen as inadequate in dealing with current topics of cultural life in China. Mao Dun's view is that there should be a new form in the vein of modern Western drama which could address current social issues. The essay thus provides information on the historical background of how Ibsen was introduced to China in the early twentieth century.

1.30

Ouyang Jingru 歐陽敬如 and Dong Xijiu 董錫玖, comp. "Ouyang Yuqian nianbiao" 歐陽予倩年表 (A chronology of Ouyang Yuqian). *Xiju yishu ziliao* 戲劇藝術資料 (Materials on dramatic arts), 4 (May 1981), pp. 19–23.

A director and playwright, Ouyang Yuqian played a very important role as a founder of modern Chinese drama. In his early plays, there is an obvious influence from Ibsen. The chronology gives useful information on Ouyang Yuqian's career in relation to the development of the modern Chinese theatre. The information on the Guangdong xiju yanjiusuo (Guangdong drama institute), which Ouyang Yuqian started in the 1920s, is of special importance, as it was one of the earliest institutional establishments that had contributed to the reform of Chinese theatre.

1.31

Pu Shao 蒲梢. "Hanyi dongxiyang wenxue zuopin bianmu — Yijiu'erjiu nian sanyue zhi" 漢譯東西洋文學作品編目 — 一九二九年三月止 (A bibliography of Chinese translations of Western and Japanese literary works — Up to March 1929). *Zhongguo xiandai chuban shiliao jiabian* 中國現代出版史料甲編 (Materials on the history of modern Chinese publishing, first series). Edited by Zhang Jinglu 張靜廬, pp. 271–323. Beijing: Zhonghua shuju 中華書局, 1954.

This is a useful bibliographical guide that gives information on how Chinese translations of Western literary works were received in China in the 1910s and 1920s. Textual information on editions and publications can be found in the book. For a study of the Chinese reception of Ibsen, the book provides the necessary sociological data about the Chinese publishing industry with regard to publications and circulation.

1.32

Ren Fangqiu 任訪秋. "Wan Qing wenxue gexin yu Wu Si wenxue geming" 晚清文學革新與五四文學革命 (Literary innovations in late Qing and the literary revolution during "May 4th"). *Wenxue yichan* 文學遺產 (Literary heritage), 1 (1983), pp. 113–122.

By tracing the source of the May 4th literary revolution to the reforms and innovations in literature in the late Qing dynasty, the essay provides a historical perspective by making a link between the Chinese tradition and the quest for modernity. Liberation of the individual from the traditional bondage of Confucianism is seen in relation not only to the influence of the West, but also to indigenous cultural change in China. It thus provides an alternative view on the context of Ibsen's influence in China.

1.33

Ruan Ruoshan 阮若珊. "Guanyu Zhongguo huaju faduan wenti de taolun" 關於中國話劇發端問題的討論 (Discussion on the genesis of modern Chinese drama). *Xiju yanjiu* 戲劇研究 (Studies on drama), 1 (1982), pp. 13–25.

In this article, the author reviews the historical beginnings of modern Chinese drama and discusses the various sources, that is, the indigenous source of change and foreign influence. In this review, the author asserts that there are both internal and external sources that caused the reform of traditional Chinese drama and called for a new drama. Ibsen and other Western dramatists that exerted a great influence in China in the early twentieth century are discussed in the context of change and continuity in the history of modern Chinese drama.

1.34

Song Chunfang 宋春舫 (Soong Chun-fang). "Jinshi mingxi baizhongmu" 近世名戲百種目 (One hundred famous modern plays). *Xinqingnian* 新青年 (New youth), 5.4 (October 1918), pp. 361–365.

Educated in France, Song Chunfang was an important figure in the introduction of Western culture to China in the 1910s and 1920s and he became a professor of French at Peking University in the May 4th era. He was noted for the advocacy of the idea to abolish traditional Chinese drama in favour of modern Western drama. In this essay, Song lists one hundred modern Western plays to be recommended to the Chinese readers. On this list is Ibsen's play *A Doll's House*.

1.35

Tam, Kwok-kan (Tan Guogen 譚國根). "Decoding Literary History: Cultural Transformation and the Chinese Reception of Ibsen." *Tamkang Review*, 22.1–4 (Autumn 1991–Summer 1992), pp. 263–286.

This is a study of how the reception of Ibsen has been related to the political movements in modern China. It shows that reception is a process of interaction between the recipient culture and the source of influence. The various interpretive paradigms in literary studies in the West have also shown their effects in the history of Chinese reception of Ibsen.

1.36

———. "Ibsen and Modern Chinese Dramatists: Influences and Parallels." *Modern Chinese Literature*, 2.1 (Spring 1986), pp. 45–62.

In this study, the focus is placed on Ibsen's influence upon modern Chinese drama. Modern Chinese playwrights ranging from Ouyang Yuqian, Guo Moruo, Tian Han and Cao Yu are discussed in the light of their indebtedness to Ibsen and of their contribution to the development of modern Chinese drama.

1.37

———. "Ibsen in China: Reception and Influence." Ph.D. thesis, University of Illinois at Urbana-Champaign, 1984.

This study traces Ibsen's influence in China from the early 1900s to the 1980s. The thesis is divided into two parts: reception and influence. In Part I, the Chinese reception of Ibsen, translation of his plays and performances were given detailed information and analysis. In Part II, the study focuses on the influence of Ibsen upon both modern Chinese fiction and drama. The formation of a modern Chinese theory of drama is also considered in relation to the influence of Ibsen.

The thesis includes the following chapters:

Part One: Reception

(1) Western Impact in the Rise of Modern Chinese Theatre: A Historical Overview;
(2) The Introduction of Ibsen to China;
(3) Ibsen the Social Reformer Versus Ibsen the Dramatist;
(4) Contemporary Chinese Reception of Ibsen;
(5) Ibsen in Chinese Translation;
(6) Ibsen on the Chinese Stage;

Part Two: Influence

(7) Ibsen in the New Literature Movement;
(8) The Nora Theme in Modern Chinese Fiction;
(9) Ibsen and Modern Chinese Dramatists: Influences and Parallels;
(10) Ibsen and Modern Chinese Dramaturgy.

1.38

———. "Iconoclasm as Ibsenism: Ibsen in the May Fourth Era." In *Interliterary and Intraliterary Aspects of the May Fourth 1919 Movement in China*. Edited by Marián Gálik, pp. 119–128. Bratislava: Publishing House of the Slovak Academy of Sciences, 1990.

As a thinker and social reformer, Ibsen has exerted a great influence in China which is not limited to that upon the theatre. In this study, it is shown that Ibsen played a significant role as an iconoclast in the May 4th

Movement in China. Evidences on the Chinese response to Ibsen are drawn from critical articles published in major magazines and journals in the period, such as *Xinqingnian* (New youth) and *Xinchao* (New trends).

1.39

———. "Self-identity and the Problematic of Chinese Modernity." *The Humanities Bulletin*, 4 (December 1995), pp. 57–64.

In this article, the cultural change from tradition to modernity in China is considered with a focus on the emergence of a new subjectivity and self-identity. The article shows the difficulties Chinese modern writers and thinkers encountered at the beginning of the century on the construction of self-identity, and on the problems Western ideas of individualism had brought forth to the Chinese through Hu Shi's introduction of Ibsenism.

1.40

Tian Han 田漢. "Jieshou 'Wu Si' de jingshen he jingyan — Chuangzao shehui zhuyi xinxiju" 接受"五四"的精神和經驗 — 創造社會主義新戲劇 (Take up the "May 4th" spirit and experience — Create a socialist new drama). *Xiju yanjiu* 戲劇研究 (Studies on drama), 2 (1959), pp. 3–13.

In Tian Han's essay, the "May 4th" spirit is considered mainly as a revolutionary concept in abandoning the tradition and in adopting the new. In the 1950s when Chinese dramatists were searching for a new mode of expression for socialist drama, Tian Han's essay was in line with the socialist problem play advocated by Li Jianwu, as well as with the interpretation of Ibsen as a revolutionary iconoclast.

1.41

Tian Han 田漢, Zong Baihua 宗白華 and Guo Moruo 郭沫若, eds. *Sanyeji* 三葉集 (Kleeblatt). Shanghai: Yadong tushuguan 亞東圖書館, 1920.

During their sojourn as students in Japan, Tian Han, Zong Baihua and Guo Moruo corresponded frequently on their ideas about Western culture, philosophy, aesthetics, and their aspirations for the future of China. These correspondences are collected in the book *Kleeblatt*, in which there is much discussion that has to do with their later contribution to modern Chinese drama. Since Tian Han and Guo Moruo are two of the founders of modern Chinese drama and have been greatly influenced by Ibsen both in style and themes, their correspondences collected in the book are useful for information on the development of modern Chinese drama.

1.42

Tian Han 田漢, et al., eds. *Zhongguo huaju yundong wushinian shiliaoji, 1907–1957* 中國話劇運動五十年史料集, 1907–1957 (Historical sources of the modern Chinese drama movement in the past fifty years, 1907–1957), 3 vols. 1958. Reprint. Beijing: Zhongguo xiju chubanshe 中國戲劇出版社, 1985.

Collected in this book are essays written by Chinese dramatists and historians on the development of modern Chinese spoken drama. There are essays on drama companies, performances, and individual dramatists. As the title of the book suggests, it is concerned mainly with the development of modern Chinese drama as a sociopolitical movement, and as a continuity of the May 4th Movement in China. In the essays there is also information on how the development of Chinese drama as an art form has been indebted to the influence of Western drama.

1.43

United College Library, The Chinese University of Hong Kong 香港中文大學聯合書院圖書館. *Zhongguo xiandai xiju cangshu mulu* 中國現代戲劇藏書目錄 (A bibliography of the modern Chinese drama collection). Hong Kong: United College Library, The Chinese University of Hong Kong 香港中文大學聯合書院圖書館, 1967, and supplement 補編, 1970.

This bibliographic catalogue lists all the holdings of modern Chinese drama, including both plays and theoretical texts, that are available in the United College Library of The Chinese University of Hong Kong. This collection has the widest coverage so far among overseas library collections of modern Chinese drama. Many of Ibsen's plays that have been translated into Chinese are also available in the collection. From this catalogue, one may obtain a view on how the reception of Ibsen in China is compared with that of other Western dramatists.

1.44

Wang Delu 王德祿. "Ping Wu Si shiqi Zhou Zuoren de wenxue zhuzhang" 評五四時期周作人的文學主張 (A critique of Zhou Zuoren's literary advocations during the May 4th era). *Shanxi daxue xuebao* 山西大學學報 (Shanxi university journal), 1 (1983), pp. 24–30.

In reviewing Zhou Zuoren's literary advocacy during the May 4th era, the article focuses mainly on Zhou Zuoren's essay, "Ren de wenxue" 人的文學 (A literature for man), which was considered by the May 4th critics as a manifesto of the new culture movement. This essay by Zhou Zuoren can in many ways be looked at as a Chinese response to Ibsen's idea of individualism.

1.45

Wang Weimin 王衛民. "Xinhai geming qianhou de xiju yundong" 辛亥革命前後的戲劇運動 (Drama movement around the 1911 Revolution). *Xiju luncong* 戲劇論叢 (Theatre studies), 4 (1981). Reprint. In *Zhongguo xiju nianjian* 中國戲劇年鑑 (Yearbook of Chinese theatre), 1982, pp. 325–330. Beijing: Zhongguo xiju chubanshe 中國戲劇出版社, 1982.

The article recounts the experiments of stage reform during the 1911 Revolution, in which the Republic replaced the Qing regime. It points out that the stage reform was both a consequence of sociopolitical changes and a cause to later and newer changes in modern China. The collapse of the Confucian order that called for a collective moral was a cause that contributed to the rise of individualistic views. The stage reform was thus meant to be experiments with contemporary themes for the stage. Historically, these experiments paved the way for the massive introduction of Western drama, particularly Ibsen, to China.

1.46

Wang Yao 王瑤. *Lu Xun yu Zhongguo wenxue* 魯迅與中國文學 (Lu Xun and Chinese literature). Xi'an: Shaanxi renmin chubanshe 陝西人民出版社, 1982.

Putting Lu Xun in historical perspective, Wang Yao, the Chinese literary historian, surveys the various foreign and native sources in Lu Xun's literary writings and shows how Lu Xun contributed to the development of modern Chinese literature. The various essays collected in the book serves to affirm the positive value of foreign influence, including that of Ibsen and his ideas of individualism, for the development of Chinese literature.

1.47

———. "'Wu Si' wenxue geming jingshen de qishi" "五四"文學革命精神的啟示 (The implication of the revolutionary spirit of "May 4th" literature), *Hongqi* 紅旗 (Red flag), 5 (1979), pp. 64–72.

This essay appeared in 1979 in *Hongqi* (Red flag), an official publication of the Chinese Communist Party, to celebrate the May 4th literary movement. In this essay, iconoclasm is taken to be the May 4th spirit. Thus, Wang Yao's essay not only deals with the revolutionary spirit of the May 4th movement and attributes it to the influence of foreign literature, it in some degree also reflects the Chinese government's new attitude toward Ibsen and Western literature in general.

1.48

———. *Zhongguo xinwenxue shigao* 中國新文學史稿 (A draft history of modern Chinese literature). 1953. Reprint. Hong Kong: Bowen shuju 波文書局, 1972.

Much useful bibliographic and socio-historical information, including the Chinese reception of foreign literature, is given in this comprehensive survey of the genesis of modern Chinese literature. The book thus serves an important role in surveying the social context of modern Chinese literature. In the book, there is information on the early Chinese reception of Ibsen.

1.49

Wang Zhefu 王哲甫. *Zhongguo xinwenxue yundongshi* 中國新文學運動史 (A history of Chinese new literature movement). Hong Kong: Yuandong shuju 遠東書局, 1965.

Similar to many literary histories published in the 1960s, Wang Zhefu's book also focuses on the development of modern Chinese literature as a social movement. It emphasizes the social context of literary works, but it also points out the quintessence of modern Chinese literature in its service of a social function. Again, the book provides information on the social context of the reception of Ibsen and the development of modern Chinese drama.

1.50

Wang Zhongxiang 王忠祥. "Yibusheng ji qi xiju zai 'Wu Si' qianhou" 易卜生及其戲劇在"五四" 前後 (Ibsen and his drama around the May 4th Movement). *Waiguo wenxue yanjiu* 外國文學研究 (Studies in foreign literature), 2 (1979), pp. 8–12.

This is a review of the Chinese reception of Ibsen in the 1910s. According to Wang Zhongxiang, Ibsenism as introduced by Hu Shi provided one of the guiding principles for the May 4th Movement. Ibsen's *A Doll's House* was widely performed in China and had exerted a great influence on the modern Chinese theatre. The review asserts that Ibsen's influence was not limited to cultural change in China and it also had a great impact upon the art of Chinese drama.

1.51

———. "Yibusheng xiju chuangzuo yu Zhongguo xiandai wenxue" 易卜生戲劇創作與中國現代文學 (Ibsen's plays and modern Chinese literature). In *Yibusheng yanjiu lunwenji* 易卜生研究論文集 (Ibsen research papers). Edited by Meng Shengde 孟勝德 and Astrid Saether, pp. 27–36, 248–257. Beijing: Zhongguo wenxue chubanshe 中國文學出版社, 1995.

In this essay, Wang Zhongxiang gives a condensed review of the reception of Ibsen in China since the early 1900s. The views of Lu Xun, Hu Shi, Guo Moruo and Mao Dun are summarized. The problem with this essay, as well as the others in this collection, is that there is no acknowledgement of sources.

1.52

Wei Zhaofeng 魏照風. "'Wu Si' shiqi Guo Moruo de xiju chuangzuo" "五四" 時期郭沫若的戲劇創作 (Guo Moruo's dramatic writings in the "May 4th" era). *Wenyi luncong* 文藝論叢 (Studies on literature and art), 2 (1981), pp. 143–156.

Putting Guo Moruo's plays in historical perspective, the author of this essay relates playwriting in the May 4th Movement to the revolutionary activities during the period. Thus the themes of individualism, female liberation and self expression in Guo's plays that are all under the influence of Ibsen are seen as ideas related to the cultural change in China toward modernity.

1.53

Wen Dayong 文大勇. "Yibusheng de shehui wentiju dui Zhongguo zaoqi huaju chuangzuo de yingxiang" 易卜生的社會問題劇對中國早期話劇創作的影響 (The impact of Ibsen's social problem plays on early modern Chinese drama). *Zhongguo xiandai wenxue yanjiu congkan* 中國現代文學研究叢刊 (Studies in modern Chinese literature), 2 (1983), pp. 215–228.

This essay focuses on the influence of Ibsen upon the emergence of the dramatic genre, the problem play, in modern China. It surveys the major dramatists that have been influenced by Ibsen's *A Doll's House* in its style as a problem play. While it points out the weakness of early Chinese drama in its mechanical and mistaken interpretation of the genre solely as social criticism in the disguise of drama, it also seeks to clarify the concept of the problem play to contemporary Chinese readers.

1.54

Wen Huo 溫䕫. "'Wu Si' xinwenxue yu wan Qing wenxue" "五四" 新文學與晚清文學 ("May 4th" new literature and late Qing literature). In *Zhongguo jindai wenxue lunwenji 1949–1979* 中國近代文學論文集 1949–1979 (Collected essays on modern Chinese literature 1949–1979), Gailun juan 概論卷 (General introduction). Edited by Zhongguo shehui kexueyuan wenxue yanjiusuo jindai wenxue yanjiuzu 中國社會科學院文學研究所近代文學研究組, pp. 61–70. Beijing: Zhongguo sheke chubanshe 中國社科出版社, 1981.

While many critics and literary historians believe that modern Chinese literature, particularly drama, is a break from the tradition, there is also the view that modern Chinese literature is a development of tradition, for the origins of the modern development can be traced back to the literature of Qing dynasty. This essay by Wen Huo follows the latter view and affirms that many of the revolutionary elements in modern Chinese literature can be found in the literature of late Qing dynasty. Thus the influence of Ibsen and other Western dramatists on the modern Chinese theatre is considered as a new development out of the need for transforming the tradition.

1.55

Wen Ling 温凌. "'Wu Si' shiqi guanyu xiqu de lunzheng "五四" 時期關於戲曲的論爭 (Debates on Chinese music-drama during the "May 4th" era). *Xiju yanjiu* 戲劇研究 (Studies on drama), 2 (1959), pp. 17–21.

Xiqu (music-drama) is a traditional form of Chinese drama with an emphasis on the performing aspects of singing and dance. The theatre reform in modern China began in the 1900s with changes in the style of music drama. In this reformed style, which has been variously called "*wenmingxi*" (enlightened drama), speech is added as an important element for the communication of revolutionary ideas to the audience. In this essay, Wen Ling surveys the different arguments on music-drama, a traditional form, and discusses the various views whether it should be abolished or reformed for the dissemination of contemporary ideas. The study of the "*wenmingxi*" provides information on an early form of modern Chinese drama, in which style Ibsen was first adapted for performance in China.

1.56

Weng Yiqin 翁義欽. "Wu Si Yundong yu waiguo wenxue" 五四運動與外國文學 (The May 4th Movement and foreign literature). *Fudan xuebao* 復旦學報 (Fudan university journal), 4 (1979), pp. 67–70.

In this essay, Weng Yiqin re-evaluates the May 4th Movement in the light of foreign influences. This is one of the earliest essays in Post-Mao China to reaffirm the positive influence of foreign literature. The historical significance of this essay lies in its positive evaluation of foreign influence before China officially reinstated its open-door policy in the early 1980s, and it served a pioneering purpose in the subsequent nationwide positive re-evaluation of Ibsen.

1.57

Wu Benxing 吳奔星. "'Wu Si' qianxi wenxue geming de xingzhi ji qi weida de lishi zhuanbian — Shilun Zhongguo xiandai wenxue de qidian wenti" "五四" 前夕文學革命的性質及其偉大的歷史轉變 — 試論中國現代文學的起點問題 (The nature of the literary revolution on the eve of the "May 4th" movement and the great historical changes — A tentative study on the genesis of modern Chinese literature). *Wenxue pinglun congkan* 文學評論叢刊 (Journal of literary criticism), 6 (1980), pp. 314–334.

Relating the call for the literary revolution in 1917 to the launch of the May 4th Movement in 1919, the author of this essay argues that the revolution in literature was instrumental to the revolution in culture. This essay serves a social and political purpose in pointing out the relation between literary revival and the cultural rejuvenation of China after the Cultural Revolution (1966–76). This reevaluation provides information on the context in which Ibsen was first introduced to China.

1.58

Xu Banmei 徐半梅. *Huaju chuangshiqi huiyilu* 話劇創始期回憶錄 (Memoirs on the formative period in modern Chinese drama). Beijing: Zhongguo xiju chubanshe 中國戲劇出版社, 1957.

In this book, the theatre historian Xu Banmei reviews the development of modern Chinese theatre in the 1900s and 1910s. Major playwrights are discussed in their relation to the reform of the theatre and to the new techniques and themes that appeared on the stage. There is useful information on the impact of Western and Japanese drama in China. Thus the reception of Ibsen in China can be assessed in the historical context given in the first-hand information provided by Xu Banmei.

1.59

Yang Yufeng 楊玉峰 (Yeung Yuk-fung). "Yijiusijiu nian yiqian Yibusheng de yijie zai Zhongguo" 一九四九年以前易卜生的譯介在中國 (Chinese translations and studies of Ibsen before 1949). *Dongfang wenhua* 東方文化 (Journal of oriental studies), 20.1 (1982), pp. 55–66.

This review essay is both historical and bibliographic in approach. It gives overall information on the historical reception of Ibsen in relation to the social change in China, in particular the movement of women's liberation. At the same time the essay also comments on the wide reception of Ibsen as a result of his revolutionary social ideas.

1.60

Yao Chunshu 姚春樹. "Lun 'Wu Si' xinwenxue yundong zhong de rendao zhuyi wenti" 論"五四"文學運動中的人道主義問題 (A study of the problem of humanism in the "May 4th" new literature movement). *Wenxue pinglun congkan* 文學評論叢刊 (Journal of literary criticism), 6 (1980), pp. 294–313.

Different from other socialist studies that emphasize the materialist aspect of the revolution that led to the May 4th Movement, this essay puts forth the view that humanism is one of the elements that called for the literary revolution in 1917. In relating the May 4th Movement to the element of humanism, the author proposes to look at the development of modern Chinese literature along the line that humanism is an important aspect of revolution. In this context, the revolutionary spirit of Ibsen's plays can be seen in its humanistic aspect.

1.61

Yi Xinnong 易新農 and Chen Pingyuan 陳平原. "*Wan'ou zhi jia* zai Zhongguo de huixiang"《玩偶之家》在中國的回響 (The Chinese response to *A Doll's House*). *Zhongshan daxue xuebao* 中山大學學報(Sun Yat-sen university journal), Zhesheban 哲社版 (Philosophy and social sciences edition), 2 (1984), pp. 129–140.

In this essay, the authors review the impact of Ibsen's *A Doll's House*, emphasizing more on its political than artistic influence. The major Chinese playwrights and thinkers who have been influenced by *A Doll's House* are mentioned. Different from the previous views that consider Ibsen as bourgeois and half-hearted in his revolutionary themes, this essay asserts the positive value of Ibsen's influence.

1.62

Yuan Zhenying 袁振英. "Yibusheng zhuan" 易卜生傳 (A biography of Ibsen). *Xinqingnian* 新青年 (New youth), 4.6 (June 1918), pp. 606–619.

In this issue of *Xinqingnian* (New youth) there are Chinese translations of *A Doll's House*, *An Enemy of the People*, and *Little Eyolf* and a biography of Ibsen written by Yuan Zhenying, one of the major Chinese exponents of Ibsen, who bases his material mainly on Edmund Gosse's study of Ibsen's life. This first Chinese biography of Ibsen runs fourteen pages and is divided into three parts. In the first two parts, Yuan Zhenying briefly describes the life of Ibsen from his youth to his mature years. In the last part of the biography, where the main focus of the study lies, Yuan concentrates on an evaluation of Ibsen's major plays.

Yuan's study of Ibsen's drama provides the Chinese with some basic ideas of the Norwegian dramatist. It is in effect a supplement to Hu Shi's essay, "Ibsenism." Taking into account that interpretations of literary works are often affected by the prevalent mode of thinking, one cannot deny that Hu and Yuan's works, though rather biased, perform a valuable service in introducing Ibsen to China. However much Ibsen is misrepresented in these two essays, Hu and Yuan should be credited for their pioneering efforts.

1.63

Yue Daiyun 樂黛雲. "Nicai yu xiandai Zhongguo wenxue" 尼采與現代中國文學 (Nietzsche and modern Chinese literature). *Beijing daxue xuebao* 北京大學學報 (Peking university journal), Zhesheban 哲社版 (Philosophy and social sciences edition), 3 (1980), pp. 20–33.

An important part of this essay deals with how Lu Xun has been influenced by Nietzsche and other Western writers. Lu Xun is one of most influential modern Chinese writers who were deeply influenced by both Nietzsche and Ibsen in his promotion of the rebellious spirit and ideas of individualism in China in the early 1900s. In this context, Ibsen's influence on Lu Xun can be seen in a broader perspective of the overall Western impact in modern China.

1.64

Zeng Xianhui 曾憲輝. "Lin Shu zhuan" 林紓傳 (A biography of Lin Shu). *Fujian shifan daxue xuebao* 福建師範大學學報 (Fujian normal university journal), 2 (1981). Reprint. In *Xinhua wenzhai* 新華文摘 (New China digest), 10 (1981), pp. 204–206.

Lin Shu is one of the earliest Chinese scholars and translators who introduced Ibsen to China through his collaborative works in translation. The biographical information given in the article is useful in understanding the social and cultural contexts in which foreign literary works were introduced to the Chinese reading public through translation. The same information may throw light on the social background under which Ibsen was introduced to China.

1.65

Zhang Geng 張庚. “Zhongguo huaju yundongshi chugao” 中國話劇運動史初稿 (A preliminary draft of the history of modern Chinese drama). In *Zhongguo jindai wenxue lunwenji 1949–1979* 中國近代文學論文集 1949–1979 (Collected essays on modern Chinese literature 1949–1979), Xiju minjian wenxue lunwen juan 戲劇，民間文學論文卷 (Section on drama and folk literature). Edited by Zhongguo shehui kexueyuan wenxue yanjiusuo jindai wenxue yanjiuzu 中國社會科學院文學研究所近代文學研究組, pp. 240–275. Beijing: Zhongguo shehui kexue chubanshe 中國社會科學出版社, 1982.

Zhang Geng, a noted theatre historian, devoted most of his life to the study of modern Chinese drama as a social movement. In this essay, he studies drama as an art form in relation to its social context and suggests that the development of drama in modern China is inseparable from its mission in education and social reform. It gives a historical overview for understanding the reception of Ibsen in China.

1.66

Zhang Hua 張華. “Lu Xun he Yibusheng” 魯迅和易卜生 (Lu Xun and Ibsen). In *Lu Xun he waiguo zuojia* 魯迅和外國作家 (Lu Xun and foreign writers), pp. 37–58. Xi’an: Shaanxi renmin chubanshe 陝西人民出版社, 1981.

Zhang Hua’s book is so far the most comprehensive survey of foreign influence on Lu Xun. In this book, there is a chapter on how Ibsen has influenced Lu Xun, whose early writings including “Moluoshi li shuo” (A discourse on the power of *Mara* poetry) and “Wenhua pianzhi lun” (On cultural extremes) that show great influence of Ibsen and other European romantic writers are discussed. The influence of Ibsen upon Lu Xun’s literary works is also studied.

1.67

———. “Xifang sichao dui qianqi Lu Xun de yingxiang” 西方思潮對前期魯迅的影響 (The impact of Western intellectual trends on young Lu Xun). In *Lu Xun he waiguo zuojia* 魯迅和外國作家 (Lu Xun and foreign writers), pp. 1–17. Xi’an: Shaanxi renmin chubanshe 陝西人民出版社, 1981.

This chapter in Zhang Hua's book relates the revolutionary spirit in young Lu Xun to his dissatisfaction with the social conditions of China and to the unhappy experience in his early life. The chapter also gives information on Lu Xun's experience as a foreign student in Japan. Thus the Western influence upon Lu Xun is considered by Zhang Hua as Lu Xun's reaction to the cultural chaos in China, and that through the promotion of Western culture Lu Xun hopes to revive China as a strong nation. When read together with the chapter on "Lu Xun and Ibsen," the reader can obtain a more detailed picture of how and why Lu Xun considers Ibsen as a model of revolutionary ideas, particularly the uncompromising spirit exemplified in Ibsen's play, *An Enemy of the People*.

1.68

Zhao Mingyi 趙銘彝. "Woguo zaoqi de huaju jiaoyu" 我國早期的話劇教育 (Theatre education in early modern China). *Xiju yishu* 戲劇藝術 (Dramatic arts), 1 (1979), pp. 105–108.

The beginning of Chinese theatre education can be dated as early as 1908 when "Chun yang she" (the Chinese Spring Willow Society) was set up in Shanghai. Right at the beginning the Chinese theatre was greatly influenced by Western and Japanese drama, among which Ibsen was one of the important sources. The drama schools established by Chen Dabei, Wang Zhongsheng and Wang Zhongxian, which all emphasized imitation of the Western dramatic tradition, are discussed to illustrate the practical aspect of theatre education in early modern China. This article gives background information on the earliest Chinese experimentation with Ibsen's plays.

1.69

Zhao Yuan 趙園. "'Wu Si' shiqi xiaoshuo zhong de hunyin aiqing wenti" "五四" 時期小説中的婚姻愛情問題 (Issues of marriage and love in "May 4th" fiction). *Zhongguo shehui kexue* 中國社會科學 (Chinese social sciences), 4 (1983), pp. 163–182.

Zhao Yuan's study outlines the issue of marriage and love as one of the major concerns of May 4th literature. Ibsen's Nora was taken as an exemplary role for many women in China in the 1910s and 1920s. This is also reflected in the literature of the period. In fiction, as well as in drama, the issue of Nora's rights and her decision to leave Helmer have been interpreted by both the Chinese dramatists and novelists as issues of freedom in marriage and love. Although the focus of Zhao Yuan's study is not placed on Ibsen's influence in drama, but Ibsen's plays and the ideas of Ibsenism advocated by Hu Shi are seen as related to the issue of women's liberation in modern China.

1.70

Zhi Fei 知非. "Jindai wenxue shang xiju zhi weizhi" 近代文學上戲劇之位置 (The place of drama in modern literature). *Xinqingnian* 新青年 (New youth), 6.1 (January 1919), pp. 21–29.

This article summarizes the social and political functions of drama in the dissemination of revolutionary ideas at the end of the nineteenth century and at the beginning of the twentieth century. Drama is the major means through which Marxist ideas, anarchism and feminist ideas were disseminated in the 1910s. In this essay, Ibsen's plays together with other playwrights' are considered as a powerful means to revolutionize the modern world. The ideas discussed are similar to those given in Emma Goldman's essay, "The Modern Drama: A Powerful Dissemination of Radical Thought" (see 1.15).

1.71

Zhong Mi 仲密 (Zhou Zuoren 周作人). "Zhongguo xiaoshuo li de nannü wenti" 中國小說裏的男女問題 (Gender in Chinese fiction). *Meizhou pinglun* 每周評論 (Weekly review), 2 February 1919, pp. 2–3.

Focusing on the gender issues in traditional Chinese fiction, Zhong Mi's (pen-name of Zhou Zuoren) article discusses the traditional Chinese concepts of gender and how the concepts have been treated in Chinese fiction. In this article, the author thus puts forth new perspectives on the issues and asks for a new treatment of these issues in modern Chinese literature. In the context of the Chinese reception of Ibsen, this article served a very important function by putting forth the feminist ideas in Ibsen's plays for the literary revolution in China in the 1910s.

1.72

Zhong Yao 仲遙 (Zhou Zuoren 周作人). "Bainian lai xiyang xueshu zhi huigu" 百年來西洋學術之回顧 (A review of Western scholarship in the past one hundred years). *Xuebao* 學報 (Academic journal), 1.10 (1908), pp. 1–12.

Ibsen is briefly mentioned by Zhong Yao (pen-name of Zhou Zuoren) in this article. After summarizing the Western intellectual and literary movements in the past century, the author turns to Norway with the following comment on Ibsen and Björnson: "In the past one hundred years, Norway produced two writers: one is Ibsen, and the other Björnson. Ibsen is a great Naturalist. His works are full of social criticism." Zhong Yao considers that Ibsen's place in literature is comparable to that of Wordsworth, Hugo, Goethe, and Tolstoy.

1.73

Zhu Wenhua 朱文華. "Ping Hu Shi de *Zhongshen dashi*" 評胡適的《終身大事》 (On Hu Shi's *The Greatest Event in Life*). *Anhui shifan daxue xuebao* 安徽師範大學學報 (Anhui normal university journal), Zhesheban 哲社版 (Philosophy and social sciences edition), 1 (1983), pp. 101–106.

Hu Shi's experimental play *Zhongshen dashi* (The greatest event in life) was written in 1920 first in English for performance at the YWCA, Beijing. But the play was not staged due to the lack of a suitable actress who dared to face criticism for being revolutionary in the pursuit of personal freedom in marriage. The play was later rewritten in Chinese and it shows the influence of Ibsen in its characterization of the female protagonist. In this article, the author studies the historical significance of the play in arousing the awareness among Chinese women of fighting for their freedom and for the rights to leave home.

2

Ibsen in the (Post-)May 4th Era 1920–1927

2.01

Chen Shouzhu 陳瘦竹. "Lun Guo Moruo de lishiju" 論郭沫若的歷史劇 (On Guo Moruo's historical plays). In *Guo Moruo yanjiu lunji* 郭沫若研究論集 (A collection of studies on Guo Moruo). Edited by Sichuan renmin chubanshe 四川人民出版社, pp. 203–220. Chengdu: Sichuan renmin chubanshe 四川人民出版社, 1980.

In this chapter of the book, Chen Shouzhu studies Guo Moruo's historical plays, some of which, such as *Zhuo Wenjun* in "Three Rebellious Women," are re-interpretations of historical women figures in imitation of the style as exemplified in *A Doll's House*. In Chen Shouzhu's study, the focus is placed on the techniques of Guo Moruo's historical drama, rather than on Ibsen and the women issues, but such a study provides a useful view on how historical drama can be considered as reinterpretations and re-presentations of history.

2.02

———. *Lun Tian Han de huaju chuangzuo* 論田漢的話劇創作 (A study of Tian Han's drama). Shanghai: Shanghai wenyi chubanshe 上海文藝出版社, 1961.

In this book, Tian Han's early plays, such as *Huo hu zhi ye* (The night a tiger was caught) and *Nan gui* (Return to the south), that bear a close resemblance to Ibsen's plays, such as *The Lady from the Sea*, are studied as a process of development in Tian Han's career as a playwright. The book provides useful materials that shed light on Tian Han's life and the historical process of his career development.

2.03

Chen Shuyu 陳漱渝. "Lu Xun yu funü wenti" 魯迅與婦女問題 (Lu Xun and the woman issue). In *Lu Xun shishi xintan* 魯迅史實新探 (A new study of the historical facts about Lu Xun), pp. 305–364. Changsha: Hunan renmin chubanshe 湖南人民出版社, 1980.

In this essay, Chen Shouru surveys the historical development of Lu Xun's views on the "women question" in China. Lu Xun's indebtedness to Ibsen, as well as his views on *A Doll's House*, is part of the focus of this essay. Lu Xun's essay "What Happens After Nora Leaves Home?" (Nuola zouhou zenyang), which was first delivered as a speech to the students in the Peking Normal College for Women, is reviewed together with the themes on women that can be found in Lu Xun's short stories.

2.04

Chen Xia 陳嘏. "Bulanduisi" 布蘭兌斯 (Brandes). *Wenxue piping yu pipingjia* 文學批評與批評家 (Literary criticism and critics). *Dongfang wenku* di liushi zhong 東方文庫第六十種 (No. 60, Eastern Library), pp. 23–40. Shanghai: Shangwu yinshuguan 商務印書館, 1923.

This is a study of Ibsen on his relation with Georg Brandes, the Norwegian literary critic and historian. The essay was at first intended to be a study of Brandes only, but since the Brandes had written widely on Ibsen, Chen Xia appended a section on Ibsen. Chen recommends to the Chinese audience Brandes's book *Henrik Ibsen* as "an exemplary work of literary criticism," indispensable to "all those who want to study Ibsen seriously." Chen highly praises Brandes's study of Ibsen as the most objective and accurate account, for he thinks that Brandes, as Ibsen's friend and enemy and more importantly a native speaker of Danish, knew Ibsen better and more thoroughly than any other critic. Chen advised the Chinese reader in the 1920s that Brandes would do more justice to Ibsen than most of the German, French, and English critics, who were awed by Ibsen's posthumous fame, as most of them came to know Ibsen after he published his major plays, and their criticism was based on the speculation they could make about Ibsen. But Brandes had the same mother tongue as Ibsen, and as a contemporary of Ibsen he was able to follow the actual course of Ibsen's development and without being blinded by his great fame. In this essay, one can already sense the diversified views on Ibsen that the Chinese had in the 1910s. Chen Xia's essay specifically aims at correcting the views of those critics who rely too much on English and French sources.

2.05

Dongbei shifan daxue waiguo wenti yanjiusuo Riben wenxue yanjiushi 東北師範大學外國問題研究所日本文學研究室. "Wu Si Yundong yilai Riben wenxue yanjiu yu fanyi mulu" 五四運動以來日本文學研究與翻譯目錄 (A bibliography of studies and translations of Japanese literature since the May 4th Movement). *Riben wenxue* 日本文學 (Japanese literature). Inaugural Number (1982), pp. 340–362; 1 (1983), pp. 332–339; 2 (1983), pp. 270–279.

This bibliography gives information on the works in Japanese literature that have been translated into Chinese since 1919. Since most Western authors, including Ibsen, were introduced to China in the early twentieth century first through Japan, the bibliography is useful to scholars who want to conduct research on Sino-Japanese literary relations, a study of which will show not only how modern Chinese literature and theatre have been influenced by Japanese experiments, but also how Western authors and playwrights, such as Ibsen, have been introduced to China.

2.06

Eide, Elisabeth. "Henrik Ibsen and Reforms in Chinese Drama." *Cambridge Approaches to Linguistics*, vol. 9 (1997), pp. 181–205.

This essay studies the influence of Ibsen on modern Chinese dramatists. Information given in this study can also be found in Kwok-kan Tam's article, "Ibsen and Modern Chinese Dramatists: Influences and Parallels," *Modern Chinese Literature*, 2.1 (Spring 1986), pp. 45–62.

2.07

Fang Xin 芳信. "Kanle *Nala* hou de lingsui ganxiang" 看了《那拉》後的零碎感想 (Random thoughts after watching *A Doll's House*). *Chenbao fukan* 晨報附刊, 12 May 1923, p. 4.

This is a review essay on the performance of *A Doll's House* in Beijing in the 1920s, a year that many Chinese young women were determined to imitate Nora and leave home to seek freedom in education and marriage. The essay singles out the message of leaving home and shows Chinese women the way to freedom.

2.08

Guo Moruo 郭沫若. *Guo Moruo juzuo quanji* 郭沫若劇作全集(Complete plays of Guo Moruo). Beijing: Zhongguo xiju chubanshe 中國戲劇出版社, 1982.

This is a collection of Guo Moruo's plays, in which the "Three Rebellious Women" (a trilogy) is included, so that readers may obtain a view of the texts that show how Guo Moruo is influenced by Ibsen in his early plays, especially in the play *Zhuo Wenjun*.

2.09

———. *Nüshen ji panni de nüxing* 女神及叛逆的女性 (Goddesses and the rebellious women). Shanghai: Guanghua shuju 光華書局, 1931.

This is a collection of Guo Moruo's creative writings produced mostly in the 1920s. Included in the collection is the trilogy "Three Rebellious Women" (San ge panni de nüxing), which shows a strong influence of Ibsen not only on literary techniques, but also on the theme of women's liberation and social responsibility.

2.10

Guo Yuheng 郭預衡. "Lu Xun bixia de aiqing, hunyin he jiating" 魯迅筆下的愛情、婚姻和家庭 (Love, marriage and the family as portrayed by Lu Xun). In *Jinian Lu Xun danchen baizhounian wenxue lunwenji ji Lu Xun zhencang youguan Beishida shiliao* 紀念魯迅誕晨百周年文學論文集及魯迅珍藏有關北師大史料 (A collection of literary essays in commemoration of Lu Xun's birth centenary and the historical materials about the Peking normal university which Lu Xun gathered), pp. 120–138. Beijing: Beijing shifan daxue chubanshe 北京師範大學出版社 , 1981.

In this essay, Guo Yuheng gives details on Lu Xun's views on the issues related to love, marriage and the family in Chinese women's pursuit for freedom in modern China in the 1920s. By putting in a historical context Lu Xun's speech on Chinese Nora which he gave at the Peking Normal College for Women in 1923, the essay provides an overview of the cultural change in China that led to the call for freedom in marriage for women.

2.11

He Yigong 何一公. "Nügaoshi yan de *Nala*" 女高師演的《那拉》 (The performance of *A Doll's House* at the Peking normal college for women). *Chenbao fukan* 晨報附刊, 17 May 1923, pp. 3–4.

Without this essay, little information can be found about the background of Lu Xun's speech on Ibsen presented at the Peking Normal College for Women in 1923. When read together with Lu Xun's speech, then the significance of this essay can be seen in the information it provides on the performance of *A Doll's House* in Beijing in 1923, a year in which many Chinese women were troubled by the dilemma between the call to leave home for freedom of education and marriage and the lack of economic and social means for independence. This review essay on the performance provides useful information on how Ibsen was received in Beijing in the general atmosphere of the quest for freedom among young women in the 1920s.

2.12

Honma Hisao 本間久雄. "Jindaiju miaoxie de jiehun wenti" 近代劇描寫的結婚問題 (Marriage in modern drama). Translated by Wei Sheng 薇生. *Funü zazhi* 婦女雜誌 (*The Ladies' Journal*), 8.7 (July 1922), pp. 50–54.

In this essay, there is discussion on how marriage is treated as a subject in modern Western drama. In taking up such a subject, Honma Hisao deals with the rise of the female subjectivity and the adoption of the female point of view in marriage. Ibsen's plays, such as *A Doll's House*, are cited as examples of women's changing attitude toward marriage.

2.13

Huang Houxing 黃侯興. "Guo Moruo lishiju shilun" 郭沫若歷史劇試論 (A tentative study of Guo Moruo's historical plays). In *Guo Moruo yanjiu lunji* 郭沫若研究論集 (A collection of studies on Guo Moruo), pp. 221–257. Chengdu: Sichuan renmin chubanshe 四川人民出版社, 1980.

This is a collection of studies which focus on the techniques and themes of Guo Moruo's historical drama. The studies also provide the sociohistorical context for an understanding of why the author Guo Moruo has written these plays and how he re-interpretes the historical figures for contemporary representations. The interaction between the historical and the contemporary in representation is of particular interest, especially the women figures in the historical plays with their contemporary aspirations.

2.14

Lavrin, Janko. "Yishujia de Yibusheng" 藝術家的易卜生 (Ibsen as artist). Translated by Jiao Juyin 焦菊隱. *Chenbao fukan* 晨報附刊, 16 & 17 February 1927, various pagination.

This essay by Jiao Juyin is a Chinese translation of Janko Lavrin's "Ibsen as Artist" from his book *Ibsen and His Creation*. According to Lavrin, his book is a psycho-critical study of Ibsen. He distinguishes between two kinds of artists, one for the sake of art, the other for the sake of life, and places Ibsen in the latter category: "Ibsen is also one of those who look upon the creation of art as a means to the creation of life. He hates mere aestheticism with its dogmatic *l'art pour l'art*, considering it as dangerous to true art as dogmatic theology is to true religion" (English original from Janko Lavrin, "Ibsen as Artist," in *Ibsen and His Creation, a Psycho-critical Study*, p. 18. London: W. Collins Sons & Co., Ltd., 1921). Lavrin quotes extensively from Ibsen's letters and the preliminary drafts of the plays to support his thesis that Ibsen "began his works as 'philosopher' and carried them out as artist." In so doing, Lavrin tries to trace Ibsen's transition from philosopher to artist. He demonstrates how in Ibsen the conflict between the artist and the philosopher is resolved and reconciled. Unlike all other Chinese theories about Ibsen, Lavrin's article places more emphasis on the relationship between philosophy and art in Ibsen's works. Jiao Juyin himself was a dramatist and director educated at the University of Chicago before he returned to China, and his interest was therefore directed more toward the artistic aspect than the social messages of Ibsen's drama.

2.15

Li Jiye 李寄野. "Yibusheng xiju zhong de funü wenti" 易卜生戲劇中的婦女問題 (The woman issue in Ibsen's drama). *Funü zazhi* 婦女雜誌 (*The Ladies' Journal*), 10.12 (December 1924), pp. 1821–1823.

In this essay, the author discusses the three plays, *A Doll's House*, *Ghosts* and *The Lady from the Sea*, in terms of the women characters in the plays and their search for personal freedom. The author reads the three plays as a sequence in Ibsen's discussion of the woman issue as a social and personal problem in the nineteenth century.

2.16

Li Zongwu 李宗武. "Jindai wenxue shang zhi liangxing wenti" 近代文學上之兩性問題 (The problem of the two sexes in modern literature). *Chenbao fukan* 晨報附刊, 23April 1925, pp. 5–6.

This newspaper essay is a survey of how the gender issues are treated in early modern Western literature, thus putting Ibsen as well as other feminist writers in the context of gender differences. *A Doll's House* and other works of a feminist nature are also discussed in the essay.

2.17

Lin Ruji 林如稷. "You kanle Nügaoshi liangtian yanju hou de zatan" 又看了女高師兩天演劇後的雜談 (Random words on watching the two-day performances at the Peking normal college for women). *Chenbao fukan* 晨報附刊, 16 May 1923, p. 3.

This is a response to the performance of *A Doll's House* at Peking Normal College for Women in 1923. It discusses the performance in the light of its message for women's liberation and freedom to pursue their own career. This two-day performance of *A Doll's House* in Beijing (Peking) was an influential and significant event in China in the history of Chinese women's movement, as the event was followed by heated discussion on the theme of women's liberation.

2.18

Liu Shaoming 劉紹銘 (Joseph S. M. Lau). "Chaoliu yu diandi" 潮流與點滴 (Tides and drops). *Mingbao yuekan* 明報月刊 (Ming Pao monthly), 201 (September 1982), pp. 97–101.

This is an essay that surveys the development and changes in modern Chinese literature, in which Hu Shi's play *The Greatest Event in Life* is discussed in relation to the development of modern drama, as well as to its indebtedness to Ibsen. The theme of women's liberation and freedom is also discussed.

2.19

Lu Xun 魯迅. "Nuola zouhou zenyang?" 娜拉走後怎樣? (What happens after Nora leaves home?). 1923. Reprint. In *Lu Xun quanji* 魯迅全集 (Complete works of Lu Xun), vol. 1, pp. 143–151. Beijing: Renmin wenxue chubanshe 人民文學出版社, 1973.

This essay was written for delivery as a speech to the students at the Peking Normal College for Women during their literary festival held on 26 December 1923. In the essay, Lu Xun warns the awakened Chinese women that the social conditions in China were still not ready for their complete liberation. After leaving home, women would lose their protection and had to face the hardships of struggling for a living, the consequence of which was that many women would return home, or they might have to become prostitutes. Lu Xun is of the view that a social revolution was needed in China so that women could be liberated. In the context of China in 1923, this essay produced a shocking effect upon the heated debates on women's liberation.

2.20

Miyamori Asataro 宮森麻太郎. "Jindaiju he shijie sichao" 近代劇和世界思潮 (Modern drama and world intellectual trends). Translated by Zhou Jianhou 周建侯. In *Xinwenyi pinglun* 新文藝評論 (New literary criticism). Edited by Liang Gong 俍工, pp. 98–104. Shanghai: Minzhi shuju 民智書局, 1923.

In this article, Miyamori surveys the development of modern drama in relation to world intellectual trends. According to Miyamori's view, modern drama can be seen as an embodiment of intellectual debates in the twentieth century, in which all the different schools of thought, such as Marxism, feminism, anarchism, are reflected. The social problem drama developed by Ibsen and Shaw is seen as part of this development.

2.21

Pu Shunqing 璞舜卿. "Yibusheng yu Sitelinbao zhi funüguan" 易卜生與斯特林堡之婦女觀 (Ibsen and Strindberg's views on women). *Funü zazhi* 婦女雜誌 (*The Ladies' Journal*), 13.9 (September 1927), pp. 19–24.

In this study, Pu Shunqing compares Ibsen with Strindberg and points out that Strindberg has a negative view about women, while Ibsen is more sympathetic with the liberation of women. Pu Shunqing believes that Strindberg's negative view may be attributed to his own misfortunes in life and that his view is a projection of his own sufferings.

2.22

Ren Tuo 仁佗. "Kanle Nügaoshi liangtian yanju yihou de zatan" 看了女高師兩天演劇以後的雜談 (Some afterthoughts on the two-day performances at the Peking normal college for women). *Chenbao fukan* 晨報附刊, 11 May 1923, pp. 3–4.

This newspaper essay provides very useful information on the performance of *A Doll's House* in China in 1923. In the same year that Lu Xun gave his famous lecture on Nora at the Peking Normal College for Women and warned Chinese women of the danger of leaving home without economic independence.

2.23

Tam, Kwok-kan (Tan Guogen 譚國根). "Feminism and Ibsenism: Portrayals of a New Female Identity in Modern Chinese Literature." In *Chinese Literature and the European Context*. Edited by Marián Gálik, pp. 113–118. Bratislava: Institute of Asian and African Studies of the Slovak Academy of Sciences, 1994.

This is a comparative study of how the influence of Ibsen upon Chinese women in the 1920s and 1930s is reflected in literature and how the issue of women's quest for a new identity became a debate in China. In the study, the author shows how Ibsen was understood as a feminist by both male and female Chinese writers, and in what ways Ibsen contributed to the shaping of the feminist movement in China.

2.24

Tam, Kwok-kan (Tan Guogen 譚國根) and Terry Siu-han Yip (Ye Shaoxian 葉少嫻). "European Influences on Modern Chinese Drama: Kuo Mo-jo's Early Historical-Problem Plays." *Journal of Oriental Studies*, 24.1 (1986), pp. 54–65.

This is a study of the European influence upon Guo Moruo's (Kuo Mo-jo) early plays. As is well known, Guo Moruo was deeply influenced by both Ibsen and Goethe in the 1920s and 1930s. This article studies how Guo Moruo treats his historical plays both thematically and formally as problem plays.

2.25

Tan Luofei 譚洛非 and Lu Wenbi 陸文璧. "Lun Guo Moruo lishiju zhong guanghui de funü xingxiang" 論郭沫若歷史劇中光輝的婦女形象 (On the brilliant images of women in Guo Moruo's historical drama). In *Guo Moruo yanjiu lunji* 郭沫若研究論集 (A collection of studies on Guo Moruo), pp. 282–298. Chengdu: Sichuan renmin chubanshe 四川人民出版社, 1980.

This article focuses on the image of women characters in Guo Moruo's historical drama, in which the women characters are presented as militant masculine figures who fight for the cause of national freedom. The purpose of Guo's drama, such as *Zhuo Wenjun* and *Nie Ying*, is to rewrite history and reconsider womanhood. However, in Guo's experiments with the new conception of womanhood, there is an adaptation of *A Doll's House* and reinterpretation of Nora as a woman fighting for national salvation.

2.26

Tang Tao 唐弢. "Funü jiefang de daolu — Jinian Lu Xun dansheng yibai zhounian tan ta jipian guanyu funü jiefang de zuopin" 婦女解放的道路 — 紀念魯迅誕生一百周年談他幾篇關於婦女解放的作品 (The path to female emancipation — A discussion of some of Lu Xun's works on women in commemoration of the centenary of his birthday). *Lu Xun yanjiu* 魯迅研究 (Studies on Lu Xun), 4 (1981), pp. 23–30.

In this study, Tang Tao surveys the history of Chinese women's movement in search of emancipation and uses it as a context for the interpretation of Lu Xun's short stories, in particular "Regret for the Past," which shows clear evidence of the influence of Ibsen.

2.27

Tung, Constantine. "Lonely Search into the Unknown: T'ien Han's Early Plays, 1920–1930." *Comparative Drama,* 2.1 (Spring 1968), pp. 44–54.

This is a study of Tian Han's (T'ien Han) plays in relation to his life. The theme of loneliness in Tian Han's early plays and his own disappointment in love are considered as related. In this way, Ibsen's influence upon Tian Han is considered not merely as a matter of literary form, but also as a matter of personal experience on the part of Tian Han.

2.28

Wang Damin 王大敏. "Lun Guo Moruo lishiju de zhandouxing he zhenshixing" 論郭沫若歷史劇的戰鬥性和真實性 (On the militant and realistic aspects of Guo Moruo's historical drama). *Guo Moruo yanjiu lunji* 郭沫若研究論集 (A collection of studies on Guo Moruo), pp. 258–281. Chengdu: Sichuan renmin chubanshe 四川人民出版社, 1980.

Guo Moruo's historical drama is a form that follows the Ibsenian mode in its structure, and is thus considered by many critics as a modern interpretation and rewriting of Chinese historical figures and themes. In this article, Wang Damin puts Guo Moruo's early plays, such as *Zhuo Wenjun* and *Nie Ying*, in the contemporary context of female liberation and individualism and reviews their sociopolitical significance.

2.29

Wu Daiying 吳黛英. "Jiuzhidu de pannizhe he xishengzhe — Lun Zijun" 舊制度的叛逆者和犧牲者 — 論子君 (The rebel and victim of the old order — On Zijun). *Heilongjiang daxue xuebao* 黑龍江大學學報 (Heilongjiang university journal), Zhesheban 哲社版 (Philosophy and social sciences edition), 4 (1979), pp. 69–72.

Wu Daiying's article is a study of Lu Xun's short story, "Shang shi" (Regret for the past), in its rebellion against the old marriage system in China in the 1910s. This story by Lu Xun is noted for its message on the influence of Ibsen that has inspired many modern Chinese women to leave home in pursuit of personal freedom in marriage.

2.30

Xin Nong 辛農. "*Kuilei zhi jiating* ping" 《傀儡之家庭》評 (A review of *A Doll's House*). *Guowen zhoubao* 國聞週報, 2.20 (31 May 1925), pp. 30–35.

Together with other essays that appeared in *Guowen zhoubao*, this essay by Xin Nong contributed to the nation-wide debate on the orientation of women's liberation in China in 1934. In reviewing Ibsen's *A Doll's House*, Xin Nong thinks that although Ibsen has been introduced to China since the 1910s, there is still room for further exploration about the message of freedom for women. However, the author also thinks that Ibsenism in a misrepresented and extreme form that places emphasis on a superficial understanding of the message of leaving home will only lead to disaster.

2.31

Yu Dafu 郁達夫. *Xiju lun* 戲劇論 (Studies on drama). Shanghai: Shangwu yinshuguan 商務印書館, 1926.

In this early work, Yu Dafu discusses Western concepts of drama with the purpose of reminding both the Chinese readers and dramatists that drama is an art form and not just a forum for social debates. Put in a historical context, the book plays an important role in its argument about the artistic nature of drama. When it is read in relation to the Chinese debate that occurred in the second half of the 1920s on whether Ibsen was an artist or mainly a social reformer, the reader will see the significance of this little book.

2.32

Yu Shangyuan 余上沅. "Guoqu ershi'er xiju mingjia ji qi daibiaozuo" 過去二十二戲劇名家及其代表作 (Twenty-two famous dramatists and their representative works). *Chenbao fukan* 晨報附刊, 9–31 October 1922, various pagination.

A reappraisal of Ibsen in the context of European drama is given by Yu Shangyuan in this essay, which forms the last part of a series collectively entitled "Guoqu ershi'er xiju mingjia ji qi daibiaozuo" (Twenty-two famous dramatists and their representative works) and was serialized in *Chenbao fukan* from October 9 to 31. In this essay, Yu puts Ibsen's plays into three categories: the historico-mythical, verse, and social. He thinks that *A Doll's House* is the most representative of the eight social plays Ibsen has written because the play shows every aspect of the techniques of modern playwriting. The play is treasured first of all for its feminist theme: "it is a tragedy of marriage and also a spiritual pillar of the modern women's movement.... The central idea of Ibsen's tragedies lies in heredity — for example, *Ghosts* — and *Ghosts* is a sequel to *A Doll's House*. Helmer is typical of the falsehood described in *The Pillars of Society*, whereas Nora is of the rebellious spirit portrayed in Selina, Mrs. Alving and Rebecca" (31 October 1922). Yu also introduces the play as a structural model for modern Chinese drama. Yu Shangyuan is a prolific theatre critic and playwright, yet perceptive as he is, he also misses the point in treating heredity as an essential element in Ibsen's tragedies. His sociological interpretation of *A Doll's House* as a play concerning women's liberation is contrary to Ibsen's declared intention.

2.33

Zeng Qingrui 曾慶瑞. "Qian lun waiguo wenxue de yingxiang he Zhongguo xiandai wenxue sichao, liupai de xiaozhang" 淺論外國文學的

影響和中國現代文學思潮，流派的消長 (A brief study of the influence of foreign literature and the growth and decline of intellectual trends and schools in modern Chinese literature). *Tianjin shehui kexue* 天津社會科學 (Tianjin social sciences) 1 (1983). Reprint. In *Xinhua wenzhai* 新華文摘 (New China digest), 7 (1983), pp. 158–160.

This is a study of the different schools of thought and literary writings that were formed in modern China as a result of foreign influence. It tries to explain the formation of schools of thought and literary writings and their decline not only in relation to the changes in the indigenous situation in China, but also in relation to the changes in political and literary discourse in the West. It serves to provide the background for an understanding of the cultural interaction between China and the West, and thus is useful in understanding the background of the Chinese reception of Ibsen.

2.34

Zhao Mingyi 趙銘彝. "Huiyi yishu jushe" 回憶藝術劇社 (A retrospect of the Art Drama Society). *Xinwenxue shiliao* 新文學史料 (Historical sources of new Chinese literature), 6 (1980), pp. 260–263.

"Yishu jushe" (Art drama society) was one of the major drama groups in China in the late 1920s and early 1930s. It had produced many plays that were adapted from foreign drama. In this review, Zhao Mingyi lists the major events and activities of the society that had contributed to the social orientation of the drama movement. The review of the society's activities serves as a case study that illustrates not only the social dimension of modern Chinese drama, but also the social context of how Ibsen has been adapted for Chinese production.

2.35

Zhen Sheng 縝生. "Beijing de jingchating zhen congmin!" 北京的警察廳真聰敏 (How clever the Beijing police!). *Chenbao fukan* 晨報附刊, 20 December 1924, p. 4.

The essay provides very useful information on how Ibsen's *A Doll's House* was experimented with on the Chinese stage in Beijing in the early 1920s. The experiment with *A Doll's House* by the "26 jushe" (26 drama society, so named after the number of its 26 founding members) took place in

1924 in Beijing. Included in the cast were the famous amateur student actress Wu Ruiyan and her male lead Wan Laitian, who played respectively Nora and Krogstad. Their performance was supported by the anti-warlord revolutionaries. Because of the play's revolutionary message, it was interrupted by the police during rehearsals. When the play was staged in YMCA, Beijing on 19 December 1924, the police once more attempted to ban the performance with the excuse that it was immoral to have actresses together with actors on the same stage. Facing protests from the audience, who were mostly university students, the police finally gave in but allowed the performance to go on for only one act. Being different from traditional Chinese drama in structure, *A Doll's House* does not require any change of scenery, and the police did not know where an act ended. Hence, the society was able to rush through all three acts without the notice of the police. However, this performance lasted only one day.

2.36

Zheng Zhenduo 鄭振鐸. "Shijiu shiji Sikande'naweiya wenxue" 十九世紀斯堪的納維亞文學 (Nineteenth-century Scandinavian literature). *Wenxue dagang* 文學大綱 (An outline of literature). vol. 4, pp. 435–454. 1927. Reprint. Hong Kong: Zhongguo wenyi liutongshe 中國文藝流通社, 1956.

An evaluation of Ibsen in the context of world literature is given in Zheng Zhenduo's *Wenxue dagang* (An outline of literature), first published in 1927. Zheng ranks Ibsen as "the greatest European dramatist in the past 150 years. All his contemporaries are no match to him. His place in literary history is comparable to that of Aeschylus, Shakespeare and Corneille." Zheng illustrates the influences Ibsen has exerted upon such dramatists as Strindberg, Hauptmann, and Shaw.

3

Ibsen in the Romantic Generation 1928–1936

3.01

Aas, Lars. "Yibosheng de shiji" 伊孛生的事蹟 (The story of Ibsen). Translated by Mei Chuan 梅川 (Wu Meichuan 吳梅川). *Benliu* 奔流 (The current), 1.3 (August 1928), pp. 347–366.

A major activity in the Ibsen centenary in 1928 appeared in a special issue of *Benliu* (The current) magazine. Under the leadership of Lu Xun and Yu Dafu, chief editors of the magazine, the special issue contains the Chinese translation of Lars Aas's "The Story of Ibsen" among others. Lars Aas's "The Story of Ibsen" was originally published in the London-based English magazine *Bookman* in March 1928, and now translated by (Wu) Mei Chuan, in which he studies Ibsen's life and ascribes Ibsen's views on society to the conditioning effects of the environment in which he grew up.

3.02

Arishima Takeo 有島武郎. "Luboke he yilina de houguo" 盧勃克和伊里納的後果 (What ended up in Rubek and Irene). Translated by Lu Xun 魯迅. *Xiaoshuo yuebao* 小說月報 (*Short Story Magazine*), 19.1 (January 1928), pp. 75–77.

The influential journal *Xiaoshuo yuebao* published in its January number Lu Xun's translation of Arishima Takeo's article: "What Ended Up in Rubek and Irene" (Rubbek to Irine no sonogo). While most other essays on Ibsen during this period are about his life and early works, Arishima Takeo's essay offers an analysis of Ibsen's later plays, which are more important than his early ones. In "What Ended Up in Rubek and Irene," Arishima discusses *When We Dead Awaken* as a projection of Ibsen's inner psyche and his answer to the world, which has been hostile to him all through his life. Arishima offers an alternative to contemporary interpretation of the play as a reflection of the author's psychological disturbances. As Michael Meyer points out, *When We Dead Awaken* is not only Ibsen's most experimental play, but also his final account of himself. Ibsen has portrayed different facets of himself in most of his plays, but none is so complete and merciless a self-portrait as the character of Rubek in *When We Dead Awaken*.

For Lu Xun, the translator and a self-appointed crusader against the evils described by Ibsen, *When We Dead Awaken* is literally an epilogue to Ibsen's dramas and life as a fighter. Lu Xun is rather disappointed with Ibsen's surrender to his enemies: "To battle alone till the end, or to hold out hands of peace to the enemies? Only after a whole life's struggle can this question arise and be answered. Unfortunately, Ibsen's answer is in the latter and thus he tastes the 'sorrows of a victor.'" Lu Xun is apparently dissatisfied with this "dramatic epilogue," by which Ibsen does not, however, mean his final word.

3.03

———. "Yibosheng de gongzuo taidu" 伊孛生的工作態度 (Ibsen's attitude toward his work). Translated by Lu Xun 魯迅. *Benliu* 奔流 (The current), 1.3 (August 1928), pp. 417–430.

Taking a different approach, Arishima Takeo, a Japanese writer and critic, attempts in his essay, "Ibsen's Attitude Toward His Work," to provide a psychological study in the light of Ibsen's reaction to adverse criticism concerning himself and his works. Portrayed as the protagonist in a drama of social attack, Ibsen becomes an isolated but courageous fighter. The six plays he wrote after *A Doll's House* are read by Arishima Takeo as an answer to society as well as an expression of personal anguish, which like a pendulum reaches its full swing in *An Enemy of the People*. With *The Wild Duck* and *The Lady from the Sea*, Ibsen's anger begins to subside. In the opinion of Arishima, Ibsen's solitude constitutes the basis of his later works. Being isolated, misunderstood, and attacked, Ibsen belongs to "the minority" as opposed to "the ignorant majority," who acts merely according to the conventions of society. Arishima believes that it requires great courage and a strong will to remain persistent and to face attacks from all sides, and it is precisely this determined attitude that makes Ibsen a great thinker. The six plays from *A Doll's House* to *The Lady from the Sea*, in Arishima's view, are the six acts of a greater dramatic verse with Ibsen himself as the protagonist. Ibsen invested his years from the age of 51 to 60, that is, the most important and mature period of his life, to the difficult strife for a single theme. It is indeed admirable that Ibsen's daringness in being an extremist persisted ten years.

3.04

Bai Wei 白薇. "Cong Molun zhongxue de youyihui chulai" 從莫倫中學的遊藝會出來 (Coming out of the Molun school fair). *Shenbao* 申報 (Shanghai news), 5 July 1934, p. 19; 6 July 1934, p. 17.

This is a review essay on the performance of Ibsen's *A Doll's House* staged by the Molun School in Shanghai in 1934. In this essay, the author comments on the character of Nora, as well as on the play's message for the women's movement in China. The author Bai Wei is a modern Chinese novelist and her works are full of images of the awakened new women in China.

3.05

Bi Yao 碧遙. "'Weiwei' yu 'Nuola'" "薇薇" 與 "娜拉" (Vivie and Nora). *Funü shenghuo* 婦女生活 (Women's life), 1.2 (August 1935), pp. 16–24.

This is a reading of Nora from the feminist perspective about the tragedy of women who do not have freedom in the quest for personal freedom. The author sees Vivie, the daughter of Mrs. Warren in Shaw's play *Mrs. Warren's Profession*, as a shadow of Nora, and reminds Chinese readers that there is the need to fight for the individual freedom of women. In the mid-1930s there was a revived interest in the theme of equality between men and women in China. Unlike the call for individual freedom for women, which was emphasized as one of the goals of the women's movement in the 1910s and 1920s, China in the 1930s was more concerned with the political orientation of the feminist movement.

3.06

Brandes, Georg. "Henrik Ibsen." Translated by Lin Yutang 林語堂 (Lin Yutang). *Benliu* 奔流 (The current), 1.3 (August 1928), pp. 431–481.

Georg Brandes's authoritative study, "Henrik Ibsen," was translated by Lin Yutang on the basis of Jessie Muir's English version published in 1899. Comprising three impressions of Ibsen recorded respectively in 1867, 1882, and 1898, Brandes's work allows the Chinese reader an overall view of Ibsen's character, ideals, obsessions, and literary pursuits and achievements. His study is much more than a critical biography. It is in actuality a psycho-moral analysis of Ibsen. As the author claims: " (It) was the earliest picture of Ibsen's intellectual personality that had been attempted in Europe." To quote William Archer in his introduction to the book, Brandes's study of Ibsen "might have for its title, not perhaps 'Ibsen Day by Day,' but certainly 'Ibsen Phase by Phase.'" Dealing with Ibsen's works in chronological order, Brandes provides the reader an opportunity to see the dramatist from the perspective of his spiritual development, for Brandes followed "every step of [Ibsen's] development from the moment when his genius attained anything like maturity." The greatest merit of this book, Archer says firmly, is that Brandes "approached the study of the poet's works with a perfectly free mind, neither overawed by a great ready-made reputation, nor wrapped into antagonism by sectarian mispraise." Through a study of Ibsen's plays and life, Brandes offers a complete and thorough portrayal of the dramatist, including his philosophical and moral sources, and literary innovations.

3.07

Cao Juren 曹聚仁. "Nuola chuzou wenti" 娜拉出走問題 (The issue of Nora's leaving). *Shenbao* 申報 (Shanghai news), 28 May 1934, p. 17.

Cao Juren reviews the performance of the play *A Doll's House* in Shanghai in that year and discusses its implication for the movement of women's liberation in China. Cao thinks that the play provides a clear message for the Chinese women, although the question of women's freedom and liberation, as Lu Xun warned in 1923, is not as simple as a matter of leaving one's home.

3.08

———. "Qishi zhong de qishi" 奇事中的奇事 (Miracle of the miracle). *Shenbao* 申報 (Shanghai news), 10 July 1935, p. 5.

This is a review essay on the performance of Ibsen's *A Doll's House* in Shanghai. The year 1935 was named "Year of Nora" in the history of modern Chinese theatre. In this essay, Cao Juren comments on the style of the performance as well as on the message of the play — the need to have an awakening in Helmer, which is a miracle of the miracle that Helmer himself can never understand.

3.09

———. "Zaikan *Nuola*" 再看《娜拉》 (Watching *A Doll's House* the second time). 1934. Reprint. In *Renshi xinyu* 人事新語 (New words on people and events), pp. 270–272. Hong Kong: Yiqun chubanshe 益群出版社, 1963.

Cao Juren reviews the performance of *A Doll's House* in 1934 and discusses its message in a new historical context. He thinks that *A Doll's*

House remains to be a memorable play because it has a rich message which leads to new interpretations in new contexts.

3.10

Chen, David Y. "The Trilogy of Ts'ao Yu and Western Drama." In *Asia and the Humanities*. Edited by Horst Frenz, pp. 26–37. Bloomington: Indiana University Comparative Literature Committee, 1959.

In this study, David Chen shows how Cao Yu is indebted to Ibsen in his play *Leiyu* (Thunderstorm). The beginning of *Leiyu* is so different from traditional Chinese drama in terms of its use of minor characters in the release of information about the protagonists, and it actually signifies the maturation of a modern form in Chinese drama.

3.11

Chen Kangshi 陳康時. "Xiaobona lun funü wenti" 蕭伯納論婦女問題 (Bernard Shaw on the woman issue). *Funü zazhi* 婦女雜誌 (*The Ladies' Journal*), 17.6 (June 1931), pp. 17–24.

In the early 1930s there was a nation-wide debate in China about how Chinese women could be truly liberated. Chen Kangshi's essay is one of those that contributed to the debate. In this essay, Chen summarizes Bernard Shaw's views on women which can be read in relation to the Ibsenian theatre tradition that deals with social-feminist topics.

3.12

Chen Shou-yi. "Hu Shih." *Yearbook of American Philosophical Society* (1962), pp. 135–143.

This is a study of Hu Shi's (Hu Shih) contribution to the "Chinese Renaissance" and his activities during his years as a student in the U.S.A. The information provided in this essay is useful in assessing how Hu Shi re-interpreted Ibsenism and traditional Chinese culture from the 1910s to the 1930s.

3.13

Chen Shouzhu 陳瘦竹. *Xiandai juzuojia sanji* 現代劇作家散記 (Essays on modern dramatists). Nanjing: Jiangsu renmin wenxue chubanshe 江蘇人民文學出版社, 1979.

In this book, there is a section on Ibsen's contribution to modern drama, which is placed in the context of his significance particularly in the first three decades of the twentieth century. In respect of Ibsen's influence in modern Chinese drama, Chen Shouzhu's study is useful in providing a broad perspective on the relation between Ibsen and Chinese drama.

3.14

Chen Xiying 陳西瀅. "Yibusheng de xiju yishu" 易卜生的戲劇藝術 (Ibsen's dramatic art). *Wenzhe jikan* 文哲季刊 (Literature and philosophy quarterly), 1.1 (April 1930), pp. 45–59.

Chen Xiying's essay "Yibusheng de xiju yishu" (Ibsen's dramatic art) is one of the most profound and provocative Chinese analyses of Ibsen's dramas. Putting Ibsen in the cultural context of European literature, Chen reevaluates his art by considering the contributions he made to the establishment of modern drama. He also traces the new elements in Ibsen's plays to Eugène Scribe and Emile Zola. Ibsen, according to Chen, is greater than his predecessors as he has modified and perfected the technique of the well-made play. His social dramas add new life to the well-made play. Illustrating his arguments with textual references from *The Pillars of Society*, *A Doll's House*, and *Ghosts*, Chen provides an excellent analysis of the development in Ibsen's method of playwriting. Nonetheless, contrary to the popular opinion in which *Ghosts* is recognized as Ibsen's greatest work, Chen claims that both *The Wild Duck* and *Rosmersholm* are much superior in regard to technique. He objects to the high opinion that Havelock Ellis and Bjornson have accorded *Ghosts*.

Following William Archer, Chen Xiying employs the dichotomy of external description of events and internal depiction of characters in his study of Ibsen's works. Regarding characterization in terms of psychological interaction as an important quality of modern drama, Chen treats *Rosmersholm* as a pioneering work in the genre of psychological drama. He grants that social plays are great in their treatment of external events and moral issues, but affirms that *Rosmersholm* and *The Wild Duck* are even greater in the direction they provide for the psychological depiction of characters in modern drama. In regard to the development of Ibsen's art, *The Wild Duck* is even more significant than *Rosmersholm*. All the works preceding *The Wild Duck* are structurally of a lineal pattern. There are too many cause-effect relations in the plots, and the endings are too much a culmination of these relations. *The Wild Duck*, however, is much more complex in its plot movement than the others. Giving up the lineal treatment of external events, Ibsen experiments with an intricate pattern involving more than ten major characters.

3.15

Chen Zhice 陳治策. "Yibusheng de *Qungui*" 易卜生的《群鬼》 (Ibsen's *Ghosts*). *Ruihu* 睿湖 (Lake of wisdom), 2 (1930), pp. 31–49.

This article by Chen Zhice can be considered as representative of the studies focusing on the dramatic techniques of Ibsen. Like Hong Shen, Chen Zhice received his education in drama and directing in the United States from 1924 to 1927. In his prologue to the essay, Chen Zhice states that it is comparatively easier to discuss Ibsenism, or Ibsen's ideas, for in so doing all one has to do is to read one of Ibsen's plays and pick out a few key sentences, than to talk about his dramatic techniques, especially those used in *Ghosts*. This is a difficult task, but since Ibsen is a dramatist, Chen Zhice believes that any study should focus on Ibsen's dramatic accomplishments, for only in this way can one do justice to the artist. Chen's statement is a critique of the popular view that Ibsen is a social revolutionist rather than a dramatist. Contrary to other Chinese critics, Chen employs the method of close reading, advocated by the American New Critics, in his analysis of the subtleties in Ibsen's drama. As he points out, Ibsen's success lies foremost in his technical innovations. The essay represents a change in focus from emphasizing Ibsen's social philosophy to an appreciation of his art.

3.16

Cui Wanqiu 崔萬秋. "Shanghai suiyue hua Jiang Qing" 上海歲月話江青 (Jiang Qing in Shanghai). *Baisheng banyuekan* 百姓半月刊 (Baisheng semi-monthly), 16–30 (1 January–16 August 1982), various pagination.

This is a long essay serialized in the Hong Kong magazine about Jiang Qing's life and career in the theatre and film industry in Shanghai in the 1930s. According to Cui Wanqiu, who was a film producer in the 1930s, Jiang Qing played the lead role when *A Doll's House* was staged in Shanghai in 1935. This essay provides very useful historical information on the theatre activities in Shanghai in the 1930s and on the production of *A Doll's House*.

3.17

Eide, Elisabeth. "Ibsen's Nora and Chinese Interpretations of Female Emancipation." In *Modern Chinese Literature and Its Social Context*. Edited by Goran Malmqvist, pp. 140–151. Stockhom: G. Malmqvist, 1977.

In this study the author surveys the various images of Nora-like female characters in modern Chinese fiction, which was used in the 1930s as a means of social debate and ideological portrayals of social life.

3.18

Ellis, Havelock. "Yibosheng lun" 伊孛生論 (Ibsen). Translated by Yu Dafu 郁達夫. *Benliu* 奔流 (The current), 1.3 (August 1928), pp. 367–415.

Yu Dafu's Chinese rendition of Havelock Ellis's "Ibsen" is based on the 1892 Scott Library edition of *The New Spirit*. In his note to the translation, Yu affirms that the essay, though written thirty-six years earlier, is still meaningful to the Chinese reader. It presents a detailed analysis of Ibsen's plays in chronological order, blending biographical information with the artistic traits of the dramatist, thus giving a sense of continuity and development in Ibsen's career. Yu Dafu reminds his readers that Havelock Ellis may have done more justice to Ibsen than many later critics who are influenced by Ibsen's posthumous fame. In 1892, the year the book was written, Ibsen was still a figure of much controversy both in his own country and in England.

3.19

Gao Lei 高磊. "Guanyu Nuola chuzou" 關於娜拉出走 (On Nora's leaving home). *Guowen zhoubao* 國聞週報, 7 May 1934, various pagination.

This is one of the series of essays that appeared in *Guowen zhoubao* in 1934, a year in which there were several stagings of *A Doll's House* in different parts of China, as well as a nation-wide debate on the woman issue that sprang up as a Chinese response to the feminist issues raised in the play. The essay makes a connection between the plight of the Chinese women in the 1930s and that of Nora, and calls for a reconsideration of action with reason.

Gao Lei's essay is an effort to provide a conclusion to the debate in

Guowen zhoubao. Gao thinks that it is more meaningful to study the causes of why Nora, as well as a large number of women, has to leave home than to argue whether or not she should return home. According to Gao, only when the basic cause of the problem is found will the family and social tragedies be solved. Gao's conclusion is that Nora's tragedy has its social causes and Helmer's attitude is a reflection of the values of male-centred society. Hence, according to Gao, it is more urgent to reform society than to seek personal freedom.

3.20

Ge Yihong 葛一虹. "Yibusheng shi lianxi Zhong-Nuo renmin de niudai" 易卜生是聯繫中挪人民的紐帶 (Ibsen: a link between Chinese and Norwegian people). In *Yibusheng yanjiu lunwenji* 易卜生研究論文集 (Ibsen research papers). Edited by Meng Shengde 孟勝德 and Astrid Saether, pp. 18–21; 238–242. Beijing: Zhongguo wenxue chubanshe 中國文學出版社, 1995.

In this essay, Ge Yihong gives a brief summary of the early productions of *A Doll's House* in China. He mentions the staging of the play by the Spring Willow Society in 1914 and by the 26 jushe (26 drama society) in 1926, and also the Year of Nora in 1935.

3.21

Gongsun Meng 公孫萌. "Nuola houhua" 諾拉後話 (An afterword on Nora). *Funü shenghuo* 婦女生活 (Women's life), 1.2 (August 1935), pp. 11–15.

In 1935 there were several stagings of *A Doll's House* in the major cities in China, including Shanghai. This essay is one of the reviews, not only on the performance, but also on a rethinking of the direction of women's liberation in China. By the mid-1930s there was already a view that women's liberation in China had gone too far and had become a fad that lost its real meaning and significance. But in this essay, the author argues that there is the need for Chinese women to seek freedom by leaving home.

3.22

Gu Jianchen 谷劍塵. "Leng fan" 冷飯 (The cold meal). *Zhongguo xinwenxue daxi: 1917–1927* 中國新文學大系 1917–1927 (A comprehensive anthology of modern Chinese literature: 1917–1927). Edited by Zhao Jiabi 趙家壁, vol. 9, pp. 295–309. Shanghai: Liangyou tushu yinshua gongsi 良友圖書印刷公司, 1936.

This short play written by Gu Jianchen in 1923 is a reaction to the fad of imitating Nora by leaving home. It satirizes the "liberated" women by portraying an anti-Nora, who is forgiven by her husband and decides to stay home. Considered in relation to the popular idea of leaving home as a sign of being modern in China in the 1920s, Gu Jianchen's play shows how a male dramatist looks at the issue.

3.23

Guo Fenyang 郭奮揚. "Yibusheng de mingju *Nuola* zai Zhongguo" 易卜生的名劇《娜拉》在中國 (Ibsen's famous play *A Doll's House* in China). *Zhongguo qingnianbao* 中國青年報 (China youth daily), 25 July 1956, p. 3.

This is an essay that recounts the various stage productions of Ibsen's *A Doll's House* in China from the beginning of the century through the 1940s. It gives the historical background about the reception, about how the Chinese looked at the play's message. What is more important in this essay is that it gives information about the stage performance of the play in Shanghai in 1934, in which Jiang Qing played the role of Nora. It also includes part of the programme notes to the 1934 performance of the play so that the views of Jiang Qing and other actors, such as Zhao Dan, are also given as illustration of the Chinese reception of Ibsen.

3.24

Honma Hisao 本間久雄. *Ouzhou jindai wenyi sichao gailun* 歐洲近代文藝思潮概論 (Trends in modern European literature and arts). Translated by Shen Duanxian 沈端先. Shanghai: Kaiming shudian 開明書店, 1928.

This book is a Chinese translation by Shen Duanxian, the dramatist and film director better known as Xia Yan. Affirming that Ibsen is not only a naturalist but also an idealist, Honma Hisao gives an outline of Ibsen's influence in Europe and summarizes his life so that the reader may have an idea of how Ibsen sees the various problems in society through his own experience. Citing Georg Brandes, Honma argues that Ibsen is a pessimist and considers humanity as basically evil. He also asserts that

Ibsen's pessimism is not of a philosophical but a moral nature. He thinks that Ibsen is convinced that human ideals can be realized if not because society is opposed to any change and for that reason Ibsen has developed a pessimism of moral indignation.

Honma puts Ibsen's major plays into the following categories: (1) religion, (2) social classes, (3) conflicts between old and new values, and (4) those between the two sexes. As for Ibsen's attitude towards life, Honma follows Wicksted's *Four Lectures on Ibsen* in demonstrating that Ibsen is a poet of skepticism and that throughout his works there is a tendency to seek a balance between self-realization and self-abnegation. As an illustration of his ideas, Honma provides a detailed analysis of *A Doll's House*, which, according to him, has exerted "great influence not only in Europe, but also in the Orient." (224). Honma Hisao's study of *A Doll's House* is in effect a supplement to the Chinese interpretation of the play as primarily a work of female emancipation from the domination of men. Honma stresses that the emancipation of women is related to the progress of mankind and that Ibsen is not a feminist at all. Quoting from Edmund Gosse's biography of Ibsen, Honma hints that Ibsen is sometimes a woman-hater.

3.25

Hu Shuhuo 胡叔和. "Cao Yu pingzhuan" 曹禺評傳 (A critical biography of Cao Yu). *Xiju yanjiu* 戲劇研究 (Studies on drama), 3 (1982), pp. 30–40.

This is a critical study of the Chinese dramatist Cao Yu's career in relation to the development of modern drama in China. In this study, there is information on how Cao Yu was inspired by his teachers at Nankai University and began to read Ibsen and Greek tragedy in his early career.

3.26

Ikuta Koji 生田長江 and Honma Hisao 本間久雄. *Shehui gaizao zhi bada sixiangjia* 社會改造之八大思想家 (Eight great theorists of social reformation). Translated by Lin Ben 林本, Mao Yongtang 毛詠棠 and Li Zongwu 李宗武. Shanghai: Shangwu yinshuguan 商務印書館, 1935.

An inquiry into Ibsen's social philosophy can be found in the Japanese critics Ikuta Koji and Honma Hisao's co-authored essay "Ibsen" (Ibusen), which is a chapter in the book *Shaki kaizo no hachidai shisoka* (Eight great theorists of social reformation) and was translated jointly into Chinese by Lin Ben, Mao Yongtang, and Li Zongwu in 1921. In this book there is a chapter on Ibsen, ranking him as a social theorist together with Karl Marx, Peter Kropotkin, Bertrand Russell, Leo Tolstoy, William Morris, Edward Carpenter, and Ellen Key. The Ibsen chapter in the book consists of six sections each dealing with a topic on the dramatist's life, major characteristics of his plays, his problem plays, his uncompromising ideal of "All or Nothing," the idea of the "Third Empire," and the women's issue. Drawing sources from Brandes and Wicksted, Ikuta and Honma present Ibsen as a fighter against social evils as well as an idealist in the pursuit of perfection. Ikuta and Honma are especially interested in Ibsen's contribution to the movement of women's emancipation: "Since John Stuart Mill, there are many people who have contributed greatly to the women's movement, but Ibsen's plays can be considered as the most important in terms of the emotional impact they have exerted on women." To illustrate Ibsen's iconoclasm, Ikuta and Honma discuss *A Doll's House* in great detail in the chapter.

3.27

Jiao Juyin 焦菊隱. "Lun Yibusheng" 論易卜生 (On Ibsen). *Chenbao fukan* 晨報附刊, 20–28 March 1928, various pagination.

Jiao Juyin's essay "Lun Yibusheng" (On Ibsen), a newspaper article subtitled "In Celebration of Ibsen's Centenary," consists of eight parts, covering Ibsen's Scandinavian background, biography, plays, and ideological inclinations. Comparing Ibsen with his Norwegian contemporaries, such as Bjornson, Jiao affirms that Ibsen is greater than them and that his success and popularity all over the world are due to the universal significance of his plays. Jiao follows Janko Lavrin, Bernard Shaw, and William Archer and stresses in his article the philosophical, artistic, and satiric aspects of Ibsen's drama. Discarding the prevailing dichotomy of treating Ibsen as an artist opposed to a social rebel, Jiao borrows from Janko Lavrin the notion of synthesis, affirming that Ibsen began as a social philosopher and ended up as an artist in his approach to drama. In terms of dramatic art, Jiao regards Ibsen as a master who contributes to the perfection of realism as a dramatic technique in his problem plays, in which there is an effort to present the social issues rather than to provide a solution for them. According to Jiao, Ibsen as a thinker wrote his plays as an emotional relief of his own personal obsessions. Jiao recapitulates the social evils rooted in the family, law, religion, traditional morals, and society, which have been treated earlier in Hu Shi's essay "Ibsenism," as a necessary part of Ibsen's views upon human civilization.

Jiao is particularly worried about the Chinese view considering Ibsen merely as a thinker, and he thinks that although China needs thinkers, art is also important and useful. Jiao suggests that the choice of art works for introduction to China should not take on the Soviet policy of rejecting foreign works because of their dissident views. One does not deny a person's art because one denies his thought. By the same token, one does not accept a person's view simply because of his art. Whether or not Ibsen's philosophy is needed in China, Jiao thinks that he cannot tell. At least he concludes that China in his time did not need egotism. As for individualism, Jiao claims that it is beneficial to Chinese society because "it means exactly the spiritual liberation and purification of the self. In China, there are many people who have lost their souls. Without a spirit, there cannot be a liberation, a purification of the self." Like Hu Shi, Jiao advocates individualism as a means to save the Chinese people from the illness of lacking a consciousness of the self.

3.28

Jin Zhonghua 金仲華. "Jinshi funü jiefang yundong zai wenxue shang de fanying" 近世婦女解放運動在文學上的反映 (Reflections of modern women's liberation movement in literature). *Funü zazhi* 婦女雜誌 (*The Ladies' Journal*), 17.7 (1 July 1931), pp. 2–13.

In this essay, there is a review on how women and the movement of women's liberation are represented in modern literature. The essay was meant to be a contribution to the debate on the issue of women's liberation in China in a nation-wide context in the early 1930s. Ibsen's plays, as well as the literary works by other Western and Chinese writers, become a focus in the review, thus making a connection between the images of literary representation and the social dimension of cultural production.

3.29

Jing Yun 景雲. "Zhongguo diyige xiju zazhi — Jieshao *Ershi shiji dawutai*" 中國第一個戲劇雜誌 —— 介紹《二十世紀大舞台》(China's first theatre magazine: *Twentieth Century Grand Theatre*). *Xiju luncong* 戲劇論叢 (Theatre studies), 2 (1958), pp. 222–223.

The essay provides historical information on theatre studies as well as on the contribution of the magazine *Twentieth Century Grand Theatre* to the development of modern Chinese theatre in Shanghai in the 1930s. In this essay the historical conditions under which the modern Chinese theatre developed are reviewed. It is a useful essay in understanding the theatre culture in Shanghai, and it provides an indispensable perspective in contextualizing the reception of Ibsen in China.

3.30

Juan Bing 鋗冰. "Nuola zouhou jiujing zenyang" 娜拉走後究竟怎樣 (What really happens to Nora after she leaves home). *Guowen zhoubao* 國聞週報, 19 March 1934, various pagination.

A further discussion of the plight of Chinese women in the 1930s, the essay reviews the situation of the Chinese women and the changes in Chinese society since the 1920s when Ibsen was introduced and *A Doll's House* was performed that led to the awakening of Chinese women to their rights. This essay was one of the many contributions to the nationwide debate on women's liberation in the 1930s.

3.31

Lavrin, Janko. "Yibusheng yu Xiaobona" 易卜生與蕭伯納 (Ibsen and Shaw). Translated by Zhang Menglin 張夢麟. *Xiandai xuesheng* 現代學生 (Modern student), 1.8 (1931), pp. 1–10; 1.9 (1931), pp. 1–12.

Zhang Menglin translated Janko Lavrin's "Ibsen and Shaw" and serialized it in the magazine *Modern Student*. The essay is originally a chapter of the book, *Studies in European Literature*, pp. 80–98 (London: Constable & Co. Ltd., 1929). Lavrin gives an illuminating study of Ibsen by contrasting him with Shaw. The latter is often treated as a disciple of the former. But with regard to their temperament, artistic concerns, and psychology, Lavrin shows that there are a number of fundamental differences. Ibsen is a moral idealist and his works are in one sense a representation of the conflicts between his ideals and the reality in which he lived. Lavrin affirms that Ibsen writes from an inner inevitability, which is the chief incentive of his works. His own spiritual fighting and experience, which he tries to embody in his plays, are the real cause. Without this urge he probably could not have created any of his plays, because he is "the very antithesis of a professional *litterateur*" (cited by Zhang Menglin from the original in Janko Lavrin's *Studies in European Literature*, p. 83). For Lavrin, what makes Ibsen different from his contemporaries in the nineteenth century is that he does not have religion as a last resort in his moral struggle. Without such a belief, all evils of life, for Ibsen, become the responsibility of the individual. Ibsen's uncompromising principle of "all-or-nothing" is an attempt at seeking the support of religion as "the ultimate justification of his own moral sense."

Lavrin's remarks were especially useful to Chinese critics and readers alike in the 1930s, who were experiencing a new form of drama different from their own tradition. In fact, to understand the idea of a play, for the average Chinese reader, is less difficult than to grasp the technique of a completely foreign literary genre. There are universal elements in themes and social problems, but much less of the universal is to be found in the technique and mode of presentation. Actually the most critical issue in the development of modern Chinese drama in the 1920s and 1930s was to find a breakthrough in technique. Hence, studies of Ibsen's dramatic techniques were particularly helpful to the experimental playwrights.

3.32

Li Hui 李輝 et al., eds. *Zhongguo xiandai xiju dianying yishujia zhuan* 中國現代戲劇電影藝術家傳 (Biographies of modern Chinese dramatists and film-makers). Nanchang: Jiangxi renmin chubanshe 江西人民出版社, 1981.

This book contains the biographical sketches of major modern Chinese dramatists and film-makers. Many of the modern Chinese film-makers were originally dramatists or actors, such as Zhao Dan and Xia Yan, who were involved in the production of Ibsen's plays. The book serves as a useful reference on the biographical and historical background for an understanding of the relation between film and theatre in modern China.

3.33

Li Xitong 李希同. *Bing Xin lun* 冰心論 (A study of Bing Xin). Shanghai: Beixin shuju 北新書局, 1932.

The book focuses on the achievements of the modern Chinese woman writer Bing Xin, but it also gives useful information on how she has been indebted to Ibsen in the early stage of her career, especially on the influence of feminist ideas in her works.

3.34

Lin Yutang 林語堂. *Yibusheng zhuan ji qi qingshu* 易卜生傳及其情書 (Ibsen's biography and love letters). Shanghai: Chunchao shuju 春潮書局, 1929.

In the years following Ibsen's birth centenary in 1928, many more studies on the dramatist appeared. In 1929 Lin Yutang translated Ibsen's love letters to Emilie Bardach and published them together with his translation of Georg Brandes's essay "Henrik Ibsen" under the Chinese title, *Yibusheng zhuan ji qi qingshu* (Ibsen's biography and love letters). This is the first Chinese translation of the letters, giving readers a glimpse of the private life of Ibsen.

3.35

Liu Baiqing 劉柏青. "Sanshi niandai zuoyi wenyi suoshou Riben wuchan jieji wenyi sichao de yingxiang" 三十年代左翼文藝所受日本無產階級文藝思潮的影響 (The influence of Japanese proletarian writers on Chinese left-wing literature in the 1930s). *Wenxue pinglun* 文學評論 (Literary review), 6 (1981), pp. 102–109.

The article provides an important source on the development of left-wing literature in China in the 1930s. Readers will thus find that Ibsen is not the only source for the development of social problem literature in China. Actually it is partly through the Japanese critics that proletarian literature was introduced to China.

3.36

Liu Dajie 劉大杰. *Yibusheng yanjiu* 易卜生研究 (A study of Henrik Ibsen). Shanghai: Shangwu yinshuguan 商務印書館, 1928.

A special contribution to the Ibsen centenary is Liu Dajie's *A study of Henrik Ibsen*, which is the first book published by a Chinese author on the dramatist. The book was partly written during Liu's stay in Japan and finally published in 1928. Divided into five chapters and with two appendices, it deals with Ibsen's life and his works, philosophy, and influence. The last chapter is devoted to Bjornson, for Liu thinks that it is impossible to treat Ibsen apart from his relations with Bjornson. In the biographical part, Liu meticulously gives interesting minor details and little anecdotes to illustrate the shaping of Ibsen's personality.

In discussing Ibsen's plays, Liu Dajie follows the usual tripartite scheme in grouping the works into the romantic, realistic, and symbolist. Liu's classification betrays the fact that he might not have read all of Ibsen's plays. Considering that in 1928 there was still no complete translation of Ibsen's works in China, Liu's inaccuracies are more a matter of carelessness than misinterpretation. As a supplement to his own interpretation, Liu includes in his book Hu Shi's essay, "Ibsenism," which though written ten years earlier, remains authoritative. Once again, Liu's study of Ibsen offers Chinese readers a moral interpretation, which prevailed in both China and Japan in the 1920s and 1930s.

3.37

Lu Gong 路工. "*Leiyu* zhiqian — Fang zhuming juzuojia Cao Yu tongzhi" 《雷雨》之前 —— 訪著名劇作家曹禺同志 (Before *Thunderstorm* — An interview with the famous playwright comrade Cao Yu). *Jutan* 劇壇 (Theatre), 1 (November 1981), pp. 6–9.

Cao Yu's play *Thunderstorm* is noted for its indebtedness to Ibsen's *Ghosts* in terms of its technique of characterization and plot design. This interview of Cao Yu focuses on how Cao Yu became interested in Western drama and in Ibsen while he was a student in Nankai University. The essay provides biographical information on Cao Yu, so that the influence of Ibsen on Cao Yu can be seen in the context of modern Chinese history.

3.38

Lu Xun 魯迅. "On Women's Liberation." *Chinese Literature*, 9 (1973), pp. 30–32.

This is an English translation of Lu Xun's essay that was first published in the 1920s, in which Lu Xun expressed his reservation about many women's decision to leave home without having any guarantee for financial independence.

3.39

———. "Regret for the Past." *Chinese Literature*, 9 (1973), pp. 3–22.

This is an English translation of Lu Xun's story "Shang shi," in which there is the portrayal of a young Chinese woman inspired by Ibsen and other Western writers to leave home and seek freedom in marriage and life. However, both she and her young lover have to suffer as a result of the lack of financial means for independence.

3.40

———. "What Happens After Nora Leaves Home?" *Chinese Literature*, 9 (1973), pp. 23–29.

This is an English translation of Lu Xun's essay by the same title that was delivered to the Peking Normal College for Women in 1923. In this essay, Lu Xun warns the enlightened Chinese women that it is important to achieve economic independence before they decide to leave home.

3.41

Lü Huang 吕璜. "Mao Dun yu Wu Si shiqi funü jiefang yundong" 茅盾與五四時期婦女解放運動 (Mao Dun and the woman's liberation movement in the May 4th era). *Zhongguo funü* 中國婦女 (Chinese women), 5 (1981), pp. 10–11.

Mao Dun is noted for his early fictional writings on modern Chinese women and their search for liberation and freedom in marriage, particularly in the novels *Hong* (Rainbow) and *Shi* (Eclipse), in which there is representation of female characters under Ibsen's influence. As one of the intellectual leaders of women's liberation, Mao Dun, together with Lu Xun and some other modern Chinese writers, has written voluminous writings (essays, short stories and novels) that attempt to search for a direction in the social and personal liberation for women. This essay shows how Mao Dun has contributed to the movement of women's liberation through his writings.

3.42

Mao Dun 茅盾. "Yibusheng de *Nuola*" 易卜生的《娜拉》 (Ibsen's *A Doll's House*). In *Hanyi xiyang wenxue mingzhu* 漢譯西洋文學名著 (Chinese translations of famous western literary works). 1936. Reprint. *Shijie wenxue mingzhu zatan* 世界文學名著雜談 (Discussions of world literary masterpieces), pp. 381–384. Tianjin: Baihua wenyi chubanshe 百花文藝出版社, 1980.

In this essay, Mao Dun discusses *A Doll's House* as a feminist work, which is a view that gained widespread influence in China in the 1930s. From this essay one can see not only the historical context of the reception of Ibsen, but also the social movement that has given Ibsen such an important place in the cultural transformation of modern China.

3.43

Nie Gannu 聶紺弩. "Tan *Nuola*" 談《娜拉》 (On *A Doll's House*). 1935. Reprint. In *Nie Gannu zawenji* 聶紺弩雜文集 (Collected essays by Nie Gannu), pp. 85–88. Beijing: Sanlian shudian 三聯書店, 1981.

This is an essay written by Nie Gannu in 1935 and reprinted in 1981, in which *A Doll's House* is discussed as a social problem play that has important implications for the women's movement in China. As a social and cultural critic, Nie Gannu highlights the feminist theme in the play as a direction for China's cultural change. The debate on the future of Nora was a striking event in China in 1934 and 1935. It served in effect as a re-evaluation of the Chinese women's liberation in the sixteen years since 1918. Lu Xun's prediction in 1923 that the lack of economic independence is a major obstacle to women's liberation is echoed in this essay, which shows doubt on how women can achieve freedom and independence.

3.44

Roberts, R. Ellis. "Henrik Ibsen." Translated by Mei Chuan 梅川 (Wu Meichuan 吳梅川). *Benliu* 奔流 (The current), 1.3 (August 1928), pp. 483–494.

R. Ellis Roberts's "Henrik Ibsen" was originally published in the London-based English magazine *Bookman* in March 1928. In one sense, Mei Chuan's (pen-name of Wu Meichuan) Chinese translation was meant to relocate the celebration of Ibsen from London to Shanghai. Roberts analyzes the cold reception of Ibsen in England and points out why his attack on falsehood was not accepted with the same zeal people showed for Shakespeare. Why did the situation in *Ghosts* seem so much more terrible to the London audience than that in Shakespeare's *Measure for Measure*? Why would *Hedda Gabler* appear heartless to the Londoners, who were familiar with Iago and Lady Macbeth? Roberts's answer is that Shakespeare presents only historical figures, who lived in the remotely dead past, but Ibsen's prose plays shocked Europe with live people on the stage. Ibsen was "too hard, too certain, too religious for an age" which was "soft, vague, and frivolious." To the people in London, Ibsen was a bleak author. The realistic effect in Ibsen's plays and the use of ordinary speech make everything on the stage seem too real and contemporaneous to the audience, whereas Shakespeare's plays are presented in poetry, which has an effect that can distance the immediacy of experience. Although Roberts is referring to the situation in England, his explanations, as the editor Lu Xun notes, may also apply to China. In other words, China in 1928 was also too "soft and vague and frivolous" to appreciate the hard facts presented in Ibsen's plays.

3.45

Ross, Terril. *The White-boned Demon: A Biography of Madame Mao Zedong*. New York: William Morrow and Company, 1984.

Information can be found in this book about Jiang Qing's role in the 1934 performance of *A Doll's House* in Shanghai. The information given in this book is that the play was performed in 1935, but actually the play was staged in both 1934 and 1935 (for details, see Kwok-kan Tam, "The Shanghai Performance of *A Doll's House* and the Mystery of Jiang Qing's Role in the Stage Production and in the Revolution: A Research Note and Review," 3.50 below).

3.46

Schwarcz, Vera. "Ibsen's Nora: The Promise and the Trap." *Bulletin of Concerned Asian Scholars*, 7.1 (Janurary–March 1975), pp. 3–5.

The focus of this essay is not placed on the historical reception of Ibsen in China, but on the issues of promise and trap that were discussed in the debates on female liberation published in *Guowen zhoubao* in 1934 and 1935.

3.47

Shi Meng 時萌. *Wen Yiduo Zhu Ziqing lun* 聞一多朱自清論 (An essay on

Wen Yiduo and Zhu Ziqing). Shanghai: Shanghai wenyi chubanshe 上海文藝出版社, 1982.

Although the essay is not a study of the reception of Ibsen in China, it provides useful information on the life of the Chinese Ibsen critic Wen Yiduo, who is noted for his attack on the superficial imitation of Ibsen in China in the 1930s and also for his critique of the Chinese social problem play.

3.48

Sichuan daxue zhongwenxi 四川大學中文系, ed. *Cao Yu zhuanji* 曹禺專集 (Special studies on Cao Yu), 2 vols. Chengdu: Sichuan daxue zhongwenxi 四川大學中文系, 1979.

This is a collection of studies on Cao Yu's life as well as his career as a modern Chinese dramatist, who has been so greatly influenced by Ibsen. All the major critical and biographical studies of Cao Yu since the 1940s are included in this book.

3.49

Song Chunfang 宋春舫 (Soong Chun-fang). *Song Chunfang lunju* 宋春舫論劇 (Song Chunfang on drama). Shanghai: Zhonghua shuju 中華書局, 1930.

This is a collection of the critical essays Song Chunfang wrote on modern Chinese and Western drama. In this collection, readers will see how modern Western drama is received by a Chinese critic, as well as how a Western-educated Chinese critic looks at Chinese drama. It provides information on how Ibsen was received among other Western playwrights introduced to China in the early twentieth century.

3.50

Tam, Kwok-kan (Tan Guogen 譚國根). "The Shanghai Performance of *A Doll's House* and the Mystery of Jiang Qing's Role in the Stage Production and in the Revolution: A Research Note and Review." *Journal of Oriental Studies*, 25.2 (1987), pp. 197–201.

This a review article on various biographies of Jiang Qing and on her role in the performances of *A Doll's House* in Shanghai in the 1930s. It compares the various biographies and essays by Terrill Ross, Roxanne Witke, Zhao Dan, Cao Juren for information about the performances.

3.51

Tan Guogen 譚國根 (Kwok-kan Tam). "Hou Wu Si huaiyi zhuyi yu Zhongguo xiandai wenxue de xiandaixing" 後五四懷疑主義與現代中國文學的現代性 (Post-May 4th skepticism and the modernity of modern Chinese literature). In *Xiandai yu duoyuan* 現代與多元 (Modernity and plurality). Edited by Zhou Yingxiong 周英雄 (Chou Ying-hsiung), pp. 155–170. Taipei: Dongda tushu gongsi 東大圖書公司, 1996.

In this article, the author identifies a strong sense of skepticism and pluralism in modern Chinese literature as a marker of modernity and discusses it in relation to the quest for a new subjectivity in modern China. The adoption of the Ibsenian technique of the "discussion scene," which offers no resolution to the dramatic conflicts, by playwrights from Guo Moruo to Tian Han is cited to illustrate the dilemma faced by Chinese intellectuals in the late 1920s and early 1930s.

3.52

———. "*Wan'ou zhi jia* yu Zhongguo erling niandai shehui wenti ju" 《玩偶之家》與中國20年代社會問題劇 (*A Doll's House* and the Chinese problem play in the 1920s). In *Mingjia lun xue* 名家論學 (Scholars on scholarship). Edited by Zong Tinghu 宗廷虎, pp. 260–269. Shanghai: Fudan daxue chubanshe 復旦大學出版社, 1988. Reprint. *Zhongguo huaju yanjiu* 中國話劇研究, 7 (1993), pp. 27–35.

A study of the Chinese reception of Ibsen in the 1920s, this essay identifies the emergence of the problem play as a dramatic genre which is indebted to the influence of Ibsen. The major playwrights of the genre who are influenced by Ibsen are discussed in the context of social change in China. At the same time, the essay also points out the artistic pitfalls of the genre.

3.53

Tian Benxiang 田本相. "Shilun xifang xiandaipai xiju dui Zhongguo xiandai huaju fazhan zhi yingxiang" 試論西方現代派戲劇對中國現代話劇發展之影響 (A preliminary study of the influence of Western modernist drama on the development of modern Chinese drama). *Nankai xuebao* 南開學報 (Nankai university journal), 2 (1983), pp. 23–34.

In this article, Tian surveys the influence of Western modernist drama on the development of modern Chinese drama. For a long time before 1979, Western modernist drama was seen as reactionary and harmful to socialist drama. But with Tian's re-assertion of the value of Western modernist drama, Chinese dramatists began in the early 1980s to appreciate the new forms of expression beyond the realistic mode. It is in this new perspective that Ibsen has been reinterpreted in China since the 1980s.

3.54

Tian Han 田漢. *Tian Han juzuoxuan* 田漢劇作選 (Selected plays by Tian Han). Beijing: Renmin wenxue chubanshe 人民文學出版社, 1981.

In this collection, many of Tian Han's early major plays are included, such as *Huo hu zhi ye* (The night a tiger was caught) and *Nan gui* (Return to the south), in which there is clear influence from Ibsen. Tian Han is one of the earliest modern Chinese playwrights who has expressed the wish to become a "budding Ibsen in China," and in his early plays, there is adaptation from Ibsen's *The Lady from the Sea*.

3.55

———. *Tian Han sanwenji* 田漢散文集 (Prose writings by Tian Han). Shanghai: Jindai shudian 今代書店, 1936.

This book includes many of the early writings by Tian Han, from which the reader can see how he interprets Ibsen as well as his own role as a playwright in China. The writings supply useful biographical information on how Tian Han looks at Ibsen and how Ibsen possibly has influenced him in his creative works.

3.56

———. *Yinse de meng* 銀色的夢 (The silvery dream). Shanghai: Liangyou tushu yinshua gongsi 良友圖書印刷公司, 1928.

This book contains important biographical information on how Tian Han began his career as a dramatist and how his dramatic works are related to his personal experience. As Tian Han is one of the modern Chinese dramatists who have been greatly influenced by Ibsen, it is useful to see how modern Chinese drama has developed as a result of changes in society and in a person's experience.

3.57

Tung, Constantine. "T'ien Han and the Romantic Ibsen." *Modern Drama*, 9.4 (February 1967), pp. 389–395.

This article studies how Tian Han (T'ien Han) came into contact with the plays of Ibsen during his sojourn in Japan, and how he in his correspondence with his friends, Guo Moruo and Zong Baihua, shows his admiration for the romantic Ibsen by calling himself "a budding Ibsen in China."

3.58

Wang Yiren 王以仁. "Guo Moruo de xiju" 郭沫若的戲劇 (The plays of Guo Moruo). In *Guo Moruo lun* 郭沫若論 (A study of Guo Moruo). Edited by Huang Renying 黃人影, pp. 55–79. Shanghai: Daguang chubanshe 大光出版社, 1936.

In this essay, Wang Yiren criticizes Guo Moruo for adapting Ibsen's revolutionary themes at the expense of his dramatic art. According to Wang Yiren, Guo Moruo's historical plays, which are made up merely of revolutionary slogans but became very influential in the 1920s, provide poor examples of drama for the development of the social problem play in China.

3.59

Wen Gan 文幹. "Cong Yibusheng de *Nuola* shuodao Zhongguo funü yundong" 從易卜生的《娜拉》說到中國婦女運動 (From Ibsen's *A Doll's House* to Chinese women's movement). *Nüzi yuekan* 女子月刊 (Women's monthly), 2.10 (October 1934), pp. 2946–2950.

The essay gives an account of how the Chinese women's movement in the 1920s and 1930s was indebted to the influence of Ibsen's *A Doll's House*. It discusses the play as an embodiment of individualistic ideas for the liberation of women. The widespread social and political influence of Ibsen as a movement in China can be seen in the information given in this essay.

Holding a revolutionary view, Wen Gan thinks that the Nora issue is a social issue. With regard to the social and political situation of China in the mid-1930s, he thinks that women should strive for liberation in society as a whole rather than just at home. His essay is a re-affirmation of the positive influence Nora has exerted upon Chinese women.

3.60

Wen Wan 文宛. "Du 'Nuola zouhou jiujing zenyang' hou" 讀〈娜拉走後究竟怎樣〉後 (After reading "What really happens to Nora after she leaves home?"). *Guowen zhoubao* 國聞週報, 9 April 1934, various pagination.

In the 1930s *Guowen zhoubao* published a series of debates on Ibsen's impact upon the women's movement in China. Wen Wan's essay is a response to Juan Bing's essay (see 3.30) and to Lu Xun's speech delivered to the Peking Normal College for Women in 1923, entitled "What Happens After Nora Leaves Home?" In this essay, Wen Wan reaffirms the need for Chinese women in the 1930s to achieve economic independence before they decide to leave home and seek their personal independence.

3.61

Wen Yiduo 聞一多. "Xiju de qitu" 戲劇的歧途 (A problematic development in drama). *Chenbao fukan* 晨報附刊, 24 June 1926, pp. 5–6. Reprint. In *Wen Yiduo quanji* 聞一多全集 (Complete works of Wen Yiduo), vol. 3, pp. 437–440. Beijing: Sanlian shudian 三聯書店, 1982.

Wen Yiduo, a noted and well-respected modern Chinese critic and scholar who received art education in the United States, criticizes the development of modern Chinese drama in the 1930s for its emphasis on the mode of the social problem play, which deviates from the original form advocated by Ibsen. The large number of social problem plays produced in China in the 1920s and 1930s in the style of Guo Moruo's propaganda plays are considered by Wen Yiduo as empty slogans.

3.62

Witke, Roxanne. *Comrade Chiang Ch'ing*. London: Weidenfeld and Nicolson, 1977.

Information about Jiang Qing's (Chiang Ch'ing) life in Shanghai in the 1930s and her involvement in the performance of *A Doll's House* can be found in this book. Unfortunately, since most of the information for the book was provided by Jiang Qing, the part on her role in *A Doll's House* has been proved to be unreliable.

3.63

Wu Yun 吳雲. *Jindai wenxue ABC* 近代文學ABC (The ABC of modern literature). Shanghai: Shijie shuju 世界書局, 1928. Reprint. 1929.

In this book, there is a chapter on the woman issue in modern literature, in which the author cites Ibsen and his plays as examples in the discussion of the feminist movement in Europe. A long section from *A Doll's House* is cited to illustrate the theme of a woman's rights in pursuit of her own freedom and education.

3.64

Xi Di 西諦 (Zheng Zhenduo 鄭振鐸). "Xiandai de Sikande'naweiya wenxue" 現代的斯堪的納維亞文學 (Modern Scandinavian literature). *Xiaoshuo yuebao* 小說月報 (*Short Story Magazine*), 20.8 (1929), pp. 1281–1308.

This is a survey of modern Scandinavian literature, in which Ibsen is considered one of the major authors. Ibsen's contribution to the modern development of Scandinavian literature is highlighted and discussed with regard to his techniques of playwriting. The four social problem plays, *A Doll's House, Ghosts, The Pillar of Society* and *An Enemy of the People*, are considered as significant contributions to modern European drama.

3.65

Xia Yingzhe 夏英喆. "Lixiang zhong de Nuola" 理想中的娜拉 (My ideal Nora). *Guowen zhoubao* 國聞週報, 16 April 1934, various pagination.

Instead of focusing on what Nora should be in the play, the author of this essay discusses how the Chinese in the 1930s should interpret Nora. The "ideal Nora" is the author's projection of an ideal heroine and an ideal image of Chinese women. Putting the essay in the context of the nationwide debates on the image of Nora, the reader will see its impact upon Chinese women's movement in the 1930s.

In Xia Yingzhe's essay, "My Ideal Nora," there is a suggestion on how Chinese Noras could preserve their own individuality after entering society. Xia proposes that Chinese women, the ideal Noras, should be healthy, independent personalities with an iron will, critical ability and at least the minimal knowledge and skill to earn a living. They would return home only if their husbands agreed that they were mistresses of the family. If they could not bear loneliness in society and had to remarry, they should also keep themselves in the position of a mistress, sharing the obligations and duties. As human beings, women have the right to do what they are entitled to, and society, family and husbands should recognize their existence. This is psychologically a thorough reform rather than something forced on men. The husband should not treat his wife as a puppet, and she should also not take herself as such. Even though the family might not be perfect, Xia believes that it is at least a really happy one. Xia thus asks: "Is it not much better to change Nora's family status by a practical psychological reform in both men and women than by restraining herself at home?"

3.66

Xian 嫻 . "Chongdu *Nuola* yihou" 重讀《娜拉》以後 (After rereading *A Doll's House*). *Shenbao* 申報 (Shanghai news), 12 August 1934, p. 17.

Similar to the many essays that appeared in *Guowen zhoubao* in the year 1934, this essay by Xian also reconsiders the political and economic implications of Nora's act of leaving home at the end of the play. It reasserts the need for Chinese women in the 1930s to fight for economic independence in order to achieve real liberation.

3.67

Xiong Foxi 熊佛西. "Lun *Qungui*" 論《群鬼》 (On *Ghosts*). *Tianjin yishibao* 天津益世報, 24 December 1929. Reprint. In *Foxi lunju* 佛西論劇 (Foxi on drama), pp. 123–133. Shanghai: Xinyue shudian 新月書店, 1931.

A noted modern Chinese dramatist and scholar, Xiong Foxi published many essays and books on drama in the 1930s. This essay collected in his book, *Foxi lunju*, is a study of the technical aspects of Ibsen's *Ghosts*. In this study, Xiong Foxi comments both on the thematic relation between the play and *A Doll's House* and on the play's techniques, especially on its opening scene, in the use of minor characters to introduce the protagonists. This is considered by Xiong Foxi as a well-controlled technique in the release of plot information and in the creation of suspense.

Different from many dramatists and critics, Xiong Foxi thinks that emphasis should be put on the technical aspect of drama.

3.68

———. "Shehui gaizaojia de Yibusheng yu xijujia de Yibusheng" 社會改造家的易卜生與戲劇家的易卜生 (Ibsen the social reformer and Ibsen the dramatist). *Tianjin yishibao* 天津益世報, 21 December 1929. Reprint. In *Foxi lunju* 佛西論劇 (Foxi on drama), pp. 115–121. Shanghai: Xinyue shudian 新月書店, 1931.

It was to combat the trend of emphasizing the social ideas of Ibsen at the expense of his art that Xiong Foxi, dramatist and director, published this essay. In his words, "Ibsen's influence in China is great, but a large part of it belongs to philosophy and social reform…. I strongly believe that our youth have been greatly influenced by Ibsen…. Now we have to consider him as a dramatist." Xiong is more concerned with Ibsen's art than with his philosophy. In this essay, he summarizes Ibsen's greatness in three aspects. Firstly, Ibsen introduces ordinary people in his drama as protagonists. Secondly, he has perfected the well-made play and invented the retrospective method in psychological exposition. Thirdly, he has demonstrated that prose dialogue is a powerful means to express the thoughts of the characters. Xiong has good reason for expressing such opinions, for most other critics tend to neglect Ibsen's achievement as a dramatist, mainly because of the shocking effects in his social plays.

3.69

Xu Gongmei 徐公美. *Xiju duanlun* 戲劇短論 (Essays on drama). Shanghai: Daguang shuju 大光書局, 1936.

Xu Gongmei's book *Xiju duanlun*, containing a long appendix on Ibsen, provides the Chinese reader with a detailed study of his plays. The appendix consists of a brief biography and synopses written by the Japanese critic Miyamori Asataro on *A Doll's House*, *Ghosts*, *An Enemy of the People*, *The Master Builder*, *The Lady from the Sea*, and *The Pillars of Society* (Miyamori Asataro, "Kindageki taikan" (An outline of modern drama), in Xu Gongmei's *Xiju duanlun* (Essays on drama), pp. 56–57). Although the part on Ibsen is an appendix, it is longer than the main body of the book. As a teacher in the Shanghai Minxin Yingxi Zhuanmen Xuexiao (Shanghai people's new school of drama and film), Xu Gongmei was enthusiastic in promoting Western-style drama in China. In one of the essays collected in the book, "Why Do We Have to Stage Western Plays?" Xu argues that it is because there are not enough good Chinese plays to be put on the stage. Furthermore, he believes that as members of the human race, both Westerners and Chinese share some common qualities. He affirms that the Chinese can also understand Western plays so long as they are not too abstract and difficult.

Miyamori's study of Ibsen is insightful in many ways. Based on English sources for his study, he argues that it is impossible for a critic to learn all languages of the world in order to study world drama. It is, of course, desirable to read Ibsen in Danish, but it is less risky for one who cannot master Danish to read a faithful translation, such as that by William Archer, than to speculate on the original. Actually, William Archer's version of Ibsen's plays has been the most authoritative in China and Japan. To a large extent, Miyamori's attitude reflects the consensus of many Chinese Ibsen critics. In the biographical part, Miyamori summarizes Ibsen's literary career and presents in a chronological order the unity of Ibsen's themes. He attributes Ibsen's sometimes pessimistic philosophy of life to the influence of Schopenhauer and Nietzsche, but asserts that Ibsen himself is an optimist in everyday life.

3.70

Yang Jialuo 楊家駱. *Minguo yilai chuban xinshu zongmu tiyao* 民國以來出版新書總目提要 (A summary bibliography of new books published since the republic), 2 vols. 1933. Reprint. Taipei: Zhongguo cidianguan choubeichu 中國辭典館籌備處, 1971.

This 2-volume book is a useful bibliography that lists most of the books published since the founding of the Republic of China in 1911, in which some of the translations and studies of Ibsen are listed. By comparing the listings of other foreign authors, the reader will see that Ibsen was much more well received during the period, and will also have an idea about the publishing industry in China.

3.71

Yang Zhensheng 楊振聲. "Nuola yu Luosimo" 娜拉與洛斯墨 (Nora and Rosmer). *Guowen zhoubao* 國聞週報, 21 May 1934, various pagination.

As one of the many contributions to the nation-wide debate on Ibsen in 1934, this essay interprets Nora as a victim of male chauvinism. Thus the message of women's right to leave home is again reiterated. The essay supports the idea that China in the 1930s was very much in need of further liberation for women.

Yang Zhensheng's essay appeared as the last essay in the debate that took place in *Guowen zhoubao*. In this essay, Yang thinks that Rosmer is in one sense a male Nora. While Nora is dissatisfied with her husband, Rosmer dislikes his wife. Yang starts out with a practical attitude and shows that there are few perfect families and even fewer perfect wives and husbands. He thinks that one way to solve the Nora problem is to be realistic about marriage and that both husband and wife should understand and respect each other. Yang does not object to Nora's having the right to leave home, but he thinks that it should be treated as the last resort in a hopeless family. Economic independence, according to Yang, is still the biggest problem in women's liberation.

3.72
"Yibusheng danchen bainian jinian" 易卜生誕晨百年紀念 (Ibsen's birth centenary). *Dagongbao* 大公報, 26 March 1928. Reprint. *Guowen zhoubao* 國聞週報, 1 April 1928, pp. 1–2.

An anonymous essay, entitled "Yibusheng danchen bainian jinian" (Ibsen's birth centenary), was published in an influential newspaper the Tianjin *Dagongbao* on March 26, 1928 and reprinted in *Guowen zhoubao* in its April 1 issue. Summarizing the reception of Ibsen in China since 1918, the writer observes that since the publication of Hu Shi's translation of *A Doll's House* in *Xinqingnian* (New youth) ten years earlier, there had been numerous writings on Ibsen and translations of his works. Every Chinese at that time was familiar with Ibsen's life and the subject of his plays. Chinese periodicals were flooded with Ibsen's biographies and chronologies of his works, as well as bibliographies of studies on Ibsen. These studies were widely circulated in China. According to this essay, Ibsen's worldwide fame can be attributed to the fact that "his dramas can appeal to most people of his age" and also that "his plays are suitable for stage performance."

The author of the essay, furthermore, points out that most problem plays are awkward in their presentation because the playwrights often put too much effort on the theme at the expense of art, and that there is a trap in didacticism, but Ibsen overcomes these difficulties and pursues the role of a detached observer of life throughout all of his plays. This essay echoes Janko Lavrin's view that Ibsen often subordinates the tendency of moralizing to his artistic inspiration. On the point of individualism, the author emphasizes that Ibsen is a Romantic who regards the self as more important than society. In this view, the self becomes a point of reference in all kinds of judgement. Following Hu Shi's view, the essay interprets Ibsen's individualism from the perspective of Confucianism and concludes that social progress depends on personal cultivation.

3.73

"1934 nian *Nuola* zai Shanghai" 1934年《娜拉》在上海 (*A Doll's House* in Shanghai 1934). *Beijing ribao* 北京日報 (Beijing daily), 28 July 1956, p. 3.

This is a report on the performance of Ibsen's *A Doll's House* in Shanghai in 1934, a year that was also named the "Year of Nora" in China. Included in this report is the information that Jiang Qing, Mao Zedong's wife, played the lead role in the performance, and also interviews with other actors and actresses who were involved in the production.

3.74

Yu Chun 雨椿. "Shi Nuola chuzou de shi shenme? — Yu Fan Zhongyun xiansheng tan funü de tianzhi" 使娜拉出走的是什麼? —— 與樊仲雲先生談婦女的天職 (What makes Nora leave home? — A discussion with Mr. Fan Zhongyun on women's natural duties). *Funü shenghuo* 婦女生活 (Women's life), 1.3 (September 1935), pp. 5–8.

In this essay, Yu Chun takes issue with Fan Zhongyun on the cause of women's decision to leave home in China since the 1910s. Fan Zhongyun comments that it is a wrong decision to leave home, as the decision creates many social problems not only for women, but also for the family. But Yu Chun argues that it is the unjust family and social system that cause many women to leave home. And if they do not leave home, they will be victimized forever. Yu Chun thinks that Ibsen's feminist ideas are not the cause for Chinese women to leave home; instead it is the social system that makes them decide to do so.

3.75

Yu Dafu 郁達夫. *Jige weida de zuojia* 幾個偉大的作家 (Some great writers). Shanghai: Zhonghua shuju 中華書局, 1935.

Included in this little book is Yu Dafu's study of Ibsen. Although Yu Dafu is more famous as a novelist, he is also a critic and translator. He has written extensively on Ibsen and has also translated critical reviews of Ibsen. In this study, he emphasizes the need to treat Ibsen as an artist rather than merely as a social reformer.

3.76

Yu Lichen 于立忱. "Nuola tuoli jiating de yuanyin yu zouhou zenyang de wenti" 娜拉脱離家庭的原因與走後怎樣的問題 (The reason why Nora leaves home and the question of what happens to her). *Guowen zhoubao* 國聞週報, 23 April 1934, various pagination.

Yu Lichen's essay attempts to provide a solution to the problem of what women must do after they leave home. Yu does not agree with Xia Yingzhe (see 3.65) particularly on the point that an emancipated woman must be a perfect woman. Yu thinks that only a few women are perfect and Chinese Noras are no different from other people. Yu especially objects to the idea of expecting Nora to be a flawlessly good woman who will not succumb to social temptations. From the viewpoint of a social movement, it is inadvisable to limit women's liberation to a few women elites. Yu reminds the reader that Nora's problem is not just her personal problem but a social issue. Analyzing the issue from a socio-historical perspective, Yu concludes that in China it became unbearable for women to stay at home. But the backward economy of China in the 1930s did not allow women to have real economic independence. Yu says in an oblique way that economic independence is a necessary means to freedom: "Because economic independence can lead to women's self-consciousness; and only career women are able to shoulder the mission of women's liberation."

3.77

Yu Shangyuan 余上沅. "Yibusheng de yishu" 伊卜生的藝術 (The art of Ibsen). *Xinyue* 新月 (Crescent moon), 1.30 (May 1928), pp. 2–16.

The *Xinyue* (Cresent moon) magazine, under the leadership of Hu Shi, Xu Zhimo and Chen Yuan and published by the Xinyue Society, dedicated an entire issue to the commemoration of Ibsen's centenary. Illustrated with a portrait of Ibsen and a scene from *Rosmersholm*, the special issue consists mainly of two articles: "The Art of Ibsen" by Yu Shangyuan and "Ibsen's Thought" by Zhang Jiazhu, which are meant to provide a balanced view of the two complementary aspects of Ibsen's drama.

Yu's article begins with two quotations in English respectively from Bergson and Schopenhauer asserting that art, being different from other spheres of human activity, cannot be judged from a utilitarian point of view. Yu states that Ibsen is basically an artist rather than a philosopher, thinker, and idealist. He points out Ibsen's achievements in dramatic technique. The greatness of Ibsen, according to Yu, lies in his artistic presentation of a complex idea. Yu even ranks Ibsen above Shakespeare. Ibsen is original in his works, but Shakespeare has the Greek, Roman, Italian, Spanish, and French as sources. Shakespeare's art is a matter of abstraction, whereas Ibsen's is one of creation. Shakespeare adopts traditional stories to present his ideas, but Ibsen creates his own stories. Yu quotes in English from Ibsen's major plays to support his argument. He accounts for Ibsen's success by his realistic treatment of contemporary issues. Ibsen's realism in characterization, dialogue, and setting is particularly powerful. Yu concludes: "Ibsen's greatness lies in his use of life as subject-matter and realism as a means for artistic achievement, and the use of technique as a medium to blend and balance thought and art."

3.78

Yuan Changying 袁昌英. "Yibusheng de *Yeya*" 易卜生的《野鴨》 (Ibsen's *The Wild Duck*). In *Shanju sanmo* 山居散墨 (Writings of a recluse in the mountain), pp. 99–116. Shanghai: Shangwu yinshuguan 商務印書館, 1937.

Yuan Changying's essay, "Ibsen's *The Wild Duck*," was written in 1936 and collected in Yuan's book *Shanju sanmo*. Contrary to the popular treatment of *The Wild Duck* as a tragedy, Yuan takes it as a serious comedy written with a "diabolical joy." In this light, Yuan studies the use of comic techniques in the play. Yuan emphasizes that suspense and the comic elements are the essential qualities to arrest the reader's attention. Yuan shows how these elements are built up through the well-knit plot structure of the play.

According to Yuan, "the reason for Ibsen's plays to be qualified as masterpieces is that, like Shakespearean drama, they possess some kind of inexhaustible quality," which never fails to command the reader's interest and imagination. The scene-by-scene analysis in Yuan's essay shows in a convincing way that Ibsen is a first-rate dramatist.

3.79

Zhang Heqin 張鶴琴. "Jiantao Sigande'naweiya wenxue" 檢討斯干的那維亞文學 (A review of Scandinavian literature). *Zhexue yu wenhua* 哲學與文化 (Philosophy and culture), new series, 7 (September 1934), pp. 39–44.

Zhang Heqin is one of the earliest Chinese scholars who studied and taught Scandinavian literature. In this study published in the 1930s, Zhang gives an overview of the development of Scandinavian literature. Ibsen and other Scandinavian writers are introduced. The major themes of Ibsen's works and his revolutionary social ideas are discussed.

3.80

Zhang Jiazhu 張嘉鑄. "Yibusheng de sixiang" 伊卜生的思想 (Ibsen's thought). *Xinyue* 新月 (Crescent moon), 1.30 (May 1928), pp. 16–17.

Zhang Jiazhu summarizes Ibsen's thought as expressed in his major plays: *The Pillars of Society*, *A Doll's House*, *Ghosts*, *An Enemy of the People*, and *The Wild Duck*. A large part of Zhang's essay, however, is about the lessons that China can draw from the plays. Zhang considers Ibsen's views on individuality, emancipation, and the fallacy of majority rule the most important. Zhang objects to the common notion of individuality as the exertion of self-will at the expense of others. Nora's will power and decision to live an independent life is especially praiseworthy, but Zhang worries whether, in the case of China, Nora's principle is applicable. For a Chinese woman, to go into society is even worse than to stay at home, and Zhang thinks that the only possible future for the Chinese Noras in the 1930s was to become prostitutes. That was the question puzzling most of the prospective Chinese Noras. But Zhang does not condemn Nora. An independent woman needs to have strong will power to counter all the various pressures of society. Following Bernard Shaw's view, Zhang is optimistic about Ibsen's notion that the minority, if they are correct, will sooner or later become the majority. In summing up, Zhang quotes Bernard Shaw and refers to Ibsen's drama as anti-idealistic: "Anti idealism is exactly what is hidden in Ibsen's plays. An idealist is just a dreamer. An idealist's ideas and dramas can make us dream.... But Ibsen wants to present to us in hard facts the sorrows of mankind."

3.81

Zhang Menglin 張夢麟. "Jindai xiju yu lihun wenti" 近代戲劇與離婚問題 (Modern drama and the problem of divorce). *Xin Zhonghua* 新中華 (New China), 1934. Reprint. In *Wenxue lunwenji* 文學論文集 (Collected essays on literature), vol. 2, pp. 35–50. Shanghai: Zhonghua shuju 中華書局, n.d.

In this article, Zhang Menglin reconsiders the subject of divorce as a social theme that has been treated in the drama written in the 1910s and 1920s. The author makes a connection between divorce, on the one hand as social issues, and literature on the other as ideological representation. Major plays and playwrights in Western drama are discussed in the article.

Zhang Menglin's essay, which first appeared in *Xin Zhonghua* (New China) in the same year that the debate in *Guowen zhoubao* broke out, is an effort to conclude the argument with modern Western opinions concerning Nora's leaving. It summarizes the plays that deal with the issue after Ibsen published *A Doll's House* and confirms that in the West it has been concluded that Nora must leave home if she desires to pursue her own education and emancipation. Zhang thinks that the arguments in the West can provide invaluable experience for Chinese women and feminist critics in their pursuit for independence.

3.82

Zhang Tianyi 張天翼. "Chuzou yihou" 出走以後 (After leaving home). *Jirenji* 畸人集 (Writings on extraordinary people), pp. 87–111. Shanghai: Liangyou tushu yinshua gongsi 良友圖書印刷公司, 1936.

This is a short story satirizing the radical interpretation of Ibsenism that led to many women's decision to leave home in the 1930s. It almost became a fashion and a sign of being modern for women to leave home. In the story, the author Zhang Tianyi mocks at the superficial interpretation of Ibsen's *A Doll's House*.

When the feminist movement went to an extreme in 1936 and leaving home became a fad, it was necessary to caution against such hypocritical practice. Zhang Tianyi expresses his view through this short story, satirizing a wealthy woman's hypocritical imitation of Nora. The story unfolds with a woman returning to her maiden home, expressing anguish over her husband's exploitation of the workers in his company. Imagining herself as a new woman, a fashionable term, the wealthy lady tells her uncle, who has been her mentor of new thoughts, that she has decided to leave her husband, and in so doing she thinks she can make herself appear to be modern.

The pressure from her parents' family is so great because the lady's brothers have financially benefited much from her wealthy husband. If she really leaves her husband, her two younger brothers will have to quit school and her elder brother, who works in her husband's company, will lose his job. Although the short story is meant to be a burlesque, it realistically presents the problems facing Chinese women. Economic dependence is still an important obstacle to the emancipation of women.

3.83

Zhang Ziping 張資平. "'Nuola zouhou jiujing zenyang' duhou" 〈娜拉走後究竟怎樣〉讀後 (After reading "What really happens to Nora after she leaves home"). *Guowen zhoubao* 國聞週報, 2 April 1934, various pagination.

This is a response to Juan Bing's essay (see 3.30) and to Lu Xun's essay, "What Happens After Nora Leaves Home?" (Nuola zouhou zenyang), written in 1923. In this essay the author reviews the development in Chinese society in the ten years from 1923 to 1934. It reasserts the rights of women in the nation-wide debate on women's liberation in 1934, the year in which several performances of *A Doll's House* were staged in Shanghai, Nanjing and Chongqing. Zhang Ziping's essay is a response to the issue whether Chinese women in the 1930s should leave home. Zhang thinks that to return home is worse than to struggle in society. His argument is based on the fact that many women had left home in 1934 and it was utterly impossible for them to return.

3.84

———. *Ouzhou wenyishi dagang* 歐洲文藝史大綱 (An outline history of European literature and art). Shanghai: Shanghai lianhe shuju 上海聯合書局, 1930.

In this book, there is a section which discusses Ibsen in the context of his place in European literature. The dramatic innovations in Ibsen plays, as well as the provocative themes in Ibsen's social drama, are summarized. The reader thus sees the contributions Ibsen has made to European literature.

3.85

Zhao Dan 趙丹. *Diyu zhi men* 地獄之門 (The gate of hell). Shanghai: Shanghai wenyi chubanshe 上海文藝出版社, 1980.

In this autobiography, Zhao Dan, a famous Chinese actor in Shanghai in the 1930s, recollects his career in the theatre and film industry. In this book there is a reference to the performance of *A Doll's House* in Shanghai in 1934, in which Zhao Dan played the role of Helmer, with Zhang Min as director and Lan Ping (the name Jiang Qing used in the theatre circles) as Nora.

3.86

Zheng Boqi 鄭伯奇. "Dongjing guanju yinxiangji" 東京觀劇印象記 (Impressions of dramatic performances in Tokyo). *Chuangzao yuekan* 創造月刊 (Creation monthly), 1.2 (July 1928), pp. 143–153.

Chuangzao yuekan (Creation monthly) published this essay in its July issue, which is a record of how Ibsen was commemorated in Japan in 1928. One of the major reasons for Zheng's trip to Tokyo was to see the production of *A Doll's House*, *Ghosts*, and *Peer Gynt* by the Tsukiji Little Theatre, an important Japanese repertory company that contributed much to the popularization of Ibsen in Japan. Thus through Zheng's trip, the Creation Society in an indirect way participated in the celebration of Ibsen's centenary. After summarizing the plot of *Ghosts*, Zheng focuses on the special Japanese style in their stage presentation of the play. The Tsukiji Little Theatre was a significant component of the shingeki movement in Japan. Its faithfulness to the original and its use of advanced stage equipment impressed Zheng. In this essay, Zheng tries to show the Chinese actors as well as audience the Japanese way of staging Ibsen.

3.87

Zhongguo dianying jia liezhuan 中國電影家列傳 (Biographies of

Chinese film-makers). Beijing: Zhongguo dianying chubanshe 中國電影出版社, 1982.

There is reference in this book on the life of the famous Chinese actor, Zhao Dan, who played Helmer in the 1934 production of *A Doll's House* in Shanghai. The cast included Lan Ping (the name Jiang Qing used in the Shanghai theatre circles) who played Nora. The director was Zhang Min.

4

Ibsen in Wartime China 1937–1948

4.01

Chen Liting 陳鯉庭. "Yanji shilun" 演技試論 (On acting techniques). *Xinhua rihao* 新華日報 (New China daily), 25 & 26 June 1942, various pagination.

Chen Liting's essay is the first of its kind in reviewing the achievements of the modern Chinese theatre in terms of performance style and techniques of directing. It is also the first review on the importance of professional directing in the theatre. In this essay, Chen commends the Chinese dramatist and director Hong Shen for his contribution for building up a tradition of professional acting and directing in the modern Chinese theatre, which is inseparable from the influence of the realistic style in Ibsen's plays.

4.02

Fan Wenhu 范文瑚. "*Wan'ou zhi jia* zai Zhongguo — jianping Hu Shi de 'Yibusheng zhuyi'" 《玩偶之家》在中國 — 兼評胡適的〈易卜生主義〉 (*A Doll's House* in China — A brief critique of Hu Shi's "Ibsenism"). *Sichuan shiyuan xuebao* 四川師院學報 (Sichuan normal college journal), 1 (1981), pp. 48–54, 65.

The essay reviews the reception of *A Doll's House* in China in the 1920s–1940s and comments on Hu Shi's interpretation of Ibsenism. It summarizes the major ideas in Hu Shi's essay and puts them in a historical context of reception.

4.03

Gu Zhongyi 顧仲彝. *Shinian lai de Shanghai huaju yundong (1937–1947)* 十年來的上海話劇運動 (1937–1947) (Drama movement in Shanghai in the past ten years (1937–1947)), 1947. Reprint. Hong Kong: Shenzhou tushu gongsi 神州圖書公司, 1976.

The book fills a very important gap in the information about the drama and theatre activities in Shanghai during the Japanese occupation in the Second World War. In the book the drama and theatre activities in Shanghai are seen as anti-Japanese activities and the anti-war theme is discussed. An interesting note about this book is that it provides the background for understanding the anti-war theatre activities during this period in Shanghai, in which *A Doll's House* was adapted into a Chinese play promoting the theme that women should leave home to join the army to fight against Japanese invasion.

4.04

Jian Chen 劍塵 (Gu Jianchen 谷劍塵) . "Sishi nian lai Zhongguo huaju de yanbian" 四十年來中國話劇的演變 (Changes in modern Chinese drama in the past forty years). *Xin Zhonghua* 新中華 (New China), new series, 2.7 (July 1944) , pp. 129–136.

The essay is a review written by the Chinese playwright Gu Jianchen (pen-name: Jian Chen), who had first-hand experience in modern Chinese theatre and could provide reliable information and professional observation on the development of modern Chinese drama. His play *Leng fan* (Cold meal) is a satire of Helmer's tyrannical attitude.

4.05

Li Changzhi 李長之. *Bei Ou wenxue* 北歐文學 (Northern European literature). Chongqing: Shangwu yinshuguan 商務印書館, 1945.

The practice of interpreting Ibsen as a moralist, though challenged by the different views in the late 1920s and early 1930s, remained the major trend in the reception of the dramatist in modern China. The years of war from 1937 to 1949 gave a further opportunity to consolidate this trend, as literature was then used as a political weapon against Japanese invasion. Except for a few general studies on Scandinavian literature or on the European problem play, such as Li Changzhi's *Bei'ou wenxue*, which contains a chapter treating Ibsen's literary achievements in the context of Norwegian literature, there was virtually no serious study of any kind on Ibsen and his drama in the 1940s.

4.06

Liu Cunren 柳存仁. *Ren wu tan* 人物談 (On people and things). Hong Kong: Dagongbao 大公報, 1952.

This book has a chapter that deals with Ibsen and his influence in China and it gives historical information on the general reception of Ibsen. As its title indicates, the book focuses on some past events and notable figures in the literary scene of modern China.

4.07

Mao Dun 茅盾. "Cong *Nuola* shuoqi — Wei *Zhujiang ribao funü zhoukan* zuo" 從《娜拉》說起 — 為《珠江日報婦女週刊》作 (On *A Doll's House* — For *The Women's Weekly* in *Zhujiang Daily)*, 1938. Reprint. In *Wenyi lunwenji* 文藝論文集 (A collection of literary essays), pp. 71–73. Chongqing: Yiqun chubanshe 益群出版社, 1942.

In this essay, the Chinese critic-novelist Mao Dun discusses *A Doll's House* from a political point of view and reinterprets the play as a message for the nationalist cause toward the liberation of China. Compared with the other authors, Mao Dun is firm in his conviction that only a social revolution will bring about changes in Chinese society. Nevertheless, in the essay, "On *A Doll's House*," first published in 1938, he confesses that he has become a bit pessimistic about the women's movement. Mao Dun thinks that the women's movement in China has been indebted to the influence of *A Doll's House*. Its introduction to China in the 1920s and 1930s had led to much discussion of the women's issue in Chinese publications. The numerous translations and stage productions of the play had not only made Ibsen popular among the Chinese but also led directly to the appearance of new women in China. The women's movement, from then on, was no longer "a term on paper." Mao Dun even sees the women's movement in the May 4th period as nothing but "Noraism." He argues that although one can find fault with the central idea of *A Doll's House*, none can deny the validity of Nora's idea that a woman is first of all "a human being" and also that there are "responsibilities she as a person has." Mao Dun believes that these ideas are valuable for Chinese women in their struggle for freedom and equality. "To be a human being" is the cause of Nora's leaving. But for Mao Dun, what matters most is still what happens to Nora afterwards. Ibsen gives no answer to this question. The reality in China over the first three decades of the twentieth century, Mao Dun thinks, proves that Chinese Noras would not succeed.

Mao Dun wrote the essay while he was taking refuge in Hong Kong and had just escaped from the Japanese occupation of Shanghai during the war. His zeal for an immediate revolution subsided. For this reason, he was able to obtain a clearer and more balanced view of the course the emancipation of Chinese women had taken. Indeed, nothing serves better than this essay as a conclusion to the debate over the women's issue in China that took place in 1934–35.

4.08

Ouyang Yuqian 歐陽予倩. *Zi wo yanxi yilai* 自我演戲以來 (Since I became an actor). Shanghai: Shenzhou guoguangshe 神州國光社, 1939.

This is Ouyang Yuqian's autobiographical account of his career, from which one will see how the modern Chinese theatre developed in the 1920s and 1930s. There are stories as well as historical information about the theatre reform movements, the enlightened drama, the introduction of western-style drama, and the formation of theatre groups and companies.

4.09

Pan Jiaxun 潘家洵. "Jindai xiyang wenti juben" 近代西洋問題劇本 (Modern western problem plays). Parts I, II, & III. *Xiyang wenxue* 西洋文學, 1 (1940) , pp. 5–8; 2 (1940) , pp. 167–172; 3 (1940) , pp. 282–287.

Pan Jiaxun's essay discusses Ibsen in the context of his influence in world literature, particularly his innovations in the social problem play.

4.10

Qu Shigong 瞿史公. *Jutan waishi* 劇壇外史 (An alternative history of the theatre). Shanghai: Yishe 藝社, 1940.

This little book by Qu Shigong gives many anecdotes about the modern Chinese theatre, some of which are based on his memory of historical facts, while others may serve as a personal observation. Many major modern Chinese playwrights and theatre directors are discussed to illustrate the development of the modern Chinese theatre. The book is useful for background information about the relation between Ibsen and modern Chinese theatre.

4.11

Yi Qiao 易喬 (Zhou Yibai 周貽白) . *Nüxing de jiefang* 女性的解放 (Female emancipation). *Xiju congshu di'er zhong* 戲劇叢書第二種 (Drama series no. 2). Shanghai: Yaxing shudian 亞星書店, 1940.

Written in 1940, this play is modelled on the structure of Ibsen's *A Doll's House* and published amidst the most difficult years during the Sino-Japanese war. Its setting is changed to China in the 1940s and the heroine (a Chinese Nora) has to struggle with her husband for the right to leave home and join the army for the salvation of the country. Much of the dialogue in this play is borrowed from *A Doll's House*. Thus the reader can see the political adaptation of Ibsen in China during the war period. The outbreak of the war between China and Japan in 1937 led to a different reception of Ibsen and subsequently gave a new impetus to the performance of his plays. Facing a critical moment in national defense, Chinese dramatists, in reaction to the government's call to mobilize women, were no longer satisfied with Ibsen's treatment of Nora. It was by means of a more radical version of *A Doll's House* that Ibsen was given a new image in wartime China. *Nüxing de jiefang* (Female emancipation), as Yi Qiao called his adaptation of *A Doll's House*, was performed in Shanghai in 1939 with the original play's ending entirely altered. The setting of the play is placed in Shanghai; the time in 1938 just before the Chinese New Year, a year after the outbreak of the Sino-Japanese war. The names of the characters are all changed to Chinese. The adapted version unfolds with the Zhuangs (Helmers) suffering from the hardships caused by the Japanese occupation of their hometown, Wuxi, where they left for Shanghai some six years ago. Unlike the original Nora who is naive, Ye Anna is portrayed as a sophisticated woman.

With regard to the atmosphere, the adaptation exhibits a complete transformation of the original. Ye Anna is a much more radical person than Nora. The domestic scope of the play is expanded to include a panoramic view of society. In the first two acts, the plot proceeds in a pace more or less the same as in the original, but the final act develops rapidly. While Nora is seeking a way to re-educate herself, Ye Anna already knows what she is going to do. The development of Ye Anna's self-confidence is too sudden and not convincing. Though the dialogue in the adaptation for a large part remains the same, the changes in the plot are so radical that the play becomes an entirely different version.

Yi Qiao thought that the play had to meet the needs of the age. The performance of *A Doll's House* could no longer take the attitude of providing "a memorandum" for Chinese women, but must serve as a pointer for future actions. He therefore made the performance a part of the cause to save China. His revision of *A Doll's House* is based on the idea of making it more suitable for presentation in wartime China.

5

Ibsen and Socialism 1949–1976

5.01

Chen Shouzhu 陳瘦竹. *Yibusheng* Wan'ou zhi jia *yanjiu* 易卜生《玩偶之家》研究 (A study of Ibsen's *A Doll's House*), Wenyi zuopin yuedu fudao congshu 2 文藝作品閱讀輔導叢書 2 (A reader's guide to works of literary arts, no. 2). Shanghai: Xinwenyi chubanshe 新文藝出版社, 1958.

The twenty years from 1956 to 1976 was a period in which Ibsen was mainly a subject of political concern in China. The only serious study of the dramatist can be found in Chen Shouzhu's book, *Yibusheng* Wan'ou zhi jia *yanjiu* (A study of Ibsen's *A Doll's House*). Without stirring political passion, Chen's book focuses on the technical aspects of the play. Relying mainly on sources from the book, *Ibsen's Workshop*, Chen introduces to the Chinese reader the process by which the play was conceived and written. Chen's treatment attempts to trace the play back to the real story behind it. His purpose is to show how art is related to real life and how Ibsen worked on the preliminary drafts before he published the play as a finished product. In this book, Chen aims at providing an example of playwriting for Chinese dramatists. As regards the ideology of Ibsen, Chen's book, however, does not deviate from the official government stance, and considers Ibsen not only as a great Norwegian dramatist, but also as the founder of modern European drama. Treating the stage as a forum for political speech, Chen argues, Ibsen honestly and courageously points out to his countrymen and to the whole of Europe the various problems in their society, ranging from politics, law, religion and morality to love and marriage. Ibsen strongly criticizes the hypocritical and selfish bourgeoisie and the corruption of the social system. Although Ibsen only raises questions and never gives scientific answers, Chen thinks that his works are enough to show that the bourgeois society is a wretched world.

5.02

Dagongbao guoji bianxie zu 大公報國際編寫組. "Nuowei juzuojia Henglike Yibusheng" 挪威劇作家亨利克・易卜生 (The Norwegian dramatist Henrik Ibsen). *1956 nian jinian de shijie wenhua mingren* 1956年紀念的世界文化名人(Commemorations of famous world cultural figures in 1956), pp. 42–45. Beijing: Zhonngguo qingnian chubanshe 中國青年出版, 1956.

This essay is very useful in revealing how Ibsen was received in China in the 1950s and how his works were interpreted according to the Chinese Marxist views. Among the many commemorative essays on Ibsen's birth centenary is this one that appeared in the Beijing newspaper *Dagongbao* (Ta kung daily) in July 1956. Putting Ibsen against the background of the politico-economic development of Europe, the essay states that Ibsen grew up in an age in which European capitalism was developing and Scandinavian literature was just beginning to establish itself, and that therefore in Ibsen's drama, "an objective course of the economic development in the capitalist society of Norway is profoundly reflected." In this essay, Ibsen is presented not as an artist but as a social reformer. It insists that in Ibsen's plays there is a strong rebellious spirit against the society in which Ibsen lived. Hence, Chinese Marxists hold that in Ibsen's later works there is the idea that "redemption of the world could only come from the labour classes," and from this idea spring the six symbolist plays, among which are *The Lady from the Sea* and *When We Dead Awaken*.

5.03

Dai Liuling 戴鎦齡. "Pipan Hu Shi de 'Yibusheng zhuyi' de cuowu guandian he fangfa" 批判胡適的〈易卜生主義〉的錯誤觀點和方法 (A critique of Hu Shi's fallacious viewpoints and methodology in his essay "Ibsenism"). *Zhongshan daxue xuebao* 中山大學學報 (Sun Yat-sen university journal), 4 (1956), pp. 126–137.

A controversy over the nature of Ibsenism is raised in Dai Liuling's essay which appeared in 1956 in response to Mao Zedong's call for a critique of Hu Shi. Representing the Marxist view then popular in China, Dai vigorously attacks Hu Shi's views of Ibsenism. Dai's definition of Ibsenism, however, stresses on literary conflicts as a method of drama. Dai Liuling points out that the fallacy in Hu Shi's essay "Ibsenism" lies in the view that Ibsen is taken merely as a preacher rather than as a playwright. Dai cites Friedrich Engels's comments on Ibsen and maintains that Ibsen's drama aims at pointing out the corruption of Norwegian society. This view is a recapitulation of Plekhanov's assertion that Ibsen's ideas originated from the semi-feudal society of Norway. The second issue Dai Liuling raises about Hu Shi's essay concerns the definition of realism. To Hu Shi, an artist's method of creation is no different from his attitude toward life. Hence, realism in Ibsen is considered by

Hu Shi as a reflection of the playwright's realistic attitude towards the world. Ibsen's plays are treated by Hu Shi as a literary reflection of his world outlook. But on the contrary Dai Liuling thinks that realism is only a method in Ibsen's plays. It is apparent that Dai Liuling makes many far-fetched assumptions in his critique of Hu Shi, particularly about Hu Shi's intentions. His argument concerning the anti-bourgeois ideas in Ibsen's plays is also groundless. It is equally strange of him to say that Hu Shi's essay is an attack of the Russian Revolution. Dai Liuling's essay is an excellent example of far-fetched interpretation and political insinuation in China in the 1950s.

5.04

Deng Suining 鄧綏甯, trans. *Xiyang xiju sixiang* 西洋戲劇思想 (Western dramatic theories). Edited by Zhongguo qingnian xiezuo xiehui 中國青年寫作協會. Taipei: Zhengzhong shuju 正中書局, 1956.

A different reception of Ibsen can be found in the Chinese communities outside the mainland. As shown in this book, the reception of Ibsen in Taiwan similar to that in the West. There have never been any large-scale commemorative activities of any kind for the dramatist, but Ibsen is very much respected as a subject of academic study in schools. In the 1960s–1980s, studies on Ibsen with respect to his general characteristics could occasionally be found in Taiwan.

5.05

———. "Yibusheng de shengping" 易卜生的生平 (Ibsen's life). *Yishu xuebao* 藝術學報 (*Bulletin of National Taiwan Academy of Arts*), 1 (October 1966), pp. 113–136.

A biographical summary of Ibsen's life and career as a dramatist, the essay gives information relating the playwright's works to his life and the themes of the major plays to social issues of Norway. The essay represents an academic orientation in the reception of Ibsen in Taiwan.

5.06

———. "Yibusheng de zuopin" 易卜生的作品 (Ibsen's works). *Yishu xuebao* 藝術學報 (*Bulletin of National Taiwan Academy of Arts*), 3 (January 1968), pp. 111–158.

A different reception of Ibsen can be found in this essay published outside the Chinese mainland. In Taiwan, the past forty years since the 1950s has seen a reception of Ibsen which focuses mainly on the art of his drama. Such a reception can be found in other essays by Deng Suining, such as "Yibusheng de shengping " (Ibsen's life) and "Yibusheng de zuopin" (Ibsen's works).

5.07

Gu Zhongyi 顧仲彝. *Bianju lilun yu jiqiao* 編劇理論與技巧 (The technique and theory of playwriting). Beijing: Zhongguo xiju chubanshe, 1981.

This is a book that covers the major Western theories of drama and theatre. At the same time, it also focuses on the drama of Ibsen and its implication for a modern theatre in China. The book was published in 1981, but it is actually a collection of the lectures Gu Zhongyi gave at the Central Academy of Drama when he was a professor there during the 1960s before the Cultural Revolution broke out. In the section on Ibsen and his drama, Gu Zhongyi offers his interpretation of the Ibsenian style of dramatic conflict, which according the socialist theory of theatre is exemplary of the model type of the socialist problem play. The book thus gives an overview of the socialist theory of drama in China and it also provides historical information on the contemporary Chinese theatre before the Cultural Revolution.

5.08

Guo Boxin 郭博信 (Kuo Po-hsin). "Yibusheng yu *Qungui*" 易卜生與《群鬼》 (Ibsen and *Ghosts*). *Zhongyang yuekan* 中央月刊 (Central monthly), 5.2 (December 1972), pp. 79–85.

There is an act-by-act analysis of Ibsen's *Ghosts* in this essay, in which Guo Boxin claims that "Ibsen is not a social reformer at all, for he does not give solutions to the questions raised in his plays." The essay is a useful study not so much in its analysis as in its approach that illustrates to the Chinese reader that there can be an alternative view of Ibsen, not as a social thinker, but as a dramatist. While on the China mainland, Ibsen is considered mainly as a social revolutionist, in Tawian, as the reader can see in Guo Boxin's essay, Ibsen is treated mainly as a dramatist.

5.09

Guo Moruo 郭沫若. *Jinxi pujian* 今昔蒲劍. Shanghai: Xinwenyi chubanshe 新文藝出版社, 1955.

This is a collection of essays that Guo Moruo wrote on the new developments in contemporary Chinese drama and theatre after 1949. Although these essays are not solely focused on Ibsen, they provide the background for an understanding of the cultural change that has led to a difference in the reception of Ibsen since the founding of the People's Republic in 1949.

5.10

Guojia chuban shiye guanliju banben tushuguan 國家出版事業管理局版本圖書館, ed. *1949–1979 fanyi chuban waiguo gudian wenxue zhuzuo mulu* 1949–1979 翻譯出版外國古典文學著作目錄 (A bibliography of Chinese translations of foreign classics in literature 1949–1979). Beijing: Zhonghua shuju 中華書局, 1980.

This is a bibliography of Chinese translations of foreign classics in literature, which gives useful information on the Chinese translations of Ibsen's plays, such as *A Doll's House*, *Ghosts*, *The Pillars of Society*, *The Master Builder*, and *Hedda Gabler*. In this bibliography, one can see not only the Chinese translations of Ibsen's works, but also the works of other playwrights so that there can be a comparison between the reception of Ibsen and that of other playwrights. The bibliography also gives full information on the circulation and editions of the translations.

5.11

Hu Yaoheng 胡耀恒 (John Yaw-herng Hu). "Yibusheng de xiju yishu" 易卜生的戲劇藝術 (Ibsen's dramatic art). *Yibusheng xiju xuanji* 易卜生戲劇選集 (Selected plays of Ibsen). Edited by Yan Yuanshu 顏元叔. *Danjiang xiyang xiandai xiju yicong* 淡江西洋現代戲劇譯叢 (Tamkang series of western plays in translation), pp. 1–10. Taipei: Jingsheng wenwu gongyingshe 驚聲文物供應社, 1970.

There appeared a considerable number of Ibsen studies in Taiwan in the 1970s. Representative of them is Hu Yaoheng's essay, "Yibusheng de xiju yishu," which was published as an introduction to the Chinese translation of *Ghosts* and *Hedda Gabler* in the *Tamkang Series of Western*

Plays in Translation. Besides being a detailed, technical analysis of the two plays, the essay also accounts for the immortality of Ibsen's art. Ibsen's innovations in plot structure, dialogue, characterization and presentation of themes are, according to Hu, the factors that contribute to his success. As a comparatist trained at Indiana University, Hu is able to highlight Ibsen's art in a short essay.

5.12

Huang Zuolin 黃佐臨. "Mantan 'Xijuguan'" 漫談戲劇觀 (On drama). *Renmin ribao* 人民日報 (People's daily), 25 April 1962, p. 5.

Huang Zuolin is a noted theatre critic and scholar of Brecht. He has credit for his contribution to the reception of Brecht in China. In this essay, he argues for an alternative theatre that is different from the Ibsenian mode that has been practised in China for more than 50 years and he advocates for a style that is close to Brecht's and to the Chinese tradition. The historical value of this essay lies in that it provides a different view from the dominant mode of theatrical representation that has been in practice in China.

5.13

Ji Shuping 冀淑平. "Wo shi zenyang banyan Nuola de" 我是怎樣扮演娜拉的 (How I play the role of Nora). *Yibusheng yanjiu lunwenji* 易卜生研究論文集 (Ibsen research papers). Edited by Meng Shengde 孟勝德 and Astrid Saether, pp. 57–62; 278–282. Beijing: Zhongguo wenxue chubanshe 中國文學出版社, 1995.

The actress Ji Shuping, who played the role of Nora in the 1956 performance of *A Doll's House* in Beijing, reviews how she understands the character and how she interprets the play. Details are given about the rehearsal and the performance.

5.14

Jie'erchawen 杰爾查文 (Konstantin Nikolaevic Derzhavin). "Yibusheng lun" 易卜生論 (A study of Henrik Ibsen). Translated by Li Xiangzhong 李祥忠 and Wang Yizhu 王以鑄. *Yilin* 譯林 (Translation), 35 (May 1956), pp. 135–156. Reprint. In *Yibusheng lun: Yibusheng shishi wushi zhounian jinian* 易卜生論：易卜生逝世五十周年紀念 (In commemoration of the 50th anniversary of the death of Ibsen). Beijing: Zuojia chubanshe 作家出版社, 1956.

The commemorative activities in Beijing in 1956 included a Chinese translation of the Russian critic Konstantin Derzhavin's essay, "Henrik Ibsen," which was originally meant to be an introductory essay to the Russian edition of Ibsen's collected works published in Moscow in 1951. Translated by Li Xiangzhong and Wang Yizhu and first published in *Yilin*, the essay adopts the arguments of Friedrich Engels and Georg Plekhanov and evaluates Ibsen from a historico-political perspective. Derzhavin points out that Ibsen started his activities as a dramatist in 1848, the year in which the whole of Europe was swept by revolutions and national liberations. It was also the year in which the *Communist Manifesto* was published. Ibsen finished his last play in 1899, and shortly thereafter, Russia through its revolution put up a new and important milestone in the social history of mankind. Ibsen was therefore identified with the proletarian revolution and uprisings in the latter half of the nineteenth century and was thus made a mouthpiece of Marxism-Leninism.

As for the political inclination of Ibsen, Derzhavin states that "a large part of the themes in his drama is derived from his controversies with bourgeois ideology." Derzhavin considers Ibsen more as a politician than as a dramatist. Contrary to the generally accepted idea that Ibsen only raises questions but does not provide answers, Derzhavin contends that at least in *Rosmersholm* Ibsen reveals his general views of the relationship between men. Rosmer's death then is seen as a result of the burden of social falsehood. *Hedda Gabler* is regarded as a declaration of the vain and empty rebellion against society. In conclusion, Derzhavin claims: "Boldly unmasking the reality of the bourgeois and false beliefs in their system, Ibsen leaves mankind a rich literary heritage, which is not only a brilliant record of his own age, but also a powerful and artistic evidence of the inner crises and inevitable destruction of his society."

5.15

Lau, Joseph S. M. (Liu Shaoming 劉紹銘). *Ts'ao Yu: The Reluctant Disciple of Chekhov and O'Neill*. Hong Kong: Hong Kong University Press, 1970.

In this monograph, there is a brief study of how Cao Yu's (Ts'ao Yu) play, *Leiyu* (Thunderstorm), was influenced by Ibsen's *Ghosts*. In the introduction, Ibsen's influence in the rise of modern Chinese drama is also mentioned. This study shows a non-socialist view on Ibsen's influence upon Cao Yu.

5.16

Li Jianwu 李健吾. "Jindai Ouzhou guanyu xiju dingyi de yichang lunzhan" 近代歐洲關於戲劇定義的一場論戰 (A debate on the definition of drama in modern Europe), 1956. Reprint. In *Xiju xintian* 戲劇新天 (New horizons in drama), pp. 277–298. Shanghai: Shanghai wenyi chubanshe, 1980.

Li Jianwu is a dramatist as well as a theatre theorist. In this essay, which was first published in the mid-1950s, he reviews the debate on the essence of drama in Europe in the latter half of the nineteenth century. The essay provides not only the historical background for the development of modern European drama, but also a reinterpretation of the debate according to the Chinese socialist view that the essence of drama lies in conflicts.

5.17

———. "Shehui zhuyi de huaju" 社會主義的話劇 (Socialist modern drama), 1956. Reprint. In *Xiju xintian* 戲劇新天 (New horizons in drama), pp. 19–54. Shanghai: Shanghai wenyi chubanshe 上海文藝出版社, 1980.

This essay was first published in the mid-1950s in an attempt to review the nature of socialist drama in China. It is a further development of Li Jianwu's view that the essence of drama lies in "conflicts," which he interprets specifically as "class conflicts." In this essay he brings forth the idea of socialist drama as a drama constituted of social conflicts, which can be formulated as stage representation in China according to Mao Zedong's principle of class analysis stated in the essay, "On Class Contradictions" (Lun jiezhi maodun).

5.18

———. "Shehui zhuyi huaju de xiju chongtu" 社會主義話劇的戲劇衝突 (Dramatic conflicts in socialist drama), 1956. Reprint. In *Xiju xintian* 戲劇新天 (New horizons in drama), pp. 55–60. Shanghai: Shanghai wenyi chubanshe 上海文藝出版社, 1980.

This essay, which was first published in the mid-1950s, is a further elaboration of Li Jianwu's view on the nature of socialist drama, which he first proposed in the essay "Shehui zhuyi de huaju" (Socialist modern drama). It helped to establish a new tradition for the Chinese theatre in the 1950s that was to politicize art forms for socialist construction, as well as to provide a formula for playwriting according to the socialist logic of class struggle.

5.19

Liu Huating 劉華庭. *Zhongguo xiandai xiju dianying qikan mulu* 中國現代戲劇電影期刊目錄 (An index to periodicals on modern Chinese theatre and film). Shanghai: Shanghai wenyi chubanshe 上海文藝出版社, 1962.

This is a reference tool that provides useful bibliographic information on periodicals concerning modern Chinese drama and film, which can be used for locating bibliographic titles regarding the reception of Ibsen in China.

5.20

Pan Shoukang 潘壽康. "Sikande'naweiya" 斯勘的納維亞 (Scandinavia). *Shijie wenxue mingzhu xinxiang cidian* 世界文學名著欣賞詞典 (A dictionary of world masterpieces), pp. 359–373. Taipei: Zhicheng chubanshe 志誠出版社, 1962.

Published in 1962, Pan Shoukang's book presents synopses of *A Doll's House*, *The Pillars of Society*, *Ghosts*, *An Enemy of the People*, *The Lady from the Sea*, and *Little Eyolf*. According to Pan Shoukang, these studies on Ibsen are no more than a chronological presentation of facts and are almost without exception devoid of critical focus or even analysis.

5.21

Ren Guilin 任桂林. "'Wu Si' Yundong he xiqu gexin" "五四" 運動和戲曲革新 (The "May 4th" Movement and reforms in Chinese music-drama). *Xiju yanjiu* 戲劇研究 (Studies on drama), 2 (1959), pp. 14–16.

This essay asserts that there is a strong link between the May 4th Movement and the reforms in traditional Chinese music-drama in that the latter serves as a source for the former. Thus the essay shows that indigenous elements of change constitute only one of the many causes but not a major cause of the May 4th Movement. Hence, the reader can find in this essay information about the context in which Ibsen was first introduced to China.

5.22

Shanghai shuju 上海書局. *Yibusheng* 易卜生 (Ibsen). Hong Kong: Shanghai shuju 上海書局, 1975.

Included in this book are biographical information of Ibsen, historical background of the modern Western theatre, Chinese translations of his major plays and criticism. The book is an item in the series "World Literary Masters," which includes Tolstoy and many other writers.

5.23

Tian Han 田漢. "Xiang xianshi zhuyi xiju dashimen xuexi" 向現實主義戲劇大師們學習 (Learn from the great masters of realistic drama). *Guangming ribao* 光明日報 (Guangming daily), 27 July 1956. Reprint. In *Tian Han lun chuangzuo* 田漢論創作 (Tian Han on creative writing). Edited by Bai Bin 柏彬, pp. 358–362. Shanghai: Shanghai wenyi chubanshe 上海文藝出版社, 1983.

Summoning the Chinese dramatists to take Ibsen and Shaw as their instructors, Tian Han, then President of the Association of Chinese Dramatists, first published this essay in *Guangming ribao* on 27 July 1956, in which he enthusiastically shows how the Chinese youth forty years earlier were influenced by Ibsen and how great Ibsen and Shaw are. Comparing Ibsen with Shaw, Tian Han thinks that Shaw is a more thorough minded revolutionist than Ibsen, for Shaw dares to attack the hypocrisy of the upper classes.

5.24

Tian Qin 田禽. *Zhongguo xiju yundong* 中國戲劇運動 (The Chinese drama movement). Shanghai: Shangwu yinshuguan 商務印書館, 1946.

The book surveys the development of modern Chinese drama and relates it to the sociopolitical movements that occurred in modern China from the 1910s to the 1940s. The title of the book shows that the approach it takes is to consider literature and the theatre arts as part of social movement. Thus the development of modern Chinese drama as an art form is discussed in relation to the May 4th Movement, the women's movement, and the national movement against Japanese invasion.

5.25

Wu Xue 吳雪. "Cong *Nuola* yanchu suo xiang dao de" 從《娜拉》演出所想到的 (Some thoughts on the performance of *A Doll's House*). *Wenyibao* 文藝報 (Literary gazette), 16 (1956), pp. 40–41.

In the year 1956 China organized many activities in memory of Ibsen on the 50th anniversary of his death. In Beijing, as well as in many other cities, there were commemorative essays that appeared in newspapers and performances of Ibsen's plays, among which the most popular was *A Doll's House*. Wu Xue's essay that appeared in *Wenyibao* not only comments on the performance of *A Doll's House*, but also reminds the Chinese audience that in China in the 1950s there was still the need to fight for the liberation of women, though in a different way, as the socialist system guaranteed freedom and liberation for all citizens.

5.26

———. "Yibusheng yiwen" 易卜生佚聞 (Anecdotes about Ibsen). *Beijing ribao* 北京日報 (Beijing daily), 27 July 1956, p. 3.

This is one of the many essays published in memory of Ibsen on the 50th anniversary of his death. It recounts the stories in Ibsen's life and also those behind his plays. Thus the essay gives the Chinese reading public biographical information on Ibsen.

5.27

Xia Dingzhi 夏定之. "Yibusheng xiandaiju *Haidan* zhi poushi" 易卜生現代劇《海妲》之剖視 (An analysis of Ibsen's modern play *Hedda Gabler*). *Fuxinggang xuebao* 復興崗學報 (Fuxinggang academic journal), 14 (March 1976), pp. 1–11.

This is an article published in a Taiwan journal. It is a study of the play with a focus on its dramatic techniques and the portrayal of a female character. In this article, the author touches on the feminist theme in the play and considers it as a social critique with a new perspective on women's frustrations in a conservative society. Thus the suicide of Hedda Gabler is interpreted as a revolt against male dominance.

5.28

Xiao Qian 蕭乾. "*Pei'er Jinte* — Yibu qingsuan geren zhuyi de shiju" 《培爾・金特》— 一部清算個人主義的詩劇 (*Peer Gynt* — A verse drama condemning individualism). *Dagongbao (Xianggang)* 大公報（香港）(Ta kung daily) (Hong Kong), Wenyiban 文藝版 (Literature and arts section), 15 August 1949, p. 5.

With increasing Soviet influence in China in the 1950s, Ibsen's plays, with an advocacy of individualism, were regarded as harmful to socialist collectivism. The unstable attitudes the Chinese showed toward Ibsen were undoubtedly a reflection of the rapid political and social changes in China that had taken place since 1949. A reconsideration of Ibsen's ideas of individualism is given in this essay by the scholar-writer Xiao Qian. Xiao believes that Ibsen is no longer needed in China, not only because Ibsen was a writer of the last century, but also because he belongs to the faraway Northern Europe, where the society is essentially different from that in China. As a forerunner of literary realism, Ibsen, Xiao says, scrutinizes the organization of society with critical eyes and points out its rotten roots. Ibsen's weakness lies in the fact that he attacks only the surface corruption of society and does not analyze its economic causes. He therefore recognizes only the existence of the individual and not the masses. He advocates the improvement of the individual but never that of society. Thus Xiao considers Ibsen an anarchist. *Peer Gynt*, according to Xiao, offers a critique of the overemphasized individualism in China. Xiao Qian thinks that the play is a caricature of selfishness as shown in the self-centred Peer Gynt.

5.29

Xu Xing 許行. "*Nuola* he Beijing guanzhong jianmian" 《娜拉》和北京觀眾見面 (*A Doll's House* will meet the audience in Beijing). *Beijing ribao* 北京日報 (Beijing daily), 25 July 1956, p. 3.

In memory of Ibsen on the 50th anniversary of his death, the play *A Doll's House* was staged in Beijing in 1956. This essay that appeared in *Beijing ribao* is a review of the performance and one of the many commemorative essays on the occasion. Besides commenting on the performance, what is interesting is that at the end of the essay there is the message that women's liberation had not achieved its task even though China had entered its socialist period.

5.30

Ye Junjian 葉君健. "Shijiu shiji Bei Ou wenxue" 十九世紀北歐文學 (Nineteenth-century Northern European literature), 1961. Reprint. In *Xilouji* 西樓集 (West house collection), pp. 129–149. Nanchang: Jiangxi renmin chubanshe 江西人民出版社, 1981.

Ye Junjian's essay, originally published in 1961, caught the attention of many Ibsen scholars. The essay is a summary of the principles of Georg Brandes's celebrated book *Main Currents in Nineteenth Century Literature*. Ye points out that the call for individuality is one of the currents in nineteenth-century thought and that Ibsen is one of the writers whose works embody the spirit of the age. Comparing Ibsen to Dr. Stockmann, Ye finds that Ibsen's final acceptance of Nietzsche's superman philosophy is evident of Ibsen's lack of confidence in the masses and consequently his failure to see the power of the masses in revolution.

5.31

Zhao Mingyi 趙銘彝. "Huaju yundong sanshi'nian gaiguan" 話劇運動三十年概觀 (An overview of the modern Chinese drama movement in the past thirty years). *Xiju luncong* 戲劇論叢 (Theatre studies), 3 (1957), pp. 24–42.

This is a historical study of the development of modern drama in China. In this study, the author, a theatre historian, emphasizes the internal dynamics of Chinese drama in its modern development and points out that it is inseparable from the social changes that occurred in China. Thus the issue of foreign influence, Ibsenism, and women's movement are all seen as related in the emergence of modern Chinese drama.

5.32

Zhou Yonghui 周永輝. "Yibusheng xiandaiju *Haidan* zhi likui" 易卜生現代劇《海妲》之蠡窺 (A glimpse into Ibsen's modern play *Hedda Gabler*). *Hualian shizhuan xuebao* 花蓮師專學報 (Hualian normal college journal), 5 (June 1973), pp. 317–334.

This is a study of Ibsen's play *Hedda Gabler* in terms of its structure and themes, in which the author raises the point of Ibsen's treatment of Hedda

Gabler as a modern reconception of female characters. The suicide of Hedda is seen as a result of her frustration with society and a protest against social injustice. In this essay, one can see the different reception of Ibsen in Taiwan.

6

Ibsen Beyond Socialism 1977–1997

6.01

A'ersaisi, Asibi'ang 阿斯比昂 • 阿爾塞斯 (Asbjorn Aarseth). "Yibusheng zuihou 12 bu xiju zhong de changjing sheji" 易卜生最後12部戲劇中的場景設計 (Scenographic patterns in Ibsen's twelve last plays). In *Yibusheng yanjiu lunwenji* 易卜生研究論文集 (Ibsen research papers). Edited by Meng Shengde 孟勝德 and Astrid Saether, pp. 63–76; 283–299. Beijing: Zhongguo wenxue chubanshe 中國文學出版社, 1995.

The author brings up the idea of the "showcase" as a principle of scenography in Ibsen's last twelve plays. Around this idea of the "showcase," Ibsen has desgined different patterns of stage movement. The essay provides a very useful study of Ibsen's plays for the purpose of stage production.

6.02

Ah Ying 阿英 (Qian Xingcun 錢杏邨). "Yibusheng de zuopin zai Zhongguo"易卜生的作品在中國 (Ibsen's works in China). *Wenyibao* 文藝報 (Literary gazette), 17 (1956). Reprint. In *Ah Ying wenji* 阿英文集 (Collected works of Ah Ying), vol. 1, pp. 738–743. Beijing: Sanlian shudian 三聯書店, 1981.

In this essay, the scholar-writer Ah Ying (pen-name of Qian Xingcun) takes issue with Hu Shi on the point of how Ibsen should be interpreted. Ah Ying argues from the socialist point of view that only in new China could the Chinese people thoroughly understand Ibsen. According to Ah Ying, the Chinese people were no longer satisfied with the bourgeois viewpoints prevalent in the May Fourth period when Ibsen was introduced. Nor could they accept the anti-historico-materialistic view that Ibsen was considered as greater than Shakespeare. Ah Ying comments that Hu Shi was one of the most reactionary of Chinese bourgeois critics, who had betrayed the Chinese people and Ibsen, and became the slave of imperialism and counter-revolutionaries. He thinks that it had never occurred to them that the long lasting brilliance of Ibsen as a great master of art lies precisely in the fact that he is a patriot, in his unfailing effort to promote world peace and welfare, and in his love of the cultural heritage of his home country. Through his works, Ibsen reveals without reservation the evils of capitalism and the corruption of the capitalists. Ah Ying argues that for this reason Ibsen would remain forever in the hearts of the Chinese people.

6.03

Aide, Yilishabai 伊麗沙白・艾德 (Elisabeth Eide). "*Wan'ou zhi jia*, *Pei'er Jinte* yu Zhongguo xiandai huaju" 《玩偶之家》、《培爾・金特》與中國現代話劇 (*Peer Gynt* and *A Doll's House*: Or One Aspect of Modern Chinese Drama). In *Yibusheng yanjiu lunwenji* 易卜生研究論文集 (Ibsen research papers). Edited by Meng Shengde 孟勝德 and Astrid Saether, pp. 77–92; 300–317. Beijing: Zhongguo wenxue chubanshe 中國文學出版社, 1995.

In this essay, the author summarizes the reception of Ibsen in China since the early 1900s. Many of the details given in the essay can be found in Kwok-kan Tam's Ph.D. thesis, "Ibsen in China: Reception and Influence" (University of Illinois at Urbana-Champaign, 1984) (see 1.37). However, there is no acknowledgement of the sources in Elisabeth Eide's essay.

6.04

Aositelude, Ailike 埃里克・奧斯特魯德 (Erik Østerud). "Henglike Yibusheng de xiju mianju" 亨利克・易卜生的戲劇面具 (Henrik Ibsen's theatre mask). In *Yibusheng yanjiu lunwenji* 易卜生研究論文集 (Ibsen research papers). Edited by Meng Shengde 孟勝德 and Astrid Saether, pp. 143–179; 376–418. Beijing: Zhongguo wenxue chubanshe 中國文學出版社, 1995.

This is a study of Ibsen's play *The Wild Duck* in terms of its technique and the common pattern of structure that the play shares with Ibsen's other later plays. The author of this essay brings up the principle of photography to illustrate the principle of truth and illusion discussed in *The Wild Duck*.

6.05

Ben Hanshen, Kaiti'er 凱梯爾・本・漢森 (Kjetil Bang-Hansen). "Dangjin yanchu Yibusheng xiju de yiyi" 當今演出易卜生戲劇的意義 (Staging Ibsen today). In *Yibusheng yanjiu lunwenji* 易卜生研究論文集 (Ibsen research papers). Edited by Meng Shengde 孟勝德 and Astrid Saether, pp. 93–105; 318–332. Beijing: Zhongguo wenxue chubanshe 中國文學出版社, 1995.

Bang-Hansen is a director who has staged Ibsen's plays. In this essay, he thinks that there is no fixed style in the production of Ibsen's plays. According to him, the most important is to have a "respect for the time" and to regard any performance of Ibsen's plays as "a meeting in time." In other words, Bang-Hansen thinks that the director of Ibsen's plays has to have his/her own interpretation.

6.06

Caitejin, Kelala 克拉拉・蔡特金 (Klara Zetkin). "Henglike Yibusheng" 亨利克・易卜生 (Henrik Ibsen). Translated by Fu Weici 付惟慈. In *Caitejin wenxue pinglunji* 蔡特金文學評論集 (A collection of Klara Zetkin's critical essays), pp. 1–12. Beijing: Renmin wenxue chubanshe 人民文學出版社, 1978.

A revival of Marxist criticism of Ibsen can be found in the Chinese translation of the German Marxist-feminist critic Klara Zetkin's essay, "Henrik Ibsen." In the editor's note, Ibsen is treated as a dramatist whose significance lies in his critique of "the hypocrisy of bourgeois morals" and whose work "brings turmoil to the capitalist world, weakens the capitalists' attack on the proletariat and is hence beneficial to proletarian liberation." According to Zetkin, Ibsen is politically more important as a feminist educator to the proletariat than as an artist. A powerful weapon for women's emancipation, Ibsen's plays are regarded by Zetkin first and foremost as a kind of drama that aims at unravelling the mentality of bourgeois women. In order to set themselves free, women have to "reject not only the false marriage system, but also the bourgeoisie and their social order." Like other socialist critics, Zetkin attempts to interpret Ibsen with a note of feminism and according to the social and political effects of his plays.

6.07

Cao Yu 曹禺. "Jinian Yibusheng danchen yibai wushi zhounian" 記念易卜生誕晨150周年 (In commemoration of Ibsen's 150th birthday). *Renmin ribao* 人民日報 (People's daily), 21 March 1978, p. 1.

Celebrating Ibsen's birthday in March 1978, Cao Yu, the foremost modern Chinese dramatist, published this essay in the Chinese government's official newspaper. In this commemorative essay, Cao Yu recalls how Ibsen was introduced to China and how Ibsen serves as a bridge linking

China and Norway. Cao Yu adds a personal remark that he has been a disciple of Ibsen since his youth. Instead of focusing on the extent to which Ibsen has influenced the Chinese, Cao Yu shifts his emphasis to the friendship between China and Norway. He sees Ibsen as "the great master of world drama who sows the seeds of art and friendship, which will germinate and bloom among the people" of the two countries. In Cao Yu's view, Ibsen is not only a dramatist but also an ambassador of friendship.

6.08

Chen Dayuan 陳達遠. "Yibusheng de jia" 易卜生的家 (Ibsen's home). In *Yuwai shuqingji* 域外抒情集 (Lyrical essays written abroad), pp. 126–127. Beijing: Beijing chubanshe 北京出版社, 1979.

A change in cultural climate occurred as a result of the turn of political atmosphere in China after 1976. The so-called Second Liberation was not limited to Chinese writers, but also extended to the reception of foreign cultural figures. The name Ibsen could be seen again in Chinese journals and newspapers. Chen Dayuan's "Yibusheng de jia" (Ibsen's home), written during the poet's visit to Skien in 1978, summarizes the reception of Ibsen in China during the Cultural Revolution.

6.09

Chen, Xiaomei. "Occidentalist Theatre in Post-Mao China: Shakespeare, Ibsen and Brecht As Counter-Others," 1993. Reprint. In *Streams of Cultural Capital: Transnational Cultural Studies*. Edited by David Palumbo-Liu and Han Ulrich Gumbrecht, pp. 155–177. Stanford: Stanford University Press, 1997.

This is a study of how the Western theatre serves as a counter current against the socialist ideology in post-Mao China. In the essay, Ibsen's drama is considered as one of the three most important forms of Western theatre in China that provide contemporary Chinese audience with alternative visions of life, art and politics.

6.10

Chen Xiufang 陳秀芳. "*Luosimo jiazu*" 羅斯默家族 (*Rosmersholm*). In *Shijie wenxue mingzhu xinxiang dadian* 世界文學名著欣賞大典 (Appreciation of masterpieces in world literature). Edited by Guo Boxin 郭博

信, pp. 38–42. Taipei: Lianjing chuban shiye gongsi 聯經出版事業公司, 1978.

This is a synopsis of the play with a focus on the main themes and the techniques. There is also information on Ibsen's life in relation to the play. Appended to the synopsis is a list of readings on Ibsen and on the play.

6.11

———. "*Shehui dongliang*" 社會棟樑 (*The Pillars of Society*). In *Shijie wenxue mingzhu xinxiang dadian* 世界文學名著欣賞大典 (Appreciation of masterpieces in world literature). Edited by Guo Boxin 郭博信, pp. 17–22. Taipei: Lianjing chuban shiye gongsi 聯經出版事業公司, 1978.

Same as the entry on *Rosmersholm*, this synopsis on *The Pillars of Society* is also an analysis of the play's themes and techniques. The reference list provided at the end of the synopsis is useful to students of Ibsen.

6.12

Chen Yongbiao 陳永標. "Zhongguo jindai xiju lilun shuping" 中國近代戲劇理論述評 (A review of modern Chinese dramatic theories). *Huanan shifan daxue xuebao* 華南師範大學學報 (South China normal university journal), Zhesheban 哲社版 (Philosophy and social sciences edition), 2 (1983), pp. 83–89.

Chen Yongbiao's article is a study of how modern Chinese theories of drama have evolved historically from the social and cultural developments in China. This article employs a contemporary perspective in its discussion of the development of modern Chinese drama as a result of Western influence, thus providing the theoretical background for a cultural re-evaluation of lbsen's role in the transformation of modern Chinese theatre and culture.

6.13

Cui Wenyu 崔文瑜. "Yibusheng de xiju" 易卜生的戲劇 (Ibsen's drama). *Xinwenyi* 新文藝 (New literature and arts), 37 (June 1983), pp. 93–98.

While most other essays published in Taiwan from 1949 to 1980 tend to treat Ibsen in brief, this article by Cui Wenyu discusses how the dramatist has been received in Europe and America. Comparing the reception of Ibsen in Taiwan with that in the West, Cui observes: "Whenever we refer to Western drama, we must read Ibsen. In the departments of foreign literature at our universities, we have the course "Selected Readings in Drama," included in which are Ibsen's *Peer Gynt*, *Rosmersholm*, *A Doll's House*, and *Ghosts*, among others. Ibsen's place in world theatre is recognized for his long lasting influence."

6.14

Deng Xingqi 鄧興器. "Tian Han xiju huodong yu chuangzuo nianpu" 田漢戲劇活動和創作年譜 (A chronology of Tian Han's theatre activities and plays). *Xiqu yanjiu* 戲曲研究 (Studies on music-drama), 3 (1980), pp. 310–328.

Although this essay is not a study of Ibsen, the information given about Tian Han's life and theatre activities shows the background of how Ibsen was received in that period, as well as how Tian Han is indebted to Ibsen in his career as a playwright.

6.15

Eide, Elisabeth. "*Peer Gynt* i Kina, 1983 og en greyende nyfortolkning av Ibsen." *Edda*, 3 (1986), pp. 221–226.

This essay studies the reception of *Peer Gynt* in China in 1983, with a focus on the change in Xiao Qian's attitude toward the play, which was previously considered by him in 1949 as a negative work promoting the harmful effects of individualism.

6.16

Fang Ping 方平. "Sange cong jiating chuzou de funü xingxiang" 三個從家庭出走的婦女形象 (The images of three women who leave home). *Dushu* 讀書 (Study), 10 (1982), pp. 67–76. Reprint. Fang Ping. "Leaving Home — Three Women in European Literature." Translated by Zhang Hong. *Cowrie*, 1.2 (1984), pp. 47–53.

In this essay, Fang Ping compares the three women who leave home for freedom, one of whom is Nora. Although it is not a historical study of the reception of *A Doll's House*, it provides a perspective on how the image of Nora is compared in a Chinese context.

6.17

Gao Zhongfu 高中甫. "Yibusheng de xingge ji qi zuopin" 易卜生的性格及其作品 (The character of Ibsen and his works). In *Yibusheng yanjiu lunwenji* 易卜生研究論文集 (Ibsen research papers). Edited by Meng Shengde 孟勝德 and Astrid Saether, pp. 37–45; 258–266. Beijing: Zhongguo wenxue chubanshe 中國文學出版社, 1995.

The author begins the essay by saying: "The writing mirrors the writer." In this essay, the focus is placed on the relation between Ibsen's plays and his personality. Thus the essay takes a biographical approach in its first part in affirming that there is a close link between Ibsen's life and his ideas of individualism. In the second part, Gao Zhongfu surveys briefly the reception of Ibsen in China.

6.18

———, ed. *Yibusheng pinglunji* 易卜生評論集 (Studies on Ibsen). Beijing: Renmin chubanshe, 1982.

This is a collection of contemporary Chinese studies on Ibsen published since the late 1970s. Many of these studies aim at a reevaluation of Ibsen from perspectives that are beyond the socialist view, such as the essays by Freud and James McFarlane.

6.19

Guo Boxin 郭博信 (Kuo Po-hsin), ed. *Shijie wenxue mingzhu xinxiang dadian* 世界文學名著欣賞大典 (Appreciation of masterpieces in world literature). Taipei: Lianjing chuban shiye gongsi 聯經出版事業公司, 1978.

In this book, there are twelve synopses of Ibsen plays, *Brand*, *Peer Gynt*, *The Pillars of Society*, *A Doll's House*, *Ghosts*, *An Enemy of the People*, *The Wild Duck*, *Romsersholm*, *The Lady from the Sea*, *Hedda Gabler*, *The Master Builder*, and *When We Dead Awaken*. In these synopses, there is analysis of the themes of the plays and their techniques, which is supplemented by biographical information on Ibsen and a list of reference readings.

6.20

———. "Yibusheng xingcheng *Pei'er Jinte* de renwu zaoxing de shangque" 易卜生形成《培爾・金特》的人物造形的商榷 (A discussion on Ibsen's technique of characterization in *Peer Gynt*). *Zhongwai wenxue* 中外文學 (*Chung-wai Literary Monthly*), 12.10 (March 1984), pp. 4–16.

Guo Boxin is one of the few scholars of Ibsen and Scandinavian literature in Taiwan. In this essay, he adopts the socio-biographical approach in an attempt to analyze *Peer Gynt* thoroughly. According to Guo, the play has three sources: Ibsen's personal experience in life and politics, Kierkegaard's influence, and the myths of Norway. Guo thinks that the ending of *Peer Gynt* is inspired by the Bible, as Peer Gynt, like the two thieves who were crucified with Christ and were saved by Christ, is also pardoned by Solveig. From other biographical evidences, Guo points out many similarities between Ibsen himself and Peer Gynt. Both of them are reckless in conduct in their youth and are easily led by immediate emotional response to events around them. Guo believes that the family misfortune that has occurred to both of them is a chief cause of their uncompromising views of life.

The Prussian annexation of Schleswig and Holstein in 1864, Guo thinks, is a reason for Ibsen to hate Norway because of its cowardice. Ibsen's love affair with his maid servant is compared to Peer Gynt's carrying Ingrid off and also to his affair with the Woman in Green. Although there is direct borrowing of Peer Gynt's character from one of the mythical figures described in Norwegian mythology, Guo argues that this only serves as a point of reference in Ibsen's characterization of Peer Gynt. On the other hand, Peer Gynt is a personification of Kierkegaard's existential philosophy as expressed in *Either/Or*. Same as in Kierkegaard's work, Peer Gynt also passes from the idealistic stage in life to the ethical and religious stages.

Guo's article represents an academic approach to Ibsen in Taiwan. Although Guo does not acknowledge his indebtedness to any previous Western scholarship on the relation between Peer Gynt and the Bible, an Ibsen scholar will notice that it is a Chinese recapitulation of Western sources.

6.21

———. "Yibusheng yu *Qungui*" 易卜生與《羣鬼》 (Ibsen and *Ghosts*). *Shijie wenxue mingzhu xinxiang* 世界文學名著欣賞 (Appreciation of masterpieces in world literature). Edited by Hou Jian 侯健, et al., pp. 28–35. Taipei: Zhongyang wenwu gongyingshe 中央文物供應社, 1979.

This study of Ibsen's *Ghosts* focuses on the literary techniques of the play. The use of minor characters in the release of information about the major characters in the opening scene is cited as an example of the good beginning of a drama. The ghostly atmosphere in the play is also discussed in relation to the theme.

This essay is the revised version of an earlier article with the same title published in 1972 (see 5.08).

6.22

Guo Jiashen 郭家申. "Yibusheng" 易卜生 (Ibsen). *Waiguo ming zuojia zhuan* 外國名作家傳 (Biographies of famous foreign authors), vol. 2. Edited by Zhang Meilun 張美倫, et al., pp. 628–635. Beijing: Zhongguo shehui kexue chubanshe 中國社會科學出版社, 1980.

This essay by Guo Jiashen is full of socialist comments, such as "dissatisfaction with the capitalist society but unable to find a breakthrough," which became a standardized evaluation of Ibsen in China in the late 1970s. Instead of seeing Ibsen as a dramatist, Guo Jiashen reads the playwright in a political context.

6.23

Hailunte, Fuluode 弗羅德・海倫特 (Frode Helland). "Ping *Haida Gaobule* zhong de foudingxing" 評《海達・高布樂》中的否定性 (Some notes on the negativity of *Hedda Gabler*). In *Yibusheng yanjiu lunwenji* 易卜生研究論文集 (Ibsen research papers). Edited by Meng Shengde 孟勝德 and Astrid Saether, pp. 106–123; 333–355. Beijing: Zhongguo wenxue chubanshe 中國文學出版社, 1995.

The author begins the essay by saying that *Hedda Gabler* is a difficult play because it has multiple messages and no two directors will agree on what the play's theme is. Instead of arguing what the play is about, the author asserts that it has an experimental nature in dealing with the postmodernist experience in fragmentation.

6.24

Hengmo, Bi'ang 比昂・亨默 (Bjorn Hemmer). "Nuowei xijujia Henglike Yibusheng" 挪威戲劇家亨利克・易卜生 (The dramatist Henrik Ibsen). In *Yibusheng yanjiu lunwenji* 易卜生研究論文集 (Ibsen research papers).

Edited by Meng Shengde 孟勝德 and Astrid Saether, pp. 124–142; 356–375. Beijing: Zhongguo wenxue chubanshe 中國文學出版社, 1995.

The author thinks that Ibsen's success lies not only in his great topical plays, but also in his techniques in skillfully unifying the three elements: the psychological, the ideological and the social. In this essay, the author points out that Ibsen has achieved an international breakthrough mainly because he is able to examine social problems from the perspective of the individual and the personal.

6.25

Huang Ruwen 黃如文. "Yibusheng xiju yu Zhongguo xinwenxue yundong" 易卜生戲劇與中國新文學運動 (Ibsen's drama and the Chinese new literature movement). *Huanan shiyuan xuebao* 華南師院學報 (Huanan normal college journal), Zhesheban 哲社版 (Philosophy and social sciences edition), 4 (1979), pp. 34–38.

This essay is a reevaluation of how Ibsen was received by the Chinese intellectuals, writers and opinion-makers during the May 4th period and how Ibsen's ideas were interpreted by the Chinese and became guiding principles of the movement in the pursuit for individuality and personal freedom.

6.26

Keleman, Haluode 哈羅德・克勒曼 (Harold Clurman). *Xiju dashi Yibusheng* 戲劇大師易卜生 (The great dramatist Ibsen). Translated by Jiang Jia 蔣嘉 and Jiang Hongding 蔣虹丁. Changsha: Hunan renmin chubanshe 湖南人民出版社, 1981.

This is a translation of Harold Clurman's *Ibsen* (London: Macmillan, 1978), in which the focus is placed on Ibsen's life and his career as a playwright. In this study, the author relates the plays to Ibsen's own experience in life.

6.27

———. "Yibusheng yu Qihefu" 易卜生與契訶夫 (Ibsen and Chekhov). Translated by Jiang Hongding 蔣虹丁. *Jiangsu xiju* 江蘇戲劇, 12 (1983), pp. 59–60.

In this essay, there is a comparison of Ibsen and Chekhov in terms of the two dramatists' achievements and their dramatic techniques. The essay shows how Ibsen and Chekhov share some common elements in their plays. It is a translation of Chapter 13 of Harold Clurman's *Ibsen* (London: Macmillan, 1978).

6.28

Li Chang 李暢. "Yibusheng de xiju he xiangxing bujing" 易卜生的戲劇和箱形布景 (Ibsen's drama and the box set). *Xiju yanjiu* 戲劇研究 (Studies on drama), 4 (1979), pp. 104–122.

A highly technical analysis of Ibsen's stagecraft, Li Chang's essay discusses how realistic setting contributes to the powerful effects of Ibsen's plays. Li's article is one of the profoundest Chinese studies of the artistic aspects of Ibsen's drama. This article is not restricted by socialist doctrines in its perspective. A number of contemporary Western studies on Ibsen, particularly those in the English-speaking world, are used as sources for the essay, which reflects a revived interest in Anglo-American criticism of Ibsen.

6.29

Li Chunxi 李春熹. "Tan liangnian lai huaju jiegou xingshi de xin tansuo" 談兩年來話劇結構形式的新探索 (On explorations in the structure of spoken drama in the past two years). *Zhongguo xiju nianjian 1982* 中國戲劇年鑑 1982 (Yearbook of the Chinese theatre 1982), pp. 294–299. Beijing: Zhongguo xiju chubanshe 中國戲劇出版社, 1982.

This essay reviews the general changes in style and structure in contemporary Chinese theatre since the 1980s. Ibsen's *Peer Gynt* and its stage production by the director Xu Xiaozhong, a professor at the Central Academy of Drama, Beijing, becomes one of the focuses of discussion in the essay. Many critics regard Xu Xiaozhong's reinterpretation and stage adaptation of Ibsen's *Peer Gynt* according to the Chinese mythological figures as the major signs of change that has brought in new elements to the contemporary Chinese theatre. The essay also discusses the use of absurdist and Brechtian techniques on the Chinese stage that has led to a new style of what is called "drama of a loose (or plotless) structure."

6.30

Li Dun 李頓 and Liu Pulin 劉普林. "Lun Wu Si xiju yundong" 論五四戲劇運動 (On the drama movement during the May 4th era). *Xiju yanjiu* 戲劇研究 (Studies on drama), 9 (1981), pp. 106–112.

The essay reviews the development of Chinese drama during the May 4th era and proposes the view to see drama as a social movement. In such a view, the development in drama is seen as having a close link with social change. Many details about the social background of early modern Chinese drama, particularly that related to the reception of Ibsen, are given in the essay.

6.31

Li Qifan 李啟範. "*Haida Gaibole*" 海達・蓋伯樂 (*Hedda Gabler*). In *Shijie wenxue mingzhu xinxiang dadian* 世界文學名著欣賞大典 (Appreciation of masterpieces in world literature). Edited by Guo Boxin 郭博信, pp. 46–50. Taipei: Lianjing chuban shiye gongsi 聯經出版事業公司, 1978.

In the synopsis, the emphasis is put on an analysis of the characterization of the protagonist Hedda Gabler, who is seen by Li Qifan as a revolutionary character. Appended to the synopsis is a list of readings for students of Ibsen.

6.32

———. "*Kuilei jiating*" 傀儡家庭 (*A Doll's House*). In *Shijie wenxue mingzhu xinxiang dadian* 世界文學名著欣賞大典 (Appreciation of masterpieces in world literature). Edited by Guo Boxin 郭博信, pp. 22–26. Taipei: Lianjing chuban shiye gongsi 聯經出版事業公司, 1978.

Same as other entries on Ibsen in Guo Boxin's book, the essay is mainly a summary of the play. Biographical information about Ibsen is also given in the essay.

6.33

———. "*Pi'er Jinte*" 皮爾・金特 (*Peer Gynt*). In *Shijie wenxue mingzhu xinxiang dadian* 世界文學名著欣賞大典 (Appreciation of masterpieces in world literature). Edited by Guo Boxin 郭博信, pp. 13–17. Taipei: Lianjing chuban shiye gongsi 聯經出版事業公司, 1978.

The synopsis offers a summary of the main themes of the play and also an analysis of its techniques. There is a list of readings provided at the end of the synopsis.

6.34

———. "*Qungui*" 群鬼 (*Ghosts*). In *Shijie wenxue mingzhu xinxiang dadian* 世界文學名著欣賞大典 (Appreciation of masterpieces in world literature). Edited by Guo Boxin 郭博信, pp. 26–30. Taipei: Lianjing chuban shiye gongsi 聯經出版事業公司, 1978.

This entry on *Ghosts* is a synopsis of its main themes, in which there is also analysis of the techniques and structure. The appendix consists of a list of readings.

6.35

———. "*Yeya*" 野鴨 (*The Wild Duck*). In *Shijie wenxue mingzhu xinxiang dadian* 世界文學名著欣賞大典 (Appreciation of masterpieces in world literature). Edited by Guo Boxin 郭博信, pp. 34–38. Taipei: Lianjing chuban shiye gongsi 聯經出版事業公司, 1978.

This synopsis of the play focuses on the theme of illusion and truth in life. At the same time there is also analysis of the play's structure. The appendix provides useful further readings on the play.

6.36

Li Qin 李欽. "'Wentiju' de wenti" "問題劇"的問題 (The problem of the "problem play"). *Renmin xiju* 人民戲劇 (People's drama), 5 (May 1982), pp. 45–47.

This is a critique of the Chinese problem play that was fashionable in the 1920s–30s and also in the 1960s–70s in its style to imitate Ibsen's social problem plays. The essay deals with the shortcomings of the Chinese imitations, most of which in general lack artistic merits. It also raises questions about art and social problems.

6.37

Li Xisuo 李喜所. "Woguo zuizao de huaju" 我國最早的話劇 (The earliest modern drama in China). *Xiju yanjiu* 戲劇研究 (Studies on drama), 9 (1982), pp. 94–95.

This is a useful article that gives information on the origin of modern Chinese drama and how it is indebted to Western sources. It provides the reader with information on how realism was interpreted and staged by the early modern Chinese dramatists, and hence also the context in which Ibsen was received.

6.38

Li Yongping 李永平. "*Da jianzhujia*" 大建築家 (*The Master Builder*). In *Shijie wenxue mingzhu xinxiang dadian* 世界文學名著欣賞大典 (Appreciation of masterpieces in world literature). Edited by Guo Boxin 郭博信, pp. 50–55. Taipei: Lianjing chuban shiye gongsi 聯經出版事業公司, 1978.

In the synopsis of the play, the author points out mainly the techniques and themes in relation to Ibsen's life and career. At the end of the synopsis, there is also a list of references.

6.39

———. "*Guomin gongdi*" 國民公敵 (*An Enemy of the People*). In *Shijie wenxue mingzhu xinxiang dadian* 世界文學名著欣賞大典 (Appreciation of masterpieces in world literature). Edited by Guo Boxin 郭博信, pp. 30–34. Taipei: Lianjing chuban shiye gongsi 聯經出版事業公司, 1978.

In the analysis of the play, the author focuses mainly on the theme of iconoclasm and individuality and discusses it as a major preoccupation in Ibsen's life, as well as in his middle plays. The reference list gives useful information on general readings about Ibsen and the play.

6.40

———. "*Haishang furen*" 海上夫人 (*The Lady from the Sea*). In *Shijie wenxue mingzhu xinxiang dadian* 世界文學名著欣賞大典 (Appreciation of masterpieces in world literature). Edited by Guo Boxin 郭博信, pp. 42–46. Taipei: Lianjing chuban shiye gongsi 聯經出版事業公司, 1978.

The entry on *The Lady from the Sea* focuses on the play's theme of personal freedom and choice in life. The biographical information on Ibsen provides the background for an understanding of the play.

6.41

Liao Kedui 廖可兑. *Xi Ou xiju shi* 西歐戲劇史 (A history of western European drama). Beijing: Zhongguo xiju chubanshe 中國戲劇出版社, 1981.

This book by Liao Kedui is a general survey of the history of European drama, from which the reader will see how Chinese scholars consider Ibsen in relation to European drama. It attempts to put Ibsen in a context that treats Ibsen more as a dramatist than as a social critic.

6.42

———. "Yibusheng he ta de juzuo *Wan'ou zhi jia*" 易卜生和他的劇作《玩偶之家》 (Ibsen and his play *A Doll's House*). *Xiju xuexi* 戲劇學習 (Drama studies), 1 (1979), pp. 29, 64–71.

Liao Kedui's essay, "Ibsen and his play *A Doll's House*," published in 1979, begins with Friedrich Engels's letter to Paul Ernst on Ibsen and claims that the letter is an important evaluation of the social conditions under which Ibsen wrote his plays. After summarizing Ibsen's representative plays to highlight his dramatic techniques, such as the well-knit structure, intense dramatic conflicts, and retrospective exposition, Liao focuses on a detailed analysis of *A Doll's House* as an illustration of these techniques.

Liao Kedui believes that politically Ibsen is a bourgeois playwright and is therefore unable to provide answers to the political issues of his day. He appreciates the fact that Ibsen has an incisive unravelling and criticism of social reality, but he thinks it a pity that Ibsen puts too much emphasis on ethical issues and often treats political issues as such because Ibsen believes that once the ethical problems are solved, all others will vanish. Resulting from this "incorrect" view is that, as Liao points out, Ibsen seldom reflects political issues in his works. All his positive figures insist on personal struggle and individual liberation. All of them emphasize spiritual struggle of the petty bourgeoisie. Ibsen tries to reform the world with his petty bourgeois outlook. He does not believe in the power of the proletariat and the masses. As a result, he gradually loses confidence in the progress of society and becomes pessimistic. Liao thinks that although Ibsen does not achieve any breakthrough in his political view, he is still a great playwright, for he has contributed tremendously to the modern theatre, especially the rise of modern social problem plays.

6.43

Liu Baiqing 劉柏青. "'Xiandai xiju zhi fu' he 'shehui wentiju'" "現代戲劇之父" 和 "社會問題劇" ("Father of modern drama" and the "social problem play"). *Jutan* 劇壇 (Theatre), 2 (1984), pp. 47–49.

This is a study of Ibsen's achievements and his place in the development of modern drama. The article outlines the development of the social problem play in relation to the contribution of Ibsen. It also deals with how drama became more and more social-oriented toward the end of the nineteenth century.

6.44

Liu Housheng 劉厚生. "Huaju heyi fanrong" 話劇何以繁榮 (How to revive modern Chinese drama). *Wenyi yanjiu* 文藝研究 (Literary studies), 1 (1981), pp. 31–40.

In this essay, Liu discusses the problems in contemporary Chinese drama and why the audience lose interest in it. He thinks that in contemporary Chinese drama too much emphasis has been put on the presentation of problems according to fixed political lines at the expense of dramatic techniques and the interest of the audience. This essay is one of the many that called for a new conception of drama, as well as a reinterpretation of Ibsen in the early 1980s.

6.45

Liu Minghou 劉明厚. *Zhenshi yu xuhuan de xuanzhe — Yibusheng houqi xiangzheng zhuyi xiju* 真實與虛幻的選擇 — 易卜生後期象徵主義戲劇 (Choice between truth and illusion: The later symbolist plays by Ibsen). Shanghai: Tongji daxue chubanshe 同濟大學出版社, 1994.

Representing contemporary Chinese scholarship on Ibsen in the 1990s, Liu Minghou's book is a publication based on her Ph.D. thesis completed at the Central Academy of Drama, Beijing. Liu Minghou is an associate professor of drama at the Shanghai Theatre Academy and her book focuses mainly on the symbolist plays by Ibsen: *The Wild Duck*, *Rosmersholm*, *The Lady from the Sea*, *Hedda Glabler*, *Little Eyolf*, *John Gabriel Borkman*, *The Master Builder*, and *When We Dead Awaken*. There is analysis of the techniques in these plays, as well as of the philosophy behind these plays which, as the author sees, is related to the social background and the life of Ibsen.

6.46

Ma Qi 馬琦. *Bianju gailun* 編劇概論 (An introduction to playwriting). Xi'an: Shaanxi renmin chubanshe 陝西人民出版社, 1981.

This is a study of playwriting techniques based on Western drama, in which the different kinds of playwriting techniques in modern drama are summarized. Examples are taken from Ibsen and other realist playwrights in modern Western drama.

6.47

Maiye, Maike'er 麥克爾・邁耶 (Michael Meyer). "Yibusheng dui xiandai xiju de yingxiang" 易卜生對現代戲劇的影響 (Ibsen's influence on modern drama). Translator anonymous. *Waiguo wenxue baodao* 外國文學報導 (Bulletin of foreign literature), 1 (1981), pp. 19–23.

Attention to Ibsen's art is provided in the Chinese translation of Michael Meyer's comments on Ibsen's contributions to modern drama. Michael Meyer is so far the most authoritative biographer of Ibsen. The translation of Michael Meyer's essay, part of the epilogue in his book *Ibsen, a Biography* (1977), represents also a new interest in Anglo-American studies of Ibsen. Through this translation the Chinese view of Ibsen's dramatic technique is broadened beyond the Russian doctrines that shaped China's literary and cultural criticism in the 1950s.

The Chinese reader is allowed to see Ibsen's threefold contribution to modern theatre, namely, the portrayal of ordinary people as protagonists, the technical innovations in dialogue, plot structure and characterization, and the understanding of human relationships.

6.48

Mao Yumei 茅于美. *Yibusheng he ta de xiju* 易卜生和他的戲劇 (Ibsen and his drama). Beijing: Beijing chubanshe 北京出版社, 1981.

The woman poet-scholar Mao Yumei's *Yibusheng he ta de xiju* (Ibsen and his drama) is the only book-length study on Ibsen published in Chinese between 1976–1981. The book is part of a series of books on foreign literature. Supplying biographical data and historical background, Mao presents a general study of the dramatist. She is no exception in affirming that Ibsen's plays are a condemnation of capitalist society. However, the book also provides some evaluation of the artistic achievements of Ibsen. Such a book-length study of Ibsen's dramatic technique, though commonplace to a Western reader, is rare in China.

6.49

Meng Shengde 孟勝德 and Astrid Saether 阿斯特里德・薩瑟, eds. *Yibusheng yanjiu lunwenji* 易卜生研究論文集 (Ibsen research papers). Beijing: Zhongguo wenxue chubanshe 中國文學出版社, 1995.

This is the proceedings of the papers presented at the Ibsen seminar jointly organized by the Norwegian Embassy in China and the Chinese Association of Translation in 1995. Included in the volume are studies on Ibsen as well as on his reception in China. Some of the studies, such as Elisabeth Eide's essay, "*Peer Gynt* and *A Doll's House*: Or One Aspect of Modern Chinese Drama," apparently share much of the research that has been done in Kwok-kan Tam's Ph.D. thesis, "Ibsen in China: Reception and Influence" (University of Illinois at Urbana-Champaign), completed in 1984. However, no acknowledgement of previous scholarship is given in these studies. Since the book is titled "Ibsen research papers," one may wonder why the papers do not follow the proper style of research in their format.

6.50

Pan Jiaxun 潘家洵, et al., eds. & trans. *Yibusheng wenji* 易卜生文集 (Collected works by Ibsen), 8 vols. Beijing: Renmin wenxue chubanshe 人民文學出版社, 1995.

This is so far the most complete collection of Ibsen's works published in Chinese translation. It includes all of Ibsen's plays, a selection of his poetry and some of his critical writings. In the appendix to volume 8 there are also Chinese translations of Western studies of Ibsen, such as Georg Lukác's and Georgii Plekhanov's studies.

6.51

Qin Zhixi 秦志希. "*Leiyu* yu *Qungui* de bijiao fenxi" 《雷雨》與《群鬼》的比較分析 (A comparative analysis of *Thunderstorm* and *Ghosts*).

Waiguo wenxue yanjiu 外國文學研究 (Foreign literature studies), 4 (1983), pp. 94–100.

A new perspective on Ibsen is given in Qin Zhixi's essay, which focuses on the thematic and technical similarities between the two plays and shows to what extent Cao Yu has been influenced by Ibsen. The author concludes that the greatness of Cao Yu's play *Thunderstorm* lies in that it has absorbed the artistic achievements of foreign literature. Qin implies that foreign literature is not necessarily antagonistic to the socialist regime. In summing up his argument, he affirms that *Thunderstorm* has its own unique qualities apart from its indebtedness to *Ghosts*, and amidst their superficial similarities, there are differences. In some places, these affinities in appearance are differences in reality. By pointing out these comparative aspects, Qin tries to show that Cao Yu has a correct attitude toward the influence of foreign culture. Qin suggests that a careful study of these similarities and dissimilarities will perhaps give the reader, as well as Chinese playwrights, some concrete and useful hints on how to assimilate the good elements in foreign culture to develop socialist art and literature.

6.52

Qu Liuyi 曲六乙. "'Wu Si' yu Zhongguo zaoqi huaju yundong" "五四"與中國早期話劇運動 ("May 4th" and early modern Chinese drama movement). *Xiju xuexi* 戲劇學習 (Drama studies), 2 (1979), pp. 7–17.

Qu Liuyi is a theatre critic as well as a theatre historian. In this essay he argues that the May 4th Movement was indebted the theatre reform that called for the treatment of contemporary topics and the use of daily life language. While the May 4th Movement was concerned with the explorations of change from tradition to a new culture in modern China, the theatre reform gave shape to these early explorations of change. Thus the reader is given information on the background relation between the reception of Ibsen and cultural change in China.

6.53

Sase, Asitelide 阿斯特里德・薩瑟 (Astrid Saether). "Yibusheng houqi zuopin zhong nüren de qiwang he nanren de yexin" 易卜生後期作品中女人的期望和男人的野心 (Female expectations and male ambitions in Ibsen's late dramas). In *Yibusheng yanjiu lunwenji* 易卜生研究論文集 (Ibsen research papers). Edited by Meng Shengde 孟勝德 and Astrid Saether, pp. 180–195; 419–436. Beijing: Zhongguo wenxue chubanshe 中國文學出版社, 1995.

This is a psychoanalytic study of Ibsen's last plays that attempts to provide an explanation for the women characters' tragedies. In this study, the author also examines the plays from a contemporary feminist perspective and discusses them in terms of the tension between the sexes.

6.54

Shanghai yishu yanjiusuo 上海藝術研究所, ed. *Zhongguo xiqu quyi cidian* 中國戲曲曲藝詞典 (A dictionary of traditional Chinese dramatic arts). Shanghai: Shanghai cishu chubanshe 上海辭書出版社, 1981.

In this dictionary which seems to have nothing to do with Ibsen, there are entries that deal with the transition from traditional Chinese theatre to the modern theatre. In the section on modern Chinese theatre, there is useful information on major playwrights and drama companies that are important for an understanding of how modern Chinese dramatists respond to the influence of the West.

6.55

Shao Jingtao 邵靜濤. "Yibusheng yu *Wan'ou zhi jia*" 易卜生與《玩偶之家》 (Ibsen and *A Doll's House*). *Jilin ribao* 吉林日報 (Jilin daily), 26 August 1979, p. 2.

Shao Jingtao's study represents an attempt to celebrate the centennial publication of *A Doll's House*, which was published a hundred years earlier in 1879. After briefly commenting on Nora, the author summarizes the major events in Ibsen's life and his concerns in the moral issues of his day.

6.56

Shen Mo 沈默. "*Wan'ou zhi jia* de jiegou yishu" 《玩偶之家》的結構藝術 (The structural art of *A Doll's House*). *Hebei xiju* 河北戲劇 (Hebei drama), 3 (1981). Reprint. In *Xiju yanjiu* 戲劇研究 (Studies on drama), 3 (1981), pp. 115–118.

This study of Ibsen's art focuses on how suspense and crises are used by Ibsen to create tensions. Shen reads *A Doll's House* from the perspective of stage art: "Drama is a performing art and therefore is different from the other art and literary forms. One of its characteristics lies in action and visual effects." In the essay, characterization, dialogue, and symbols are analyzed in detail in their relation to the plot. Shen is one of the few Chinese critics who give attention to the art of Ibsen's drama.

6.57

———. "Yibusheng de liansuo fanying" 易卜生的連鎖反應 (Ibsen's chain reactions). *Suibi* 隨筆 (Random notes), 16 (May 1983), p. 45.

In this short note, the author discusses Ibsen's plays *A Doll's House* and *Ghosts* together and considers the latter as a sequel to the former. This is a biographical-historical approach to the two plays and it tries to put them in the political context of the argument in Europe over the issue of whether or not Nora should stay at home. Thus *Ghosts* is seen as Ibsen's response to the attack from the critics.

6.58

Shi Shuqing 施叔青. "*Dang shizhe fusheng*" 當死者復生 (*When We Dead Awaken*). In *Shijie wenxue mingzhu xinxiang dadian* 世界文學名著欣賞大典 (Appreciation of masterpieces in world literature). Edited by Guo Boxin 郭博信, pp. 55–59. Taipei: Lianjing chuban shiye gongsi 聯經出版事業公司, 1978.

The synopsis follows the same pattern as in other entries that the play is analyzed in terms of themes and techniques in relation to the Ibsen's life and career. The theme of art and truth is discussed. The list of references provides useful readings for students of Ibsen.

6.59

Sun Jun 孫俊. "Shitan 'Shangshi' — Cong Zijun de beiju kan Lu Xun sixiang fazhan de yige cemian" 試談《傷逝》 — 從子君的悲劇看魯迅思想發展的一個側面 (A brief discussion of "Regret for the past" — A glimpse of Lu Xun's intellectual progress through the tragedy of Zijun). *Ningxia daxue xuebao* 寧夏大學學報 (Ningxia university journal), Zhesheban 哲社版 (Philosophy and social sciences edition), 3 (1982), pp. 23–26.

Though this essay focuses on the intellectual development of Lu Xun, it puts the issue in the perspective of the women's movement in China and reconsiders Lu Xun's position toward the liberation of women in China in the 1920s. The short story "Regret for the Past" explores the theme of a woman, named Zijun, leaving home in the style of Nora in pursuit of freedom in marriage, but without the economic means for independence. The hardships of life experienced by Zijun are meant to remind Chinese women that a more practical approach has to be adopted in the pursuit of freedom.

6.60

Sun Wei 孫葳. "Yige chuantong de wujie — Xiaoyi Yibusheng shi de jiegou" 一個傳統的誤解 — 小議易卜生式的結構 (A traditional misinterpretation — A brief note on the Ibsenian structure). *Waiguo xiju* 外國戲劇 (Foreign theatre), 3 (1983), pp. 97–99.

A protest against the negligence of Ibsen's art is registered in Sun Wei's essay which sums up the situation of Ibsen criticism in contemporary China, in which Sun remarks: "Up till today, the evaluation of Ibsen as demonstrated in a large number of essays is mainly on his social plays, whereas for the other plays there is inadequate treatment with regard to both subject-matter and form."

6.61

Suo'ersida, dage 達格・索爾斯達 (Dag Solstad). "Yiwei xiandai Nuowei zuojia bixia de Yibusheng" 一位現代挪威作家筆下的易卜生 (A modern Norwegian writer's use of Ibsen in his novels). In *Yibusheng yanjiu lunwenji* 易卜生研究論文集 (Ibsen research papers). Edited by Meng Shengde 孟勝德 and Astrid Saether, pp. 196–207; 437–452. Beijing: Zhongguo wenxue chubanshe 中國文學出版社, 1995.

The Norwegian novelist Dag Solstad recounts his experience in adapting Ibsen's plays, particularly *The Wild Duck*, for his novels. In this essay, Solstad gives the reader information on how he has incorporated the Norwegian small-town life in his novels.

6.62

Tam, Kwok-kan (Tan Guogen 譚國根). "From Social Problem Play to

Socialist Problem Play: Ibsen and Contemporary Chinese Dramaturgy." *The Journal of the Institute of Chinese Studies of The Chinese University of Hong Kong*, 17 (1986). pp. 387–402.

This is a study of how Ibsen was received in China in the 1950s–1970s, and how Ibsen's social problem play was reinterpreted as socialist problem play that provided the foundation for the formation of socialist drama in China. It reviews the various positions that contemporary Chinese dramatists and theorists have toward Ibsen and his dramaturgy.

6.63

———. "Marxism and Beyond: Contemporary Chinese Reception of Ibsen." *Edda*, 3 (1986), pp. 205–220.

This is a study of Chinese scholarship on Ibsen in 1949–1985. It discusses how the reception of Ibsen in contemporary China has been affected by the changes in political climate in China, as well as by the international scholarship on Ibsen. The reception of Ibsen in contemporary China has actually become a site of contestation between socialist interpretations and Anglo-American academic studies.

6.64

Tan Guogen 譚國根 (Kwok-kan Tam). "Bashi niandai Zhongguo jutan de xingshi chuangxin yu yishi xingtai de zhuanbian" 八十年代中國劇壇的形式創新與意識形態的轉變 (Theatrical innovations and ideological change in China in the 1980s) (unpublished conference paper), 17 pp. Taipei: Bijiao wenxue xuehui 比較文學學會, 1992.

A study of the ideological changes in China since the early 1980s, the paper focuses on how the theatre responds to such changes by experimenting with new modes of exploration. The various Western forms of theatre, such as the Brechtian and Absurdist, were staged in China in the early 1980s. Following the stagings with Western techniques, Chinese dramatists begin to experiment with different combinations of such modes, which are seen as a reaction to the Ibsenian theatre in China, as well as a breakthrough in social vision. The paper surveys the historical development of the realistic theatre in China as background to the discussion of the new modes and experiments.

6.65

———. "Yibusheng xiju yu dangdai Zhongguo xiju lilun de xingcheng" 易卜生戲劇與中國當代戲劇理論的形成 (Ibsen and the formation of contemporary Chinese dramatic theory). In *Wenxue yu biaoyan yishu* 文學與表演藝術 (Literature and the performing arts). Edited by Chen Bingliang (Chan Ping-leung) 陳炳良, pp. 140–163. Hong Kong: Lingnan xueyuan zhongwenxi 嶺南學院中文系, 1994.

This is a comprehensive review of Ibsen's contribution to the theory of contemporary Chinese drama, which is modelled on Ibsen's problem play. The article surveys the Chinese reception of Ibsen in the 1910s and discusses how Ibsen has been understood as a realistic playwright by Hu Shi and other May 4th intellectual leaders in China. In this review article, the Chinese socialist problem play is shown to have a close relation with Ibsen's social problem play. The Marxist theory of class conflict has been applied to contemporary Chinese drama by the Chinese playwright and theorist Li Jianwu to replace the French theory. Thus drama is seen to be a reflection of class conflicts in the contemporary Chinese socialist problem play.

6.66

Tan Peisheng 譚霈生. *Lun xijuxing* 論戲劇性 (On dramaticity). Beijing: Beijing daxue chubanshe 北京大學出版社, 1981.

In this book, Tan Peisheng reconsiders dramaticity in relation to the concept of dramatic conflict. In his discussion, he redefines dramaticity as an effect of dramatic climax rather than as dramatic conflict. The examples he cites are mainly from *A Doll's House*. Thus his book can be read as the Chinese reinterpretation of *A Doll's House* in the 1980s, following a reevaluation of socialist drama.

6.67

Tian Benxiang 田本相. "*Leiyu* lun" 《雷雨》論 (On *Thunderstorm*). *Xiju yishu luncong* 戲劇藝術論叢 (Studies on dramatic art), 1 (1979), pp. 141–158.

Tian Benxiang discusses Cao Yu's innovation in his play *Thunderstorm* and reads it in relation to Western influence on modern Chinese drama. As is well known, *Thunderstorm* is indebted to Ibsen's *Ghosts* in its exposition and characterization. Tian's reading signifies the adoption of a new approach to drama and the theatre in 1979, a time when China was ready for a more relaxed cultural policy.

6.68

Ting Li-hsin. "Mrs. Alving as Portrayed by Henrik Ibsen." *Mingzhi gongzhuan xuebao* 明志工專學報 (Mingzhi (Ming-chih) technical college journal), 8 (June 1976), pp. 57–108.

Representing the academic treatment of Ibsen in Taiwan is this English article "Mrs. Alving as Portrayed by Henrik Ibsen," which offers a textual analysis of *Ghosts*. The article is originally part of an M.A. thesis. Ting believes that through an analysis of Ibsen's characters the reader can understand better the nature of his drama. He argues that the best approach to an Ibsen play, which is marked by its hidden ideas and spirit, rests with a correct reading of the characters. "The chief clue to Ibsen's complete personality lies in the characters he portrays in his works, for there is a part of himself in literally all of them." Ting thinks that the true Ibsen, especially his ideological inclinations, can be found in these two plays. In other words, Ting sees in Ibsen's characters a projection of Ibsen's inner self. *Ghosts* is treated as its author's protest against hypocrisy and self-deception. Ting adds: "Almost entirely self-inspired, Ibsen is a rare genius who requires no outside influence for his work. Self-analysis and social realism are two of his life principles. In each play he expresses his constant introspection; and in each play especially of his later period, he reflects realistic social problems."

6.69

Tong Daoming 童道明. "Zaitan xijuguan" 再談戲劇觀 (Again on the concept of drama). *Xiju yishu* 戲劇藝術 (Theatre arts), 1 (1984), pp. 10–17.

In this article, the author Tong Daoming, a contemporary Chinese theatre critic and professor of drama at the Shanghai Theatre Academy, discusses the nature of drama as an art form which should be distinguished from political slogans. It reviews the different theories and views of modern drama, including the Ibsenian form that has become popular in modern China.

6.70

Wang Ning 王寧. "Yibusheng juzuo de duochong daima" 易卜生劇作的多重代碼 (Multiple codes in Ibsen's drama). In *Yibusheng yanjiu lunwenji* 易卜生研究論文集 (Ibsen research papers). Edited by Meng Shengde 孟勝德 and Astrid Saether, pp. 46–56; 267–277. Beijing: Zhongguo wenxue chubanshe 中國文學出版社, 1995.

In this essay, Wang Ning mentions the different reception of Ibsen mainly because there is the use of multiple codes in his plays. A similar view can be found in Kwok-kan Tam's article, "Decoding Literary History: Cultural Transformation and the Chinese Reception of Ibsen," *Tamkang Review* 22.1–4 (Autumn 1991–Summer 1992), pp. 163–286 (see 1.35).

6.71

Wang Xinmin 王新民. "Huaju yishu yao chuangxin — Cong huaju *Wuwai you nuanliu* tan qi" 話劇藝術要創新 — 從話劇《屋外有暖流》談起 (We need innovations in the art of spoken drama — On the play *Warm currents outside the house*). *Guangming ribao* 光明日報 (Guangming daily), 4 July 1980, p. 3.

The play *Wuwai you nuanliu* (Warm currents outside the house) is an experiment that aims at a new stage production beyond the "revolutionary model plays" developed during the Cultural Revolution in 1967–1976. The historic significance of the production lies in its break with the socialist realistic style and in its turn toward the artistic production of drama. Thus the play can be considered as a turning point in the history of contemporary Chinese theatre that calls for the subsequent Chinese reevaluation of Ibsen's art in playwriting since the early 1980s.

6.72

Wang Zhenzhong 王臻中. "*Wan'ou zhi jia* de beijumei" 《玩偶之家》的悲劇美 (Tragic aesthetics in *A Doll's House*). *Jiangsu xiju* 江蘇戲劇 (Jiangsu drama), 9 (1982), pp. 16–18.

Viewed in relation to the trend of reevaluating Ibsen with an emphasis on his dramatic art that has occurred in China since 1980, Wang Zhenzhong's essay is one of the early efforts in considering Ibsen as an artist, and not just as a social reformer. In the practice of socialist literary criticism in contemporary China, *A Doll's House* has been considered mainly from the perspective of class struggle between Helmer and Nora. But now in Wang Zhenzhong's study, *A Doll's House* is reconsidered with regard to its art form.

6.73

Wang Zhongxiang 王忠祥. "Yibusheng he ta de wenxue chuangzuo" 易卜生和他的文學創作 (Ibsen and his literary writings). In *Yibusheng wenji* 易卜生文集 (Collected works by Ibsen), vol. 1. Edited by Zhang Fusheng 張福生, pp. 1–28. Beijing: Renmin wenxue chubanshe 人民文學出版社, 1995.

This is an introduction to the Chinese translations of Ibsen's plays collected in the *Yibusheng wenji*. In this essay, Wang Zhongxiang reviews the reception of Ibsen in the West as well as in China, and also comments on the contemporary significance of Ibsen and Ibsenism, not only to social change, but also to the development of modern drama. There is a summary of Ibsen's innovations in dramatic techniques.

6.74

———. "Yibusheng 'shehui wenti ju' juyu" 易卜生"社會問題劇"舉隅 (Examples of Ibsen's "social problem plays"). *Huazhong shiyuan xuebao* 華中師院學報 (Central China normal college journal), 2 (1982), pp. 64–69.

Wang Zhongxiang's essay shows a break from the orthodox literary criticism that has been in practice in China since the late 1950s. In this essay, the author does not completely give up the Marxist-socialist interpretation of Ibsen, but he is able to point out the technical innovations in the plays, such as the techniques of the discussion scene, retrospective exposition, and dramatic crisis. All these aesthetic considerations point to a new reception deviated from the mere political interpretation of Ibsen.

6.75

Wei Zhaofeng 魏照風. "Zhongguo huaju shihua" 中國話劇史話 (Notes on the history of modern Chinese drama). *Xiju yanjiu* 戲劇研究 (Studies on drama), 12 (1982), pp. 111–119.

It traces the historical genesis of modern Chinese drama to the influence of Western forms, particularly that of Ibsen, and to the indigenous need for change in China. This essay serves a political purpose of re-evaluating the development of modern Chinese drama so as to shed light on the relation between social change and the revolution in art form.

6.76

Wen 雯. "*Pei'er Jinte* jianjie" 《培爾・金特》簡介 (A brief note on *Peer Gynt*). *Xijubao* 戲劇報 (Theatre news), 8 (1983), p. 45.

As the title of the essay suggests, it summarizes the plot of Ibsen's early play, *Peer Gynt*, in the purpose of reintroducing individualism to China. The play was severely attacked in China in the 1950s for its advocacy of individualism. However, after the Cultural Revolution people begin to see the need to reaffirm the positive value of this play.

6.77

Wen Xiliang 溫希良 and Zhu Dongyu 朱東宇. "Shitan waiguo wenxue dui Zhongguo xiandai wenxue de jiji yingxiang" 試談外國文學對中國現代文學的積極影響 (A preliminary discussion of the positive influences foreign literature exerted on modern Chinese literature). *Zhongguo xiandai wenxue yanjiu congkan* 中國現代文學研究叢刊 (Modern Chinese literature studies series), 7 (Febuary 1981), pp. 276–297.

Similar to the views expressed in many other essays published in the early 1980s, Wen Xiliang and Zhu Dongyu argue in their essay that foreign influences should be considered constructive for the development of China, for many new ideas and elements in modern Chinese literature and culture come first from foreign influences. Examples in this essay are drawn from the works of the major modern Chinese writers, such as Lu Xun and Mao Dun, who have been considered as masters and are also greatly influenced by foreign writers in their works. In this light, one can see the tendency to reevaluate the influence of Ibsen, which has been considered previously from the socialist point of view as "not progressive enough."

6.78

Wu Lichang 吳立昌. "Yibusheng" 易卜生 (Ibsen). In *Wenyi xiao baike* 文藝小百科 (A concise encyclopedia of literature and arts). Edited by Wu Lichang 吳立昌 et al., p. 252. Shanghai: Xuelin chubanshe 學林出版社, 1982.

A dictionary discussion of Ibsen and his social plays is given in this entry in *A Concise Encyclopedia of Literature and Arts*, in which Ibsen is described as follows: "Through the creation of artistic figures, the dramatist attacks the evils of capitalist society from the viewpoint of the petty bourgeoisie and raises a number of stimulating questions concerning religion, law, morality, education, and the status of women. Yet he fails to show a correct way to solve them and relies only on moral power and individual rebellion for social reform."

6.79

Wu Wenhui 吳文輝, Yi Xinnong 易新農, and Zhang Guopei 張國培, eds. *Waiguo wenxue* 外國文學 (Foreign literature), vol. 2. Beijing: Waiguo wenxue chubanshe 外國文學出版社, 1979.

The relaxation of government censorship in China in 1978–79 allowed the emergence of unorthodox opinions. Representing a new view on Ibsen, which pays a considerable degree of attention to his art, is this book by Wu Wenhui, Yi Xinnong, and Zhang Guopei, in which Ibsen is criticized as a "bourgeois writer who is discontented with the capitalist world but does not totally repudiate it." And as for the violent social conflicts, "he simply takes them as moral issues and tries to find breakthroughs in morality. He thinks that heredity has a determining effect in human behaviour and his works are tinted with the colours of Naturalism." Ibsen is thus regarded as representative of critical realism, which, according to the authors of the book, has been "on the way to decline."

6.80

Wu Zuguang 吳祖光. "*Pei'er Jinte*" 培爾・金特 (*Peer Gynt*). *Wenyibao* 文藝報 (Literary gazette), 8 (1984), pp. 74–75.

Wu Zuguang is a noted modern Chinese playwright. In this reading of *Peer Gynt*, Wu asserts that the play should be read in a positive light and its message of individualism should be seen as useful to the revival of Chinese culture. In this essay, Wu Zuguang analyzes the play's theme and reinterprets individualism as "being responsible for one's action."

6.81

Xiao Man 蕭曼. "Kan *Pei'er Jinte* yanchu suibi" 看《培爾・金特》演出

隨筆 (Random notes on the performance of *Peer Gynt*). *Waiguo xiju* 外國戲劇 (Foreign theatre) , 4 (1981), pp. 154–156.

This is a review of the stage production of *Peer Gynt*, which was directed by Xu Xiaozhong for the China Youth Art Theatre, Beijing. Xu is a famous director at the Central Academy of Drama, who also staged the play in Hong Kong in 1985. The review praises the production as innovative in stage adaptation and at the same time successful in bringing out the theme of individualism to the Chinese audience.

6.82

Xiao Qian 蕭乾. "Cong 'Nuola chuzou yihou zenmeban' zhijin" 從〈娜拉出走以後怎麼辦〉至今 (From "What happens after Nora leaves home" to now). *Zhongguo qingnian* 中國青年 (Chinese youth), 11 (1982), pp. 16–17.

Beginning with a reconsideration of the status of Chinese women outlined in Lu Xun's essay, "What Happens After Nora Leave Home?," which was delivered as a speech on the movement of women's liberation at the Peking Normal College for Women in 1923, Xiao Qian reviews the history of Chinese women's struggle for independence up to the 1980s. His view is that the major obstacle to women's independence lies in their lack of an independent mind, that is, a sense of individuality. Thus he thinks that the idea of individualism in Ibsen's plays should be reintroduced to the Chinese in the 1980s.

6.83

———. "*Pei'er Jinte* yizhe qianji" 《培爾・金特》譯者前記 (The translator's preface to *Peer Gynt*). *Shijie wenxue* 世界文學 (World literature), 3 (1978), pp. 69–72.

In this preface, Xiao Qian, the famous Chinese writer, Ibsen scholar and translator who won several prizes for his translations of Ibsen, reviews his first encounter with the plays of Ibsen and how he interprets Ibsen as reactionary in his early years. After the disastrous Cultural Revolution (1966–76) in China which occurred mainly as a result of mass hero-worship, Xiao begins to see the positive value of individualism and thus obtains a new vision of the play *Peer Gynt*. This essay is very useful for a knowledge about the history of the Chinese reception of Ibsen and how it is related to the politics of contemporary China.

6.84

———. "Tiqi Yibusheng" 提起易卜生 (Random thoughts on Ibsen). In *Yibusheng yanjiu lunwenji* 易卜生研究論文集 (Ibsen research papers). Edited by Meng Shengde 孟勝德 and Astrid Saether, pp. 16–17; 235–237. Beijing: Zhongguo wenxue chubanshe 中國文學出版社, 1995.

In this short essay, Xiao Qian reviews the reception of Ibsen in China. According to him, Ibsen's influence in China is much greater than Shakespeare's, although the latter is more famous. Xiao Qian also briefly mentions how he translated Ibsen's *Peer Gynt* in the 1980s.

6.85

———. "Yibusheng de *Pei'er Jinte*" 易卜生的《培爾・金特》 (Ibsen's *Peer Gynt*). *Waiguo xiju* 外國戲劇 (Foreign theatre), 4 (1981), pp. 72, 74–77.

A reconsideration of Ibsen's individualism can be found in this article by Xiao Qian. Early in 1949, Xiao Qian thought that *Peer Gynt* was an attack on individualism and could serve as a weapon against bourgeois thought in the intellectual reform movement. But in 1978 Xiao read the play from a different perspective. Expressing his contempt of the Gang of Four in 1978 when he completed the Chinese translation of acts one and five of the play, Xiao considered it a ridicule of political opportunists. According to Xiao's interpretation, the play's theme provides a contrast between the human and the devil: "a 'human being' should have his own self, his beliefs and principles, and is not opportunistic, whereas a 'devil' does not and will avoid difficulties and yield to temptation. The devil's judgement is purely based on personal advantages, not on the consideration of what is right and what is wrong." In 1981, however, Xiao was able to notice that all his previous interpretations of the play and, consequently, of Ibsen, were very much affected by his personal emotions and political naiveté, which, he now thinks, is not a correct attitude toward a literary work. Refuting his previous position, Xiao recommends a rereading of Ibsen in terms of a broader philosophical perspective that can shed light on ideals in life and personal integrity.

6.86

———. "Zhe bu jinjin shi yichuxi — *Pei'er Jinte* gongyan yougan" 這不僅僅是一齣戲 — 《培爾・金特》公演有感 (This is not only a drama — My thoughts on the performance of *Peer Gynt*). *Xiju bao* 戲劇報 (Theatre news), 6 (June 1983), p. 10.

In this essay, Xiao Qian reminds the readers that the Chinese stage production of *Peer Gynt* by the China Youth Art Theatre, Beijing in 1983 should not be seen merely as a drama and that the social and political messages on individualism should be fully grasped. According to Xiao Qian, the collectivism in traditional Chinese culture and in the socialist system is the cause of mass disasters during the Cultural Revolution (1966–76). This should be remedied by promoting individualism.

6.87

Xinhuashe jizhe 新華社記者. "Yibusheng guxiang fangwenji" 易卜生故鄉訪問記 (A visit to Ibsen's hometown). *Xinhua ribao* 新華日報 (New China daily), 23 Febuary 1979, p. 3.

Published anonymously under the authorship of "Reporter of the New China News Agency," the essay comments on why the Chinese had to celebrate Ibsen's 150th birthday in 1978. According to the essay, Ibsen represents a close cultural exchange between China and Norway. It also gives the reader a glimpse of Ibsen's hometown and the house Ibsen lived in when he was young.

6.88

Xu Xiaozhong 徐曉鍾. "Zaixian Yibusheng — Daoyan *Pei'er Jinte* de sikao" 再現易卜生 — 導演《培爾・金特》的思考 (Recreating Ibsen — My thoughts on staging *Peer Gynt*). *Xijubao* 戲劇報 (Theatre news), 8 (1983), pp. 44–49.

Xu Xiaozhong is a professor and currently president of the Central Academy of Drama, Beijing. In 1983 he directed Ibsen's *Peer Gynt* for the China Youth Art Theatre. In this essay, Xu Xiaozhong reveals that he had never seen any production of *Peer Gynt* before he decided to direct the play. Thus many of the mythological figures in the play are represented in forms similar to those in the classical Chinese novel *Journey to the West*. Yet, for the director what is important is not the superficial staging of the play, but a mastery of its spirit and theme, that is, the play as a satire of conformity, hypocrisy, and the lack of individuality.

6.89

Xu Zhichao 徐志超. "Waiguo wenxue he woguo xinwenxue" 外國文學與我國新文學 (Foreign literature and modern Chinese literature). *Jiangxi daxue xuebao* 江西大學學報 (Jiangxi university journal), 2 (1979), pp. 79–85.

This is a historical study of the impact of foreign literature upon the development of modern Chinese literature up to the 1940s. In this study, the author emphasizes the positive value of the impact and asserts that there is the need for an open-door policy in the field of arts and literature. The basic argument in the essay is that cultural exchange is necessary for the development of any nation's literature. Thus the essay can be seen as one of the background works that led to the relaxation of state control of the arts, and eventually to the reinterpretation of Ibsen's plays and his ideas of individualism in the 1980s.

6.90

Xue Xingguo 薛興國. "*Bolangde*" 勃朗德 (*Brand*). In *Shijie wenxue mingzhu xinxiang dadian* 世界文學名著欣賞大典 (Appreciation of masterpieces in world literature). Edited by Guo Boxin 郭博信, pp. 1–13. Taipei: Lianjing chuban shiye gongsi 聯經出版事業公司, 1978.

This is a synopsis of the play, in which the author points out mainly the techniques and themes. In this synopsis the author also gives information about Ibsen's career. At the end of the synopsis, there is also a list of references.

6.91

Yan Zheng 嚴錚. "Jianlun Yibusheng de mingju *Wan'ou zhi jia*" 簡論易卜生的名劇《玩偶之家》 (A brief study of Ibsen's famous play *A Doll's House*). *Henan shida xuebao* 河南師大學報 (Henan normal university journal), 6 (1979), pp. 78–83, 95.

Yan Zheng's essay is a recapitulation of the Chinese view that the play reflects Ibsen's attack on bourgeois society. Yan analyzes the play from a Marxist-feminist point of view and recognizes its great contribution to the advent of women's emancipation. As an attack on bourgeois values, Yan thinks, the play is a satire on the male-centred values represented by Helmer, who is a typical example of intellectuals struggling upward on the social ladder of Norway. Helmer is a representative of male-centred ideology and a supporter of traditional social beliefs. Taking a Marxist-feminist approach, Yan emphasizes that it is the social system that enables Helmer to achieve his social status and all the benefits and he therefore supports it. Helmer is a hypocrite and does not have true love. He struggles hard for his career. "For his own future, he does not care about his wife and sacrifices his friend. His sole purpose in life is to gain fame and material success. Deep in his mind are the evils of an egotist." In this way, Yan Zheng regards Nora as a contrast to Helmer and the play as a "song praising the emancipation of women." As for the social effects of the play, Yan Zheng asserts that they are not simply about women's emancipation but also about the capitalist social system, and the play repudiates the values that are built on money. Yan believes that this is the reason why Ibsen does not want the play to be considered solely about women's emancipation.

6.92

———. "Yibusheng de *Wan'ou zhi jia*" 易卜生的《玩偶之家》 (Ibsen's *A Doll's House*). In *Waiguo wenxue wushiwu jiang* 外國文學五十五講 (Fifty-five lectures on foreign literature), vol. 2. Edited by Waiguo wenxue wushiwu jiang bianweihui 外國文學五十五講編委會, pp. 298–317. Guiyang: Guizhou renmin chubanshe 貴州人民出版社, 1980.

Yan Zheng's essay asserts that Ibsen's social plays are a mirror of his discontent with capitalism and his characters are mostly "intellectuals who isolate themselves from the masses and claim themselves 'saviours' who can help the poor to solve their problems." Yan concludes with confidence that *A Doll's House* is "a protest against capitalism" and has "a great social effect," but "the limitation of the play lies in Ibsen's inability to find a way out of the declining capitalism." In other words, to Yan Zheng, Ibsen is only a half-hearted revolutionist.

6.93

You Fuxi 游復熙. "*Wan'ou zhi jia* bainianji" 《玩偶之家》百年記 (The centenary of *A Doll's House*). *Lianhebao* 聯合報 (United daily news), 27 April 1978, p. 20.

While the 150th anniversary of Ibsen's birth was celebrated on the Chinese mainland in 1978, a commemorative essay, entitled "The centenary of *A Doll's House*," appeared in the influential newspaper, *Lianhebao* (United daily) in Taiwan on April 27. The author, You Fuxi, states that there has been an unfailing interest in *A Doll's House*, which has become popular in China since 1937. In the past seven decades, the Chinese family, society, and women's movement were all in one way or another influenced by this play. It is hardly an exaggeration to say, You Fuxi holds, that *A Doll's House* has been the most important play in the twentieth century. The reason for celebrating Ibsen's *A Doll's House* is clearly stated by You Fuxi: its lasting social effects. In the essay, You attributes the play's success to its being a simple but significant domestic drama, its straightforward presentation of the problem, and its unexpected ending with Nora leaving home. Whether or not the play is misinterpreted, You Fuxi holds the view that it has in effect become an important document in feminism, as well as a footnote to "Ibsenism," which is regarded as synonymous with "equality between men and women."

6.94

Yu Qiuyu 余秋雨. "Lishiju jianlun" 歷史劇簡論 (A brief study of historical drama). *Wenyi yanjiu* 文藝研究 (Studies on literature and art), 6 (1980). Reprint. In *Zhongguo xiju nianjian* 中國戲劇年鑑 (Yearbook of the Chinese theatre), 1981, pp. 205–208. Beijing: Zhongguo xiju chubanshe 中國戲劇出版社, 1981.

In this study of historical drama, Yu Qiuyu makes the point that the purpose of historical drama is to present new views, which might not necessarily be based on historical truth. The most typical of such writings can be found in Guo Moruo's drama written in the 1920s, especially those plays that are modelled on Ibsen's social problem plays. However, the abuse of the genre of historical drama as exemplified in Guo Moruo's historical plays has caused much argument among Chinese critics and scholars. Wen Yiduo is of the view that drama is an art form and should not be mere presentation of slogans. It is true that there should be new insights or new perspectives in historical drama, which, however, should also be based on historical truth.

6.95

Zhang Fusheng 張福生. "Zhong-Nuo wenhua jiaoliu zhong de yijian shengshi" 中挪文化交流中的一件盛事 (A grand event in Sino-Norwegian exchange). In *Yibusheng yanjiu lunwenji* 易卜生研究論文集 (Ibsen research papers). Edited by Meng Shengde 孟勝德 and Astrid Saether, pp. 22–26; 243–247. Beijing: Zhongguo wenxue chubanshe 中國文學出版社, 1995.

In this essay, Zhang Fusheng gives details about how Renmin wenxue chubanshe (People's literature publishing house) planned to publish the Chinese translation of Ibsen's plays and poetry. The plan has now been realized in the eight-volume edition of *Yibusheng wenji* (Collected works by Ibsen), published in 1995.

6.96

Zhang Heqin 張鶴琴. "Yibusheng" 易卜生 (Ibsen). In *Nuowei wenxueshi* 挪威文學史 (A history of Norwegian literature), pp. 49–65. Taipei: Liming wenhua shiye youxian gongsi 黎明文化事業有限公司, 1980.

Zhang Heqin's book *Nuowei wenxueshi* (A history of Norwegian literature), published in 1980, provides an example of reading Ibsen in the context of Norwegian literary history. Treated in the context of Norwegian literary history, Ibsen's works are presented by Zhang in factual accounts in a chronological order.

6.97

Zhang Yun 張雲. "*Haida Gaobule* suixiang" 《海達・高布樂》隨想 (Thoughts on *Hedda Gabler*). *Waiguo wenxue* 外國文學 (Foreign literatures), 9 (1987), pp. 68–72.

This is an essay on Ibsen's controversial play *Hedda Gabler*. According to the author, Hedda Gabler commits suicide at the end of the play because she has been victimized by the conservative society in Norway in the nineteenth century. Thus there is a note of feminism in the play.

6.98

Zhao Mingyi 趙銘彝. "Yetan waiguo xiju zai Zhongguo" 也談外國戲劇在中國 (Again on foreign drama in China). *Waiguo xiju* 外國戲劇 (Foreign theatre), 3 (1980), pp. 133–134.

This essay affirms the value of adaptations of foreign drama for the

Chinese theatre. It begins with a historical review of the Chinese reception of foreign drama since the May 4th Movement, but it concludes that in the contemporary period foreign drama still plays an important role in the development of Chinese theatre. The essay is meant to rectify the previous view which was prevalent during the Cultural Revolution that foreign drama was harmful to socialist construction. Thus read, the essay served a role to pave for the way of reevaluating Ibsen in China in the 1980s.

6.99

Zhu Weizhi 朱維之 and Zhao Li 趙理. *Waiguo wenxue jianbian* 外國文學簡編 (An outline of foreign literature). Beijing: Zhongguo renmin daxue chubanshe 中國人民大學出版社, 1980.

In this book, there is such a statement: "Ibsen is a strong opponent to the capitalist institution and its moral values. From the stance of a bourgeois democrat, he unreservedly criticizes the various aspects of bourgeois social life, politics, law, religion, and marriage." As for *A Doll's House*, the authors assert that family tragedy is an inevitable result of the capitalist social and marriage system: "In order to develop the theme to its full and to thoroughly condemn the evils of capitalism, Ibsen portrays Krogstad, Mrs. Linde, and Dr. Rank whose tragic fate combined with Nora's further reveals the corruption of bourgeois social system."

7

Chinese Translations and Adaptations of Ibsen's Plays, Poetry and Critical Essays

I. Plays

Lady Inger of Ostraat (1855)

7.01

Pan Jiaxun 潘家洵, trans., *Esiteluote de Yingge furen* 厄斯特羅特的英格夫人 (*Lady Inger of Ostraat*). In *Yibusheng wenji* 易卜生文集 (Collected works by Ibsen), vol. 1. Edited by Zhang Fusheng 張福生, pp. 204–309. Beijing: Renmin wenxue chubanshe 人民文學出版社, 1995.

There is a synopsis of the play before the translation. In the synopsis, the translator Pan Jiaxun summarizes the main themes of the play. There is no indication whether the translation is based on English or other versions.

7.02

Shi Ling 石靈 (Sun Shiling 孫石靈), trans. *Yingge'er furen* 鷹革爾夫人 (*Lady Inger of Ostraat*). In *Yibusheng xiquji* 易卜生戲曲集 (A collection of Ibsen's plays). Shanghai: Jinxing shudian 金星書店, 1941.

Shi Ling's (pen-name of Sun Shiling) effort in Ibsen translation is represented by his Chinese version of *Lady Inger of Ostraat*, which is highly faithful to the English version. As suggested in his "Afterword" to the adaptation of *John Gabriel Borkman*, Shi Ling probably is personally more favourably inclined to literal or faithful translation than to adaptation.

Peer Gynt (1867)

7.03

Xiao Qian 蕭乾, trans. *Pei'er Jinte* 培爾・金特 (*Peer Gynt*). *Waiguo xiju* 外國戲劇 *(Foreign theatre)*, 4 (1981), pp. 78–154. Reprint. Chengdu: Sichuan renmin chubanshe 四川人民出版社, 1983. Reprint. In *Yibusheng wenji* 易卜生文集 (Collected works by Ibsen), vol. 3. Edited by Zhang Fusheng 張福生, pp. 287–448. Beijing: Renmin wenxue chubanshe 人民文學出版社, 1995. Reprint. In *Yibusheng xijuxuan* 易卜生戲劇選 (Selected plays by Ibsen), pp. 1–160. Beijing: Renmin wenxue chubanshe 人民文學出版社, 1997.

Notwithstanding that Ibsen had already achieved fame in China early in the 1920s, only in 1981 did the first Chinese translation of *Peer Gynt* appear. The translator, Xiao Qian, also an Ibsen critic, recalls how he came to the idea of undertaking such a project at the age of seventy. After watching a performance of the play in London in the mid-1940s, he began to collect its various English translations. In the early 1950s, he met Pan Jiaxun, the Chinese William Archer, at a dinner held by Ye Shengtao, a famous Chinese writer. He asked Pan if he planned to translate the play and tried to push him to take up the task. Pan was intrigued by his suggestion. Afterwards, he sent Pan the four English versions in his collection. This occurred around 1956. The next year, because of the anti-rightist movement in China, Xiao was deprived of the freedom and rights of a writer and was shunned by all his friends. In 1973, when Xiao returned to Beijing from the reform school, he learned that Pan was looking for him. Later Pan returned the four English translations of *Peer Gynt* to him and apologized for not being able to keep his promise of translating the play.

In 1978, with the relaxation of political control over intellectuals, Xiao was invited by the journal *Shijie wenxue* (World literature) to translate the play (Source: Xiao Qian, "Yibusheng de *Pei'er Jinte*" (Ibsen's *Peer Gynt*), *Waiguo xiju* (Foreign theatre), 4 (1981) , p. 74). The difficulty the translators of Ibsen had during the Cultural Revolution (1966–76) is clearly depicted in Xiao's confession. He frankly admits that he is not an ideal person to translate *Peer Gynt* because he does not know Norwegian and is not a poet. As a matter of fact, he can only translate the play in prose. He prefers it to reach the reader in a plain form rather than in a fancy but awkward way. Except for a few short verses, he has used the vernacular throughout the translation. He hopes that in the future some poet, especially one who knows Norwegian, will translate it again in verse form. The four English translations Xiao Qian refers to in his own rendition are the 1944 stage text by Norman Ginsbury (published in London in 1946), William Archer's 1906 version, and the Everyman (London) and Blue Ribbon (New York) editions.

The League of Youth (1869)

7.04

Pan Jiaxun 潘家洵, trans. *Qingnian tongmeng* 青年同盟 (*The League of Youth*). In *Yibusheng wenji* 易卜生文集 (Collected works by Ibsen), vol. 4. Edited by Zhang Fusheng 張福生, pp. 1–136. Beijing: Renmin wenxue chubanshe 人民文學出版社, 1995.

This is a revised version of Pan Jiaxun's translation which was first published in 1926 under the title *Shaoniandang*. In this version, the translator has made some stylistic changes.

7.05

———. *Shaoniandang* 少年黨 (*The League of Youth*). In *Yibusheng ji* 易卜生集 (Ibsen's plays), vol. 2. 1926. Reprint. Shanghai: Shangwu yinshuguan 商務印書館, 1928.

The first two-volume Chinese collection of Ibsen's works, including *Nuola* (*A Doll's House*), *Qungui* (*Ghosts*), *Guomin gongdi* (*An Enemy of the People*), *Shaoniandang* (*The League of Youth*), and *Dajiang* (*The Master Builder*), was published by Shangwu yinshuguan in 1926 as a part of *Shijie congshu* (World series). The publication of the collection was made possible through the conscientious effort of Pan Jiaxun. As an introduction to these translations, Pan published a biography of Ibsen, which was first written in 1921. Hu Shi's "Ibsenism," which was originally published in *Xinqingnian* in 1918, is also appended to the collection, while a portrait of Ibsen is given on the opening page. Presenting Ibsen's major plays in Chinese vernacular, the collection represents a significant event in the reception of Ibsen. In 1928, to celebrate Ibsen's birth centenary, Pan Jiaxun's two-volume collection of Ibsen's plays was reprinted by Shangwu yinshuguan.

7.06

Wu Qirui 巫啟瑞, trans. *Shaonian tongmeng* 少年同盟 (*The League of Youth*). *Chenbao fukan* 晨報附刊, 5–26 January 1923, various pagination.

Wu translated *Shaonian tongmeng* (*The League of Youth*) in 1923 and serialized it in the *Chenbao fukan* from January 5 to 26. This translation is based on English versions.

Emperor and Galilean (1873)

7.07

Huang Yushi 黃雨石 and Gao Rongsheng 高榮生, trans. *Wangdi yu Jialiliren* 皇帝與加利利人 (*Emperor and Galilean*). In *Yibusheng wenji* 易卜生文集 (Collected works by Ibsen), vol. 4. Edited by Zhang Fusheng

張福生, pp. 137–448. Beijing: Renmin wenxue chubanshe 人民文學出版社, 1995.

This is the first Chinese translation of the play. A synopsis is provided at the beginning of the play, in which the main themes are summarized. In the translation, the style follows that of contemporary Chinese.

7.08

Lin Xianghua 林驤華, trans. *Wangdi yu Jialiliren* 皇帝與加利利人 (Emperor and Galilean). In *Yibusheng xijuxuan* 易卜生戲劇選 (Selected plays by Ibsen), pp. 333–643. Beijing: Renmin wenxue chubanshe 人民文學出版社, 1997.

This is a translation done in contemporary Chinese. In general, the dialogue is closer to the spoken language and is therefore more suitable for stage presentation.

The Pillars of Society (1877)

7.09

Pan Jiaxun 潘家洵, trans. *Shehui zhizhu* 社會支柱 (*The Pillars of Society*). In *Yibusheng wenji* 易卜生文集 (Collected works by Ibsen), vol. 5. Edited by Zhang Fusheng 張福生, pp. 1–112. Beijing: Renmin wenxue chubanshe 人民文學出版社, 1995.

This version is a reprint of the translation previously published under the title *Shehui zhushi* in 1959.

7.10

———. *Shehui zhushi* 社會柱石 (*The Pillars of Society*). 1959. Reprint. Beijing: Renmin wenxue chubanshe 人民文學出版社, 1978.

In 1959, a collection of the four social plays, *The Pillars of Society*, *A Doll's House*, *Ghosts*, and *An Enemy of the People*, was published by Renmin wenxue chubanshe. The number of copies printed for each of these editions varied from 3,750 to 5,000 (Source: Guojia chuban shiye guanliju banben tushuguan 國家出版事業管理局版本圖書館 (Textual studies library, National Bureau for the publishing industry), ed. *1949–1979 fanyi chuban waiguo gudian wenxue zhuzuo mulu* 1949–1979 翻譯出版外國古典文學著作目錄 (A bibliography of Chinese translations of foreign classics in literature 1949–1979), pp. 20–21. Beijing: Zhonghua shuju, 1980). On the celebration of the 150th anniversary of Ibsen's birth in 1978, the collection was republished by Renmin chubanshe.

7.11

Sun Xu 孫煦, trans. *Shehui dongliang* 社會棟樑 (*The Pillars of Society*). In *Shijie wenxue mingzhu* 世界文學名著 (Masterpieces in world literature). Shanghai: Shangwu yinshuguan 商務印書館, 1938.

An industrious translator of Ibsen, Sun Xu published in 1938 and 1939 Chinese texts of *The Pillars of Society*, *The Wild Duck*, and *Hedda Gabler*.

7.12

Zhou Shoujuan 周瘦鵑, trans. *Shehui zhushi* 社會柱石 (*The Pillars of Society*). *Xiaoshuo yuebao* 小說月報 (*Short Story Magazine*), 1–12 (1920), various pagination. Reprint. In *Shuobu congshu* 說部叢書 (Fiction series), 4.5. Shanghai: Shangwu yinshuguan 商務印書館, 1921.

Zhou Shoujuan's rendition of *Shehui zhushi* (*The Pillars of Society*) was published in 1921 in book form by Shangwu yinshuguan. In his preface to this edition, Zhang Shewo urges Chinese dramatists to arouse the awareness of the people in order to reform society and to show that society is the origin of evils. Since society is made up of people, Zhang says, dramatists should attack the evildoers if they want to attack the social evils. He believes that the best way to correct a person is to reveal his evilness to other people so that the wrongdoer will feel that he is like an ugly person in front of a mirror and will know that he has to "improve" himself. This is what Zhang calls realism. This kind of drama is, he asserts, realistic literature and the author is a realistic author. Although Zhang thinks Ibsen's plays unsuitable for the Chinese stage, their merits, especially the well-structured plots, might serve as models for the Chinese playwrights (Source: Zhang Shewo, "Xu" (Preface), *Shehui zhushi* (*The Pillars of Society*), trans. Zhou Shoujuan, pp. 1–3. Shanghai: Shangwu yinshuguan, 1921).

A Doll's House (1879)

7.13

Cao Kaiyuan 曹開元, trans. *Kuilei jiating* 傀儡家庭 (*A Doll's House*). Taipei: Hualian chubanshe 華聯出版社, 1969.

This is a Chinese-English bilingual edition, in which the translation is meant as a reading for students to learn English. There is no indication whose translation the English version is.

7.14

Chen Xia 陳嘏, trans. *Kuilei jiating* 傀儡家庭 (*A Doll's House*). *Shuobu congshu* 說部叢書 (Fiction series), 3.51. Shanghai: Shangwu yinshuguan 商務印書館, 1918.

It was not until 1918 that the first full text of *A Doll's House* translated by Chen Xia was made available to the reading public in response to the call for promoting Western drama in China by Song Chunfang in the mid-1910s. The title Chen Xia gave to the play is *Kuilei jiating*, meaning the puppet family. As is the case with the Chinese translation of other Western texts in the early twentieth century, there is no indication of the sources on which the translation is based. Presumably Chen has William Archer's English version as source. In this light, *Kuilei jiating* is highly faithful to the English version. Concerning Archer's translation, some critics may agree that there are certain places which are not accurate or even incorrect. However, it is unfair to judge Archer's translation according to modern standards or to compare it with those by James Walter MacFarlane and Michael Meyer, simply for the reason that in Archer's time very few Englishmen knew Norwegian well enough to do the job. Archer should be given credit for his effort, however inaccurate his translation is. It is in this light that Chen Xia and other Chinese translators of Ibsen are commendable for what they have done in introducing Ibsen to China. At any rate, the fact that Chen's text is written in elegant modern Chinese, and does not show the awkwardness common to early translations, does help popularize Ibsen in China.

7.15

Liu Jinmei 柳津美, adapt. and trans. *Kuilei jiating* 傀儡家庭 (*A Doll's House*). Taipei: Wuzhou chubanshe 五洲出版社, 1960.

In Taiwan, there is a daring attempt by Liu Jinmei to adapt *A Doll's House* into a novel, with the Chinese title *Kuilei jiating*, published by Wuzhou chubanshe in 1960. The novel employs an omniscient third person narrator. Much of the dialogue in the play is retained, but the most crucial change occurs in the descriptions of Torvald and Nora. In this adaptation, a great deal of the details in the original are left out. In fact, Liu Jinmei's Nora is presented as a woman much stronger than Ibsen's. The implication of hope, by the metaphor of sunlight and flower buds, at the end is heavily loaded with feminist messages which may not necessarily be what Ibsen means in the original. Nevertheless, it shows the translator's optimistic view of women's emancipation.

7.16

Luo Jialun 羅家倫 and Hu Shi 胡適, trans. *Nuola* 娜拉 (*A Doll's House*). *Xinqingnian* 新青年 (New youth), 4.6 (1918), pp. 508–572.

The translation of Ibsen's plays was given a new impetus when the Ibsen number of *Xinqingnian* came out in June 1918. *A Doll's House*, *An Enemy of the People*, and *Little Eyolf* were translated and serialized in the magazine. None of the translators knows Norwegian or Danish. The source they rely on is William Archer's 1906 edition of Ibsen's works. Archer was then an Ibsen authority both in the English-speaking world and in China.

7.17

Ouyang Yuqian 歐陽予倩, trans. and adapt. *Kuilei zhi jiating* 傀儡之家庭 (*A Doll's House*). *Xiju xieshe juben* 戲劇協社劇本 (Performance text of the Drama Association). *Guowen zhoubao* 國聞週報, 19 April 1925, pp. 33–47; 26 April 1925, pp. 26–37; 3 May 1925, pp. 29–40.

An attempt to put *A Doll's House* on the Chinese stage led to Ouyang Yuqian's adaptation of the play with the Chinese title *Kuilei zhi jiating*. The play was successfully produced by Hong Shen in May 1925 for the Shanghai Stage Society. Ouyang's adaptation is a bold task as it is a complete departure from the original. Everything in the play is made to sound Chinese except the plot. The names of the characters are modified to become Chinese ones. Some other details such as the setting are also changed to suit the taste of the Chinese audience. The adaptation was published in *Guowen zhoubao* on May 3, 1925.

7.18

Pan Jiaxun 潘家洵, trans. *Nuola* 娜拉 (*A Doll's House*). Shanghai: Shangwu yinshuguan 商務印書館, 1926. Reprint. *Wan'ou zhi jia* 玩偶之家 (*A Doll's House*). In *Yibusheng ji* 易卜生集 (Ibsen's plays), vol. 1. Shanghai: Shangwu yinshuguan 商務印書館, 1928. Reprint. Beijing: Renmin wenxue chubanshe 人民文學出版社, 1959; reprint 1978. Reprint. In *Waiguo juzuoxuan* 外國劇作選 (Selected foreign plays), vol. 5. Shanghai: Shanghai wenyi chubanshe上海文藝出版社, 1981. Reprint. In *Yibusheng wenji* 易卜生文集 (Collected works by Ibsen), vol. 5. Edited by Zhang Fusheng 張福生, pp. 113–208. Beijing: Renmin wenxue chubanshe 人民文學出版社, 1995. Reprint. In *Yibusheng xijuxuan* 易卜生戲劇選 (Selected plays by Ibsen), pp. 161–252. Beijing: Renmin wenxue chubanshe 人民文學出版社, 1997.

Pan Jiaxun's translation of *A Doll's House* was first published in book form together with his other social plays, such as *Qungui* (*Ghosts*), *Guomin gongdi* (*An Enemy of the People*), *Shaoniandang* (*The League of Youth*), and *Dajiang* (*The Master Builder*) by Shangwu yinshuguan in 1926 as a part of *Shijie congshu* (World series). Ibsen's major plays, especially those on social problems, were all translated into Chinese prior to the 1950s. In later years, various reprints or new translations came from the press. In 1956, to commemorate Ibsen on the fiftieth anniversary of his death, Renmin wenxue chubanshe in Beijing planned to publish a new four-volume edition of Pan Jiaxun's Ibsen translations. The first and third volumes, which came out in 1956, include *The League of Youth*, *The Pillars of Society*, *A Doll's House*, *The Wild Duck*, *Rosmersholm*, and *The Lady from the Sea*. The second volume, containing *Ghosts*, *An Enemy of the People*, and *Hedda Gabler*, was published a year later, and the fourth volume, comprising *The Master Builder*, *Little Eyolf*, *John Gabriel Borkman*, and *When We Dead Awaken*, appeared in 1959. Later in the same year, a collection of the four social plays, *The Pillars of Society*, *A Doll's House*, *Ghosts*, and *An Enemy of the People*, was also published by Renmin wenxue chubanshe. The number of copies printed for each of these editions varied from 3,750 to 5,000 (Source: Guojia chuban shiye guanliju banben tushuguan 國家出版事業管理局版本圖書館, ed. *1949–1979 fanyi chuban waiguo gudian wenxue zhuzuo mulu* 1949–1979 翻譯出版外國古典文學著作目錄 (A bibliography of Chinese translations of foreign classics in literature 1949–1979), pp. 20–21. Beijing: Zhonghua shuju 中華書局, 1980). On the celebration of the 150th anniversary of Ibsen's birth in 1978, a collection of *The Pillars of Society*, *A Doll's House*, *Ghosts*, and *An Enemy of the People* was published by Renmin chubanshe. Pan Jiaxun's version of *A Doll's House* also appeared in Beijing in the form of a pocket-size book with 10,000 copies printed by Renmin wenxue chubanshe (source: ibid, p. 21). It was evident that the book was meant to reach a general audience (workers and high school students) rather than intellectuals.

7.19

Shen Peiqiu 沈佩秋, trans. *Nuola* 娜拉 (*A Doll's House*). *Shijie xiju mingzhuxuan* 世界戲劇名著選 (Masterpieces in world drama). Shanghai: Qiming shuju 啟明書局, 1937.

With the outbreak of the Sino-Japanese war in 1937, the literary scene in China drastically changed. Conceived as a powerful intellectual weapon, drama was presented by the Chinese government as part of the national defense program. Included in *Shijie xiju mingzhu xuan* (Masterpieces in world drama) published by Qiming shuju in 1937 is Shen Peiqiu's *Nuola* (Nora), a Chinese version of *A Doll's House*. In the preface to this edition, the editors, Qian Gongxia and Xie Bingwen maintains that the purpose of the drama series was to save China from disaster through the theatre, which was a useful means to mobilize the masses (Source: Qian Gongxia and Xie Bingwen, "Preface." In *Nuola* (Nora). Translated by Shen Peiqiu, p. 1. Shanghai: Qiming shuju, 1937). Shen Peiqiu states, in a note to the translation, that *A Doll's House* is the greatest of Ibsen's social plays. He further thinks that it is because Ibsen saw in his time that women's status was so low, and the so-called love and family commitments had taken away their soul and individuality, that he was motivated to write *A Doll's House*, in which he outspokenly urges women to fight for their own rights. This is, to Shen, the central theme of the play. *A Doll's House* was written in 1879, but the questions Ibsen raises, Shen thinks, still exist in China. Hence, Shen believes that it is a meaningful job to translate the play into Chinese, with the hope of popularizing it to his countrymen. Unlike the other Chinese translations, Shen's version of *A Doll's House* presents a Nora who is strong and resolute. The dialogue is so strong that it can arouse the emotions of the reader.

7.20

Shen Zifu 沈子復, trans. *Wan'ou furen* 玩偶夫人 (*A Doll's House*). In *Yibusheng xuanji* 易卜生選集 (A collection of Ibsen's plays), vol. 1. Shanghai: Yongxiang yinshuguan 永祥印書館, 1948.

The trend to compromise between literal translation and adaptation was followed by Shen Zifu when in 1948 he published a new version of *A Doll's House*, despite the fact that Pan's authoritative two-volume collection, *Yibusheng ji*, had been reprinted in the previous year in Shanghai. In fact, what sounds unacceptable to Chinese readers is the usual awkward transliteration of Western names by other Chinese translators. Thus, in his new translation, Shen has altered mainly the titles and names of the characters. *A Doll's House* is made *Wan'ou furen* (literally, a doll lady). Shen Zifu had an ambitious project of translating all the works of Ibsen, yet he succeeded with only five. Shen had a special liking for Ibsen's plays, particularly the lively characters and their rebellious spirit.

7.21

Zhai Yiwo 翟一我, trans. *Kuilei jiating* 傀儡家庭 (*A Doll's House*). Shanghai: Shijie chubanshe 世界出版社, 1947. Reprint. Taipei: Hualian chubanshe 華聯出版社, 1969.

The year 1963 was marked by the publication of an English-Chinese bilingual edition of *Kuilei jiating* (*A Doll's House*) in Hong Kong by Shijie chubanshe. While the English text follows the 1928 New York Blue Ribbon edition, the Chinese is only a reprint of Zhai Yiwo's 1947 translation, which was published by Shanghai's Shijie chubanshe. Appended to the book is Zhu Junyun's Chinese version of Archer's story about Laura Kieler, on whom Ibsen's portrayal of Nora is based. A noteworthy point about this book is that comments on Nora by the famous writers Lu Xun and Guo Moruo are cited as an epigraph to the play. Both Lu Xun and Guo Moruo agree that Nora's leaving home raises more questions than it solves for the cause of women's liberation. Guo even goes so far as to assert that Nora's decision is the beginning of her fight for economic rights and independence. The didactic purpose of the translation is, therefore, obvious. In the epigraph, the translator cites Lu Xun and Guo Moruo to affirm the significance of Ibsen to Chinese society. Zhai Yiwo's English-Chinese parallel edition of *A Doll's House* was reprinted in Taiwan in 1969 by Hualian chubanshe, but ascribed to different authorship. Everything in this reprint remains the same except that the original preface containing quotations from Lu Xun and Guo Moruo has been deleted and in the appendix Zhu Junyun's name is also removed so that the story of Laura Kieler appeares as an anonymous translation. The reason for such alterations was perhaps to avoid any unnecessary political complications, as many modern Chinese writers had been banned in Taiwan until the late 1980s.

Ghosts (1881)

7.22

Fang Letian 方樂天, annot. *Gui* 鬼 (*Ghosts*). *Ou-Mei mingjuxuan* 歐美名劇選 (Selected famous European and American plays). Shanghai: Shangwu yinshuguan 商務印書館, 1930.

An English edition of *Ghosts*, with Chinese annotations made by Fang Letian, was published in 1930 by Shanghai's Shangwu yinshuguan. The work was part of the series, *Selected Famous European and American Plays* (see *Shangwu tushu mulu 1897–1949* 商務圖書目錄 1897–1949 (A catalogue of Shangwu yinshuguan publications 1897–1949), p. 227. Beijing: Shangwu yinshuguan, 1982).

7.23

Lin Shu 林紓 and Mao Wenzhong 毛文鐘, trans. and adapts. *Meinie* 梅孽 (*Ghosts*). *Shuobu congshu* 說部叢書 (Fiction series), 4.13. Shanghai: Shangwu yinshuguan 商務印書館, 1921.

This is an adaptation of *Ghosts* done in elegant classical Chinese. Opposing the general belief that classical Chinese is a dead language, Lin demonstrates through his translation of Western masterpieces that the classical language is as useful as the vernacular. Lin himself does not know any Western language, and his translations are all based on what his collaborators told him. *Ghosts* is adapted by Lin into a novel with the assistance of Mao Wenzhong. Lin does not follow the plot organization of the original, and he retells the story according to his own understanding. The Chinese title he gives to the adaptation is *Meinie* (literally, the sin of syphilis). In brief remarks added here and there, Lin expresses his own judgement on the moral issues in the story. An interesting point about the adaptation is that Lin has mistaken Ibsen as a German author.

Despite these pitfalls, Lin's lively translation has made the work quite popular.

7.24

Pan Jiaxun 潘家洵, trans. *Qungui* 群鬼 (*Ghosts*). *Xinchao* 新潮 (New tide), 1.5 (May 1919), pp. 823–877. Reprint. In *Yibusheng xuanji* 易卜生選集 (A collection of Ibsen's plays), vol. 1. Shanghai: Shangwu yinshuguan 商務印書館, 1926; reprint 1928; reprint 1931. Reprint. Beijing: Renmin wenyi chubanshe 人民文藝出版社, 1959; reprint 1978. Reprint. In *Yibusheng wenji* 易卜生文集 (Collected works by Ibsen), vol. 5. Edited by Zhang Fusheng 張福生, pp. 209–290. Beijing: Renmin wenxue chubanshe 人民文學出版社, 1995. Reprint. In *Yibusheng xijuxuan* 易卜生戲劇選 (Selected plays by Ibsen), pp. 253–332. Beijing: Renmin wenxue chubanshe 人民文學出版社, 1997.

Only until 1919 did a full translation of *Ghosts* by Pan Jiaxun appear in *Xinchao*, a journal run by students at the Peking University. The translation would otherwise be excellent if not for that in some footnotes Pan has added his own comments which are misleading. In the opening scene of *Ghosts*, for example, Regina uses some French words, such as "rendezvous," "bon voyage," and "pied de mouton." Ibsen portrays Regina as a maid who has been in love with her young master Oswald and is learning French because she wants to go to Paris with Oswald. For the purpose of explaining the special flavour of French in the translated text, Pan makes the following comment in his note to "rendezvous," the first French word in the play: "She (Regina) uses French words in order to show that she has contacts with the upper class" (Source: Pan Jiaxun 潘家洵, trans., *Qungui* 群鬼 (Ghosts), *Xinchao* 新潮 (New tide), 1.5 (May 1919), p. 824. Reprint. In *Yibusheng xuanji* 易卜生選集, vol. 2, p. 3. Shanghai: Shangwu yinshuguan 商務印書館, 1931). This obviously contradicts what Oswald says later in Act Two: "And then I got it out of her that she'd taken the whole thing seriously, that she'd been going around here thinking about me the whole time, and that she'd begun to learn French" (Source: Michael Meyer, trans., *Ghosts*, *Ibsen Plays: One*, pp. 78–79. London: Eyre Methuen, 1980). How different the message becomes as a result of Pan's misinterpretation. This at the same time reveals the subtlety in Ibsen's plays that is difficult for the translators. Even such able English translators as Michael Meyer also misses the message and makes "rendezvous" appear as an English word in his translation. Pan's continuous efforts in translating Ibsen through the 1920s and 1930s have made him, nevertheless, an authoritative figure comparable to William Archer in England.

7.25

Shen Zifu 沈子復, trans. *Gui* 鬼 (*Ghosts*). In *Yibusheng xuanji* 易卜生選集 (A collection of Ibsen's plays). vol. 2. Shanghai: Yongxiang yinshuguan 永祥印書館, 1948.

With the translation of *Ghosts*, Shen intends to show his readers that social conventions are the cradle of evils: "The old and dead beliefs have poisoned the people, and thus Mrs. Alving cannot free herself even though she wishes to. She is poisoned and cannot emancipate her own self" (p. 105). Shen remarks that he has been awestruck by the terrible ending in *Ghosts*. But he expects that the horror would lead his readers to an awareness of their own situation. The afterword to each of the five plays shows clearly that there is a moral purpose in Shen's translations.

7.26

Yan Yingyou 嚴影悠 (Yen Ying-yu), trans. *Qungui* 群鬼 (*Ghosts*). In *Yibusheng xiju xuanji* 易卜生戲劇選集 (A collection of Ibsen's plays). Edited by Yan Yuanshu 顏元叔, pp. 1–111. *Danjiang xiyang xiandai xiju yicong* 淡江西洋現代戲劇譯叢 (Tamkang collection of modern western plays in Chinese translation). Taipei: Jingsheng wenwu gongyingshe 驚聲文物供應社, 1970.

In 1970 there witnessed a new translation of *Ghosts* and *Hedda Gabler* in Taiwan. *Ghosts* was translated from Eva le Gallienne's English version by Yan Yingyou, while *Hedda Gabler* was done by Gao Tian'en. Both of these translations are put together in *Yibusheng xiju xuanji*, which is part of the Tamkang collection of modern western plays in Chinese translation, published under the auspices of Tamkang College (now Tamkang University). In his preface to the book, Yan Yuanshu, a professor of English literature at the National Taiwan University, justifies the project as follows: "Each of the translations has been reviewed carefully so as to ensure, firstly, faithfulness to the original and, secondly, intelligibility" (p. 2). Obviously, the translations are only faith to the English versions, on which they are based, rather than to the original. Preceding the translation is an introductory essay which deals with the theme, structure, characterization, and imagery of the plays. Such a critical essay is necessary as introduction to Western literature. Otherwise, even with the translation in hand, the reader may still have the difficulty to reconstruct the cultural context. These two works are good examples to illustrate the criteria set by Yan Yuanshu in the introduction of Western authors.

An Enemy of the People (1882)

7.27

Pan Jiaxun 潘家洵, trans. *Guomin gongdi* 國民公敵 (*An Enemy of the People*). In *Yibusheng ji* 易卜生集 (Ibsen's plays), vol. 1. Shanghai: Shangwu yinshuguan 商務印書館, 1926. Reprinted as *Renmin gongdi* 人民公敵. In *Waiguo juzuoxuan* 外國劇作選 (Selected foreign plays), vol. 5. Shanghai: Shanghai wenyi chubanshe 上海文藝出版社, 1981. Reprint. In *Yibusheng wenji* 易卜生文集 (Collected works by Ibsen), vol. 5, pp. 291–400. Edited by Zhang Fusheng 張福生. Beijing: Renmin wenxue chubanshe 人民文學出版社, 1995.

The first two-volume Chinese collection of Ibsen's works, including *Nuola* (*A Doll's House*), *Qungui* (*Ghosts*), *Guomin gongdi* (*An Enemy of the People*), *Shaoniandang* (*The League of Youth*), and *Dajiang* (*The Master Builder*), was published by Shangwu yinshuguan in 1926 as a part of *Shijie congshu* (World series). As an introduction to these translations, Pan published a biography of Ibsen, which was first written in 1921.

From 1979 to 1981, a series of books known as *Waiguo juzuoxuan* (Selected foreign plays) was edited by Shanghai xiju xueyuan (Shanghai Theatre Academy) and published by Shanghai wenyi chubanshe. Both *A Doll's House* and *An Enemy of the People* are included in Volume 5 of the series. Preceding the two plays is an introductory essay on Ibsen. From the Marxist viewpoint, the essay reviews Ibsen's career as a dramatist.

7.28

Tao Lügong 陶履恭, trans. *Guomin zhi di* 國民之敵 (*An Enemy of the People*). *Xinqingnian* 新青年 (New youth), 4.6 (June 1918); 5.1 (July

1918); 5.2 (August 1918); 5.3 (September 1918); 5.4 (Oct. 1918), various pagination.

The translation of Ibsen's plays was given a new impetus when the Ibsen number of *Xinqingnian* came out in June 1918. *A Doll's House*, *An Enemy of the People*, and *Little Eyolf* were translated and serialized in the journal. Like other translators who did not know Norwegian or Danish, the source Tao Lügong relied on is William Archer's 1906 edition of Ibsen's works.

The Wild Duck (1884)

7.29

Pan Jiaxun 潘家洵, trans. *Yeya* 野鴨 (*The Wild Duck*). In *Yibusheng wenji* 易卜生文集 (Collected works by Ibsen). Edited by Zhang Fusheng 張福生, vol. 6, pp. 1–124. Beijing: Renmin wenxue chubanshe 人民文學出版社, 1995.

There is no indication of the source of the translation, though critics know that Pan Jiaxun relied on English versions in his previous translations of Ibsen.

7.30

Sun Xu 孫煦, trans. *Yeya* 野鴨 (*The Wild Duck*). *Shijie wenxue mingzhu* 世界文學名著 (Masterpieces in world literature). Shanghai: Shangwu yinshuguan 商務印書館, 1938.

An industrious translator of Ibsen, Sun Xu published in 1938 and 1939 Chinese texts of *The Pillars of Society*, *The Wild Duck*, and *Hedda Gabler*.

7.31

Xu Gudi 徐鵠荻, trans. *Yeya* 野鴨 (*The Wild Duck*). Shanghai: Xiandai shuju 現代書局, 1929.

In 1929, a year after the celebration of Ibsen's birth centenary, there was a new translation of *The Wild Duck* by Xu Gudi, which is an improvement on the basis of previous translations.

7.32

Yang Jingci 楊敬慈, trans. *Yeya* 野鴨 (*The Wild Duck*). *Chenbao fukan* 晨報附刊, 11 February–8 March 1924, various pagination.

In 1924, Yang Jingci's translation of *The Wild Duck* was serialized in *Chenbao fukan* from 11 February to 8 March 1924. This translation was published a year after *A Doll's House* was staged in the Peking Normal College for Women and also a year after Lu Xun gave his famous speech on the prospects of Chinese women's liberation. Published in an influential newspaper, this translation became very popular in the 1920s.

Rosmersholm (1886)

7.33

Liu Boliang 劉伯量, trans. *Luoshimazhuang* 羅士馬莊 (*Rosmersholm*). Shanghai: Xueshu yanjiuhui 學術研究會, 1927; reprint 1930.

Rosmersholm was rendered into Chinese for the first time by Liu Boliang in 1923 and published in 1927. Liu translated the play during his stay in Berlin; and according to the preface, the translation is based on William Archer's English version. As background information, Liu summarizes in the preface the historical events related to the play and states that its purpose is to ridicule the political corruption in Norway. His remarks suggest that China was then as corrupt as Norway was in Ibsen's time. Obviously, Liu translated the play for political insinuation.

7.34

Pan Jiaxun 潘家洵, trans. *Luosimozhuang* 羅斯莫莊 (*Rosmersholm*). In *Yibusheng wenji* 易卜生文集 (Collected works by Ibsen). Edited by Zhang Fusheng 張福生, vol. 6, pp. 125–224. Beijing: Renmin wenxue chubanshe 人民文學出版社, 1995.

This is the only translation of the play in contemporary China. In the synopsis given at the beginning of the play, the translator outlines the main themes of the play.

The Lady from the Sea (1888)

7.35

Pan Jiaxun 潘家洵, trans. *Haishang furen* 海上夫人 (*The Lady from the*

Sea). In *Yibusheng wenji* 易卜生文集 (Collected works by Ibsen). Edited by Zhang Fusheng 張福生, vol. 6, pp. 225–330. Beijing: Renmin wenxue chubanshe, 1995.

This translation in contemporary Chinese provides an alternative to Shen Zifu's version which was translated in the 1940s. The main themes of the play are summarized in the introduction.

7.36

Shen Zifu 沈子復, trans. *Haifu* 海婦 (*The Lady from the Sea*). In *Yibusheng xuanji* 易卜生選集 (A collection of Ibsen's plays). vol. 3. Shanghai: Yongxiang yinshuguan 永祥印書館, 1948.

In his new translation, Shen has altered mainly the titles and names of the characters. *The Lady from the Sea* is turned into *Haifu* (literally, the sea lady). As an attack on "the bourgeois marriage system," Shen explains, *The Lady from the Sea* is constructive in showing a way to happiness in life. He sighs, however, that there is still a long way for China to develop in order to reach that goal (p. 143). The afterword to each of the five plays shows clearly that there is a moral purpose in Shen's translations.

7.37

Yang Xichu 楊熙初, trans. *Haishang furen* 海上夫人 (*The Lady from the Sea*). *Gongxueshe wenxue congshu* 共學社文學叢書 (Gongxue society literature series). Shanghai: Shangwu yinshuguan 商務印書館, 1920; reprint 1939. Reprint. In *Yibusheng xiju xuanji* 易卜生戲劇選集 (A collection of Ibsen's plays). Hong Kong: Jianwen shuju 建文書局, 1959.

In this translation, Yang Xichu aims to exhort Chinese women to consider their role as wives and in so doing, he cautiously reminds the reader in the introduction that there are three messages in *The Lady from the Sea*: "First, marriage involves the two sexes and their future life; second, marriage should be based on free will; third, one has to be responsible for the consequences of marriage. If we are not aware of these three lessons, or the nature of marriage, and do not go through a correct procedure, then the marriage is stupid, meaningless and nothing more than prostitution." In other words, Yang wishes to provide a moral lesson for the reader through his translation.

Hedda Gabler (1890)

7.38

Gao Tian'en 高天恩 (Kao Tien-en). *Haida Gaibole* 海達・蓋伯樂 (*Hedda Gabler*). In *Yibusheng xiju xuanji* 易卜生戲劇選集 (A collection of Ibsen's plays). Edited by Yan Yuanshu 顏元叔, pp. 113–258. *Danjiang xiyang xiandai xiju yicong* 淡江西洋現代戲劇譯叢 (Tamkang collection of modern western plays in Chinese translation). Taipei: Jingsheng wenwu gongyingshe 驚聲文物供應社, 1970.

In 1970 there appeared in Taiwan a new translation of *Hedda Gabler* by Gao Tian'en. There is no indication of the sources on which Gao's translation is based. The translation is put together with *Ghosts* in *Yibusheng xiju xuanji*, which is part of the Tamkang collection of modern western plays in Chinese translation, published under the auspices of Tamkang College (now Tamkang University). Preceding the translation is an introductory essay which deals with the theme, structure, characterization, and imagery of the plays.

7.39

Pan Jiaxun 潘家洵, trans. *Haide Jiabolei* 海得加勃勒 (*Hedda Gabler*). *Xiaoshuo yuebao* 小說月報 (*Short Story Magazine*), 19.3 (1928), pp. 331–353; 19.4 (1928), pp. 487–504; 19.5 (1928), pp. 622–645.

As the influence of Ibsen began to spread in China, more and more of his plays were translated. In 1928, to celebrate Ibsen's birth centenary, Pan Jiaxun's two-volume collection of the dramatist's plays was reprinted by Shangwu yinshuguan. In addition, Pan also serialized his translation of *Haide Jiabolei* (Hedda Gabler) in *Short Story Magazine*. This is the first Chinese text of the play.

7.40

Sun Xu 孫煦, trans. *Haidan* 海妲 (*Hedda Gabler*). *Shijie wenxue mingzhu* 世界文學名著 (Masterpieces in world literature). Shanghai: Shangwu yinshuguan 商務印書館, 1939.

An industrious translator of Ibsen, Sun Xu published the Chinese texts of *The Pillars of Society*, *The Wild Duck*, and *Hedda Gabler* in 1938 and 1939.

7.41

Wu Lümei 鄔侶梅, trans. *Heda furen zhuan* 赫達夫人傳 (*Hedda Gabler*). Shanghai: Wenxing shudian 文星書店, 1945.

A different translation of *Hedda Gabler* was done by Wu Lümei in 1945 under the title, *Heda furen zhuan* (literally, a biography of Lady Hedda). The play was published in Shanghai, then under Japanese occupation. Unlike Pan Jiaxun's version, Wu alters the title and makes it sound more like Chinese than just a transliteration of the title as "Haide Jiabolei." Wu's effort indicates a tendency to compromise between literal translation and adaptation.

The Master Builder (1892)

7.42

Pan Jiaxun 潘家洵, trans. *Dajiang* 大匠 (*The Master Builder*). In *Yibusheng ji* 易卜生集 (Ibsen's plays), vol. 2. Shanghai: Shangwu yinshuguan 商務印書館, 1926; reprint 1928.

Pan Jiaxun's translation of *The Master Builder* was published in book form together with Ibsen's other social plays by Shangwu yinshuguan in 1926 as part of *Shijie congshu* (World series). Presenting Ibsen's major plays in Chinese vernacular, the collection is a significant event in the reception of Ibsen. As the influence of Ibsen began to spread in China, more and more of his plays were translated. In 1928, to celebrate Ibsen's birth centenary, Pan Jiaxun's two-volume collection of Ibsen's plays was reprinted by Shangwu yinshuguan.

7.43

———, trans. *Jianzhushi* 建築師 (*The Master Builder*). In *Yibusheng wenji* 易卜生文集 (Collected works by Ibsen), vol. 7. Edited by Zhang Fusheng 張福生, pp. 1–96. Beijing: Renmin wenxue chubanshe 人民文學出版社, 1995.

This is a reprint of Pan Jaixun's previous translation of the play. In this reprint, some changes, such as the new title, are made to follow the standardized usage and translation of Ibsen in contemporary China. In the introduction, the main themes of the play are summarized.

7.44

Shen Zifu 沈子復, trans. *Jianzhushi* 建築師 (*The Master Builder*). In *Yibusheng xuanji* 易卜生選集 (A collection of Ibsen's plays), vol. 5. Shanghai: Yongxiang yinshuguan 永祥印書館, 1948. Reprint. Taipei: Wenxing shudian 文星書店, 1956.

In his afterword to the translation of *The Master Builder*, Shen expresses his sympathy for Halvard Solness who is ruined by his dreams. A reprint of Shen Zifu's 1948 translation of *The Master Builder* appeared in Taiwan in 1965. The publisher, Wenxing shudian, replaced Shen's afterword in the original edition with some brief notes on the life and philosophy of Ibsen. In the general foreword to the book, Xiao Mengneng explains to the reader that the purpose of the reprint is to preserve Chinese culture in Taiwan. In other words, Ibsen's plays are considered by the publisher as an important part of the cultural heritage of China that needs to be preserved.

7.45

Wu Qirui 巫啟瑞, trans. *Jianzhushi* 建築師 (*The Master Builder*). *Chenbao fukan* 晨報附刊, 1–31 October 1922, various pagination.

Ibsen's *The Master Builder*, translated by Wu Qirui, appeared in 1922 in *Chenbao fukan* on 1–31 October 1922. In this translation, the translator does not provide any introduction or notes to explain his purpose, but the translation is done in fluent modern Chinese.

Little Eyolf (1894)

7.46

Pan Jiaxun 潘家洵, trans. *Xiao Aiyoufu* 小愛友夫 (*Little Eyolf*). In *Yibusheng wenji* 易卜生文集 (Collected works by Ibsen). Edited by Zhang Fusheng 張福生, vol. 6, pp. 97–174. Beijing: Renmin wenxue chubanshe 人民文學出版社, 1995.

In this version, which is the only Chinese text of the play published in contemporary China, Pan Jiaxun follows the style of translation he uses in other Ibsen plays. The translation is done in fluent contemporary Chinese.

7.47

Wu Ruonan 吳弱男, trans. *Xiao Aiyoufu* 小愛友夫 (*Little Eyolf*). *Xinqingnian* 新青年 (New youth), 4.6 (June 1918) & 5.3 (September 1918), various pagination.

The translation of Ibsen's plays was given a new impetus when the Ibsen number of *Xinqingnian* came out in June 1918. Together with *A Doll's House* and *An Enemy of the People*, *Little Eyolf* was serialized in the journal. The source of translation is William Archer's 1906 edition of Ibsen's works.

John Gabriel Borkman (1896)

7.48

Pan Jiaxun 潘家洵, trans. *Ruohan Gaibolü'er Bokeman* 約翰・蓋勃呂爾・博克曼 (*John Gabriel Borkman*). In *Yibusheng wenji* 易卜生文集 (Collected works by Ibsen). Edited by Zhang Fusheng 張福生, vol. 6, 175–264. Beijing: Renmin wenxue chubanshe 人民文學出版社, 1995.

This is a new translation of the play published in contemporary China and the translation is done in fluent contemporary Chinese. In the synopsis given at the beginning of the play, the main themes are summarized.

7.49

Shen Zifu 沈子復, trans. *Bukeman* 卜克曼 (*John Gabriel Borkman*). In *Yibusheng xuanji* 易卜生選集 (A collection of Ibsen's plays), vol. 4. Shanghai: Yongxiang yinshuguan 永祥印書館, 1948. Reprint. Taipei: Wenxing shudian 文星書店, 1965.

Borkman, Shen thinks, represents in his character a kind of courage and noble ambition. This is contrary to the usual interpretation of Borkman as a tragic figure who destroys his own ability to love by devoting himself to the attainment of power. The afterword shows clearly that there is a moral purpose in Shen's translations.

A reprint of Shen Zifu's 1948 translation of *John Gabriel Borkman* and *The Master Builder* appeared in Taiwan in 1965. The publisher, Wenxing shudian, replaced Shen's afterword in the original edition with some brief notes on the life and philosophy of Ibsen.

7.50

Shi Ling 石靈 (Sun Shiling 孫石靈), trans. and adapt. *Bao Zhiyuan* 鮑志遠 (*John Gabriel Borkman*). *Wenyi xinchao she xiao congshu* 文藝新潮社小叢書 (Wenyi xinchao society series), no. 5. Shanghai: Wenyi xinchao she 文藝新潮社, 1940.

An adaptation of *John Gabriel Borkman* was made by Shi Ling (the pen-name of Sun Shiling) in 1940. In the "Afterword," Shi Ling notes that he did the translation at the request of Li Jianwu, a professor of drama in Shanghai. He says that Li had translated the first few pages and that he had to finish the rest by following the principles adopted by Li at the beginning (p. 139). In this adaptation, the names and the locale are all altered so that the play sounds like a Chinese one. John Gabriel Borkman becomes Bao Zhiyuan, a name carrying the meaning of being ambitious and with a high ideal, and so does the title. Instead of taking place in the Norwegian capital, the action is moved to Beijing. The plot, however, follows closely that of the original. The play is altered to make it more readily acceptable to the average Chinese reader. In the 1940s, it was not unusual for the Chinese translators to modify a work in order to suit the taste and standard of the reader. Li Jianwu is one of the famous playwrights who objected to the direct translation of plays without considering the expectations and needs of the readers.

When We Dead Awaken (1899)

7.51

Pan Jiaxun 潘家洵, trans. *Women siren zaixing shi* 我們死人再醒時 (*When We Dead Awaken*). *Xiaoshuo yuebao* 小説月報 (*Short Story Magazine*), 20.10 (1929), pp. 1595–1613; 20.11 (1929), pp. 1785–1801; 20.12 (1929), pp. 1947–1954.

As the influence of Ibsen began to spread in China, more and more of his plays were translated. In 1928, to celebrate Ibsen's birth centenary, Pan Jiaxun's two-volume collection of the dramatist's plays was reprinted by Shangwu yinshuguan. In the year following, Pan furthermore translated Ibsen's last play, *Women siren zaisheng shi* (*When We Dead Awaken*), which was also published in *Short Story Magazine* in 1929.

7.52
———. *Zamen siren xinglai de shihou* 咱們死人醒來的時候 (*When We Dead Awaken*). In *Yibusheng wenji* 易卜生文集 (Collected works by Ibsen). Edited by Zhang Fusheng 張福生, vol. 7, pp. 265–333. Beijing: Renmin wenxue chubanshe 人民文學出版社, 1995.

Similar to other plays collected in this book, the translation is done in fluent contemporary Chinese. In the synopsis preceding the translation, the main themes of the play are summarized.

II. Poetry

7.53
Lü Yuan 綠原, Lu Yong 盧永 and He Dong 賀東, trans. "Shi xuan" 詩選 (Poems by Ibsen). In *Yibusheng wenji* 易卜生文集 (Collected works by Ibsen). Edited by Zhang Fusheng 張福生, vol. 8, pp. 3–160. Beijing: Renmin wenxue chubanshe 人民文學出版社, 1995.

Included in this volume of the collection are sixty-one poems written by Ibsen in different periods of his life. The selection is a fair sample of his poetry.

III. Critical Essays

7.54
Liu Huakai 劉華開, trans. "Wen lun" 文論 (Essays by Ibsen). In *Yibusheng wenji* 易卜生文集 (Collected works by Ibsen). Edited by Zhang Fusheng 張福生, vol. 7, pp. 163–238. Beijing: Renmin wenxue chubanshe 人民文學出版社, 1995.

These essays include the speeches and theatre criticism written by Ibsen throughout his life. From these twenty-five essays, the reader gets a glimpse of Ibsen's views about politics and the theatre.

8

Chinese Stage Productions of Ibsen's Plays

Peer Gynt (1867)

8.01

Xianggang huajutuan 香港話劇團 (Hong Kong Repertory Theatre), Hong Kong, 1990. Director: Xu Xiaozhong 徐曉鍾. (Sources: Xu Xiaozhong 徐曉鍾, *Xu Xiaozhong daoyan yishu yanjiu* 徐曉鍾導演藝術研究 (Studies on Xu Xiaozhong's art of directing). Beijing: Zhongguo xiju chubanshe 中國戲劇出版社, 1991; Yang Shipeng 楊世彭 (Daniel S. P. Yang), "What Does a Stage Director Do?" — Speech given at New Asia College monthly dinner lecture, 27 February 1998.)

This production was based on Xu Xiaozhong's previous experience in staging the play in Beijing in 1983. According to Xu's memoire, he was invited by Yang Shipeng (Daniel S. P. Yang), artistic director of the Hong Kong Repertory Theatre, to direct the production of *Peer Gynt*.

8.02

Zhongyang xiju xueyuan 中央戲劇學院 (Central Academy of Drama), Beijing, 1983. Director: Xu Xiaozhong 徐曉鍾. (Source: Xu Xiaozhong 徐曉鍾. "Zaixian Yibusheng — Daoyan *Pei'er Jinte* de sikao" 再現易卜生 — 導演《培爾・金特》的思考 (Recreating Ibsen — My thoughts on staging *Peer Gynt*). *Xiju bao* 戲劇報 (Theatre news), 8 (1983), pp. 44–49.)

In May 1983, Zhongyang xiju xueyuan (Central Academy of Drama) presented a stage production of *Peer Gynt*. The preparation and rehearsal took seven months from September 1982 to March 1983. The performance was based on Xiao Qian's 1981 translation of the text. It is reported that the play was produced under very difficult circumstances. The performance was a recreated experience based on contemporary Chinese understanding of the play: "None of the directors, stage designers and actors had seen any production of the play before. They had only very little knowledge about the play. It was staged according to the Chinese interpretation in the 1980s and was a creative performance with Chinese characteristics." The Chinese indeed had no other experience in the production of Ibsen than *A Doll's House* and *Ghosts*. Even the text of *Peer Gynt* was not translated until 1981. The chief director, Xu Xiaozhong, admits the difficulties in staging *Peer Gynt* for the Chinese audience. The first time he read the play, he was puzzled by it and wondered whether it was really written by Ibsen, who once seemed to be so familiar to him.

Yet this time Ibsen became a complete stranger not only to him but also to the actors. Through this production, Xu learned that there was "another Ibsen" who was unfamiliar to most of the Chinese. The allegorical theme and the spectacular stage effects of the play presented an entirely new Ibsen to China. Although the original is a verse drama, this production followed Xiao Qian's prose translation. The changes in the production include the omission of some minor scenes for compression. The added Chinese characteristics, so called by Xiao Qian, refer to the portrayal of the Troll King. For fear that the Chinese audience was unable to comprehend such a Western mythological figure, the directors decided to present it in the image of the Chinese legendary animal god Pigsy described in *Xiyouji* (Journey to the west). The marriage horse in the original was turned into a traditional Chinese dancing lion. It is no wonder that some critics, such as Wang Meng, comment that the production looked more like a Chinese opera than a Western play.

A Doll's House (1879)

8.03

Beijing nügaoshi 北京女高師 (Peking normal college for women), Beijing, 5 May 1923. (Source: Ren Tuo 仁佗, "Kanle Nügaoshi liangtian yanju yihou de zatan" 看了女高師兩天演劇以後的雜談 (Some afterthoughts on the two-day performances of the Peking normal college for women), *Chenbao fukan* 晨報附刊, 11 May 1923, pp. 3–4.)

On May 5, 1923, *A Doll's House* was staged to commemorate the fourth anniversary of the May Fourth Movement. In the essay published in *Chenbao fukan*, Ren Tuo praises *A Doll's House* as a highly successful production. His impression is that it was an excellent performance. The actors were faithful to the play. He even brought along Pan Jiaxun's translation to check the performance when he watched it . He finds that on the whole it was highly faithful. Ren Tuo considers the actress who played Nora as best in recapturing the atmosphere of the play. Her expressions and movements, Ren Tuo says, were able to show the resolute character of Nora. Her acting was especially exquisite in the second half of the third act, which is the most important scene of the play. It is impossible to judge by present-day standards how faithful the performance was, but according to Ren Tuo it was an accurate production of Pan Jiaxun's translation, which was comparable to William Archer's English version.

On the next day, May 12, *Chenbao fukan* published another review article on the same performance. Entitled "Kanle *Nala* hou de lingsui ganxiang" 看了《那拉》後的零碎感想 (Random thoughts after watching *A Doll's House*) (*Chenbao fukan* 晨報附刊, 12 May 1923), p. 4), Fang Xin's article reveals how the play was received by most of the audiences, who were not satisfied with the performance. Many critics believe that any presentation of such plays as *A Doll's House* before a Chinese audience at that time was doomed to failure. In some respect, this performance was a failure, as it failed to keep the interest of the audience. Fang Xin blames the audience for not being able to see the social significance of the play in China. As she puts it in retrospect, "Some people may not agree with my comments on the audience. But why did some people take up their hats and shawls and leave at the second act of the play? When Nora was confronting Torvald, there were only a few spectators left. Did the actors fail, or did the audience know that they did not deserve watching the play?"

8.04

Ershiliu jushe 26劇社 (26 drama society), Beijing, 1924. (Source: Zhen Sheng 縝生. "Beijing de jingchating zhen congmin!" 北京的警察廳真聰敏 (How clever the Beijing police!). *Chenbao fukan* 晨報附刊, 20 December 1924, p. 4.)

Another experiment with *A Doll's House* took place in 1924 in Beijing by the "Ershiliu jushe" (26 drama society). Included in the cast were the famous amateur student actress Wu Ruiyan and her male lead Wan Laitian, who played respectively Nora and Krogstad. Their performance was supported by the anti-warlord revolutionaries. Because of the play's revolutionary character, it was interrupted by the police during rehearsals. When the play was staged in the YMCA, Beijing on 19 December 1924, the police once more attempted to stop the performance with the excuse that it was immoral to have actresses together with actors on the same stage. Facing protests from the audience, who were mostly university students, the police finally gave in but allowed the performance to go on for only one act. Structurally contrary to the traditional Chinese drama, *A Doll's House* does not need any change of scenery, and the police did not know where an act ended. Hence, the society was able to rush through all three acts without the notice of the police. However, this performance lasted only one day.

8.05

Guanghua jushe 光華劇社 (Bright China drama society), Shanghai, 1935. (Sources: Guo Fenyang 郭奮揚. "Yibusheng de mingju *Nuola* zai Zhongguo" 易卜生的名劇《娜拉》在中國 (Ibsen's famous play *A Doll's House* in China), *Zhongguo qingnianbao* 中國青年報 (China youth daily), 25 July 1956, p. 3; Yi Xinnong 易新農 and Chen Pingyuan 陳平原. "*Wan'ou zhi jia* zai Zhongguo de huixiang" 《玩偶之家》在中國的回響 (The Chinese response to *A Doll's House*). *Zhongshan daxue xuebao* 中山大學學報 (Sun Yat-sen university journal), Zhesheban 哲社版 (Philosophy and social sciences edition), 2 (1984), pp. 129–140.)

In 1935, the Guanghua jushe staged *A Doll's House* in Shanghai to celebrate the "Year of Nora," and also to support the promotion of feminist ideas of women's rights in China.

8.06

Jinan minjiaoguan 濟南民教館 (Jinan people's education house), Jinan, 1935. (Sources: Guo Fenyang 郭奮揚. "Yibusheng de mingju *Nuola* zai Zhongguo" 易卜生的名劇《娜拉》在中國 (Ibsen's famous play *A Doll's House* in China), *Zhongguo qingnianbao* 中國青年報 (China youth daily), 25 July 1956, p. 3; Yi Xinnong 易新農 and Chen Pingyuan 陳平原. "*Wan'ou zhi jia* zai Zhongguo de huixiang" 《玩偶之家》在中國的回響 (The Chinese response to *A Doll's House*). *Zhongshan daxue xuebao* 中山大學學報 (Sun Yat-sen university journal), Zhesheban 哲社版 (Philosophy and social sciences edition), 2 (1984), pp. 129–140.)

In 1935, the "Year of Nora" in China, the Jinan minjiaoguan (Jinan people's education house) staged *A Doll's House* with the purpose to promote women's rights and disseminate ideas of feminism.

8.07

Mofeng she 磨風社 (Windmill society), Nanjing, 1935. (Sources: Guo Fenyang 郭奮揚. "Yibusheng de mingju *Nuola* zai Zhongguo" 易卜生的名劇《娜拉》在中國 (Ibsen's famous play *A Doll's House* in China), *Zhongguo qingnianbao* 中國青年報 (China youth daily). 25 July 1956, p. 3; Zhao Mingyi 趙銘彝. "Yetan waiguo xiju zai Zhongguo" 也談外國戲劇在中國 (Again on foreign drama in China). *Waiguo xiju* 外國戲劇

(Foreign theatre), 3 (1980), pp. 133–134; Kwok-kan Tam, "The Shanghai Performance of *A Doll's House* and the Mystery of Jiang Qing's Role in the Stage Production and in the Revolution: A Research Note and Review," *Journal of Oriental Studies*, 25.2 (1987), pp. 197–201.)

Encouraged by the success of the Shanghai performance in 1935, Mofeng she (Windmill society) presented *A Doll's House* at Tao Tao Theatre, Nanjing, in February 1935. The performance was directed by Zhang Min with Wang Ping, then a primary school teacher and an amateur actress (later in the 1970s and 1980s a director in the August 1 Film Studio in Beijing), playing the role of Nora. The presentation was less fortunate than that in Shanghai, for it was abruptly terminated after three days when the leading actress, Wang Ping, was dismissed from the school by education officials. The Nanjing Board of Education regarded Wang's participation in the performance as a role morally unsuitable for a school teacher and harmful to the image of other teachers. The event became a national scandal when it was reported in newspapers, and literary organizations protested against the unreasonable action of the city government.

8.08

Molun zhongxue 莫倫中學 (Molun school), Shanghai, 1934. (Source: Bai Wei 白薇, "Cong Molun zhongxue de youyihui chulai" 從莫倫中學的遊藝會出來 (Coming out of the Molun school fair), *Shenbao* 申報 (Shanghai news), 5 July 1934, p. 19; 6 July 1934, p. 17.)

This production of *A Doll's House* was staged by Molun school, Shanghai in 1934, so-called the "Year of Nora." In this performance, Nora was represented as a resolute character in confronting her husband, as well as in fighting for her own freedom in education.

8.09

Nankai zhongxue 南開中學 (Nankai middle school), Tianjin, 1928. Director: Zhang Pengchun 張彭春. (Source: Tian Benxiang 田本相, *Cao Yu zhuan* 曹禺傳 (A biography of Cao Yu), pp. 80–86. Beijing: Shiyue wenyi chubanshe 十月文藝出版社, 1988.)

In the Ibsen performance at the Nankai Middle School, Tianjin in October 1928, Cao Yu played Nora. The school was one of those that were greatly influenced by Western liberal ideas. The 1928 performance of *A*

Doll's House was one of the activities in celebration of the school's anniversary and Ibsen's centennial birthday. This production was done in a professional way with a system of directing and rehearsal.

8.10

Peidu jushe 陪都劇社 (Chongqing drama society), Chengdu, 1941; Chongqing, 1948. (Source: Guo Fenyang 郭奮揚. "Yibusheng de mingju *Nuola zai Zhongguo*" 易卜生的名劇《娜拉》在中國 (Ibsen's famous play *A Doll's House* in China), *Zhongguo qingnianbao* 中國青年報 (China youth daily), 25 July 1956, p. 3.)

In 1941, an adaptation of the play was staged in Chengdu with Ouyang Hongying playing the lead role. But it did not arouse the attention of the critics, for Chengdu, located in the mountains, was a much smaller city than Shanghai, and the audience was very limited. In 1948, the theme of national liberation was taken up in the performance of another version of *A Doll's House* at the Kangjian Tang Theatre in Chongqing. The theatre company, Peidu jushe (Chongqing drama society), was a socialist affiliate. In this performance, Lai Qing was the director, and the major roles of Nora and Helmer were played by Bai Ling and Zhang Yang. Owing to its sensitive theme, the Nationalist government did not approve the presentation. With no other choice, the company had to agree to omit the political speeches. When it came to actual performance, however, the actors and actresses spoke their original lines. On the third day of presentation, the theatre company's secretary, Chen Qianmou, was arrested for violation of the law. As a protest and because of curiosity, more and more people flocked to see the play and the production established a record of lasting over a month. In this way, the play became not only a weapon in national defense but also a means of struggle between the Nationalists and Communists in China.

8.11

Qingnianhui 青年會 (YMCA), Shanghai, 1939. Director: Yi Qiao 易喬. (Source: Yi Qiao 易喬, "Xie zai *Nüxing de jiefang* gongyan qian" 寫在《女性的解放》公演前 (On the performance of *Female Emancipation*), *Xiju zazhi* 戲劇雜誌 (Theatre magazine), 3.4 (1939), p. 124.)

The outbreak of the war between China and Japan in 1937 led to a different reception of Ibsen and subsequently gave a new impetus to the performance of his plays. Facing a critical moment in national defense, Chinese dramatists, in response to the government's call to mobilize women, were no longer satisfied with Ibsen's treatment of Nora. They required a more positive ending. It was by means of a more radical version of *A Doll's House* that Ibsen was given a new image in wartime China. *Nüxing de jiefang* (Female emancipation), as Yi Qiao calls his adaptation of *A Doll's House*, was performed in Shanghai in 1939 with the play's ending entirely altered. The setting of the play is placed in Shanghai; the time in 1938 just before the Chinese New Year, a year after the outbreak of the Sino-Japanese war. The names of the characters are all changed to Chinese ones. The adapted version unfolds with the Zhuangs (Helmers) suffering from the hardships caused by the Japanese occupation of their hometown, Wuxi, which they left for Shanghai some six years previously. Instead of celebrating Christmas, a Western festival, Ye Anna (Nora) is preparing for the Chinese New Year. Then the story proceeds as that of *A Doll's House*. When Jiang Hengfu (Krogstad) suddenly appears, Ye Anna leads her daughter Little Anna to play a game of war against the Japanese invaders in order to occupy her so that Ye Anna can deal with Jiang Hengfu. In the original, the children play hide-and-seek. The game of war, according to Yi Qiao, is meant to provide a background for the play and also to foreshadow Ye Anna's anti-war sentiments. *Nüxing de jiefang* was presented by the YMCA in Shanghai to raise funds for the education of underprivileged people, and it was sponsored by the Literary Society and Christian Fellowship at the Shanghai Hujiang University. Yi Qiao was the director, while Ping Gu played the role of Ye Anna. According to the comments and reviews published in *Xiju zazhi* (Theatre magazine) (No. 3, 1939), the performance was highly successful.

8.12

Shanghai chunyang she 上海春陽社 (Shanghai spring willow society), Shanghai, 1914. (Source: Ge Yihong 葛一虹, "Guanyu waiguo xiju zai Zhongguo qingkuang de san feng xin" 關於外國戲劇在中國情況的三封信 (Three letters on foreign drama in China), *Xiju yanjiu* 戲劇研究 (Studies on drama), 12 (1982), pp. 65–67.)

The earliest production of an Ibsen play in China took place in 1914 with the performance of *A Doll's House* by the Shanghai Spring Willow Society. Owing to the heavy influence of the Spring Willow Society in

Tokyo, this production in Shanghai was probably done in the Japanese shingeki style.

8.13

Shanghai xiju xueyuan 上海戲劇學院 (Shanghai theatre academy), Shanghai, 1962. Director: Xiong Foxi 熊佛西. (Source: archive of Shanghai Theatre Academy.)

This production of *A Doll's House* was directed by Xiong Foxi, with Cao Lei and An Zhenji playing the roles of Nora and Helmer, respectively. Xiong Foxi was president of the Shanghai Theatre Academy in the early 1960s. This production was an attempt to reproduce the play in a style as close and faithful to the original as possible.

8.14

Shanghai yeyu juren xiehui 上海業餘劇人協會 (Shanghai amateur actors association), Shanghai, 1934. Stage manager: Zhang Min 章泯; director: Wan Laitian 萬賴天. (Sources: "1934 nian *Nuola* zai Shanghai" 1934 年《娜拉》在上海 (*A Doll's House* in Shanghai, 1934), *Beijing ribao* 北京日報 (Beijing daily), 28 July 1956, p. 3; Cui Wanqiu 崔萬秋, "Shanghai suiyue hua Jiang Qing" 上海歲月話江青 (Jiang Qing in Shanghai), *Baisheng banyuekan* 百姓半月刊 (Baisheng semi-monthly), 16–30 (1 January–16 August 1982), various pagination.)

A significant event in the history of Ibsen performance in China occurred in 1934 when a presentation of *A Doll's House* took place in Shanghai. The play was for the first time presented in a spectacular manner by the Shanghai yeyu juren xiehui (Shanghai amateur actors association). All the important personalities of the association took part in the performance. A production committee was formed, including the notable stage manager Zhang Min and director Wan Laitian, who had already played Krogstad ten years earlier in Beijing. The famous actors and actresses Lan Ping (Jiang Qing, who later went to Yan'an, and became Mao Zedong's wife), Zhao Dan, Jin Shan, and Wei Heling played Nora, Helmer, Krogstad, and Dr. Rank respectively.

In the programme notes, there are pictures of the major actors and actresses accompanied by short passages describing each one's feelings about his/her roles. Lan Ping (Jiang Qing) talks about her experience as

Nora. When she first read *A Doll's House*, she was still a young girl who had no experience of the world. Yet Nora gradually became her heroine. She enthusiastically admired Nora and wished all women who were treated as playthings by men would become Noras. Soon she also left family, though in a different situation from that of Nora's. But she took Nora's words: "I must try to become a real human being!" In this way, a problem arose. Lan Ping thinks that although women should be grateful to Ibsen for giving them a brave Nora, he, however, does not tell them what happens to Nora after she leaves home. Hence, Lan Ping suggests that they have to ask: "Is it really true that Nora can be free from being a plaything after she leaves home?"

A Doll's House was a shocking event to the Shanghai audience. It was the spectacularly realistic effect that distinguished the production from all previous ones which were in one way or another tinted by the colours of traditional operatic performance. In this play, the director Zhang Min for the first time introduced the Stanislavsky Method to the Chinese theatre. Zhao Dan, the actor who played Helmer, recalls how they were at first influenced by the concepts of class analysis practised and subjected the roles to critical examination, which brought about a repudiation of Helmer who was thus "portrayed with the purpose of revealing his bourgeois nature." The result was that the performance became a critique of Helmer and the class values he represented. Such an analysis, however, made the performance a mechanical illustration of the class theory. Through practice, the actors and the director Zhang Min found that a good performance should not be a political sermon. They began to study Stanislavsky and learned how to be immersed in one's role and finally overcame any mechanical and doctrinal interpretation of the play.

The performance, marked by its character as a left-wing production, is not devoid of social purpose. As the production committee claims: "Although in Europe people have nearly forgotten the name Nora, they have reason to do so, for they have produced numerous Noras, not only on the stage, but also in real life. They even have greater personalities than Nora. In China, Nora is still an unusual name, and there are not many real Noras. This is the reason for their endeavour and they hope that their presentation of *A Doll's House* will serve as a memorandum for Chinese women. It is no exaggeration to say that China is still in the age of Nora." The performance was regarded by the production team not as an entertainment but as an educational experience for both the actors and the audience. The serious preparation for the performance can be seen in its tight rehearsal schedule, which at times allowed the actors just enough time to eat only two pieces of cake for lunch.

8.15

Shanghai yeyu shiyan jutuan 上海業餘實驗劇團 (Shanghai amateur experimental drama troupe), Shanghai, 1935. (Source: Guo Fenyang 郭奮揚. "Yibusheng de mingju *Nuola* zai Zhongguo" 易卜生的名劇《娜拉》在中國 (Ibsen's famous play *A Doll's House* in China), *Zhongguo qingnian-bao* 中國青年報 (China youth daily), 25 July 1956, p. 3.)

The Shanghai yeyu shiyan jutuan (formerly called "Shanghai yeyu juren xiehui" 上海業餘劇人協會 (Shanghai amateur actors association)) staged *A Doll's House* at the Jincheng (Golden city) Theatre in Shanghai in June 1935. Everything in acting style remained more or less the same as the one they staged a year earlier, perhaps, with the exception that it became a monumental performance signifying the maturity of the Chinese stage. In commending Lan Ping's (Jiang Qing) acting as "very successful in presenting the strong character of Nora," the theatre critic Cao Juren comments that "all the spectators were moved." Ge Yihong, a theatre historian who witnessed the performance, describes the production as "a great achievement in directing, acting and stage management, with fantastic scenery and spectacular lighting effects," and affirms that it was praised as "a world standard presentation." The play was received with applause from both the critics and the audience. Numerous review articles were published in the Shanghai newspapers and journals in response to the performance. The year 1935 was thus named the "Year of Nora" in the history of Chinese theatre.

8.16

Shanghai zhirenyong jushe 上海智仁勇劇社 (Shanghai wisdom-benevolence-bravery drama society), Shanghai, 1935. (Source: Guo Fenyang 郭奮揚. "Yibusheng de mingju *Nuola* zai Zhongguo" 易卜生的名劇《娜拉》在中國 (Ibsen's famous play *A Doll's House* in China), *Zhongguo qingnianbao* 中國青年報 (China youth daily), 25 July 1956, p. 3.)

A Doll's House was staged by the Shanghai zhirenyong jushe in

Shanghai in 1935 to celebrate the "Year of Nora" in China, and to promote ideas of feminism and women's rights in China.

8.17

Siding jushe 思定劇社 (Augustin drama group), Hong Kong, 1996. Director: Gao Jixiang 高繼祥. (Source: Zhang Bingquan (Cheung Ping Kuen) 張秉權 and Zhu Qiong'ai (Chu King Oi) 朱瓊愛, eds. *Xianggang jutan 360 du* 香港劇壇360度 (Hong Kong theatre 360 degrees), p. 105. Hong Kong: Guoji yanyi pinglunjia xiehui (Xianggang fenhui) 國際演藝評論家協會 (香港分會) (International Association of Theatre Critics (H.K.), 1998.)

The performance was done in Shatin Town Hall, Hong Kong, on 22–24 November 1996. The actors included Zhong Xuejian, Du Weichang, Zhuang Yongkang and many others. According to the statistics given, there were four performances with a total audience of 450.

8.18

Xianggang qingnian jutuan 香港青年劇團 (Hong Kong Youth Theatre Company), Hong Kong, 1985. Director: Huang Haoyi (Wong Ho-I) 黃浩義. (Source: Programme notes on the performance by Xianggang qingnian jutuan.)

This is a Cantonese performance of the play, set in the 1920s. All the characters are given Chinese names and the actors wear Chinese costumes. If the title of the play was not given, the audience would not know that it was an adaptation of Ibsen's *A Doll's House*.

8.19

Xianggang yingshi jutuan 香港影視劇團 (Hong Kong Movie and TV Theatrical Company), Hong Kong, 1997. Director: Bai Yaocan 白耀燦. (Source: Programme notes on the performance by Xianggang yingshi jutuan.)

This is a highly faithful production of *A Doll's House*. It is faithful in the sense that the production captures the original spirit of the play. In terms of adaptation, the ending is moved to the beginning so that the audience is given a shock about the confrontation between Nora and Helmer before they see what leads to the confrontation. Such a beginning produces a strong effect of suspense. Though the dialogue is in Cantonese, the furniture and the costumes are in Norwegian style and the audience knows that it is Ibsen's play.

8.20

Zhongguo qingnian yishu xueyuan 中國青年藝術學院 (China youth arts academy), Beijing, 1956. (Source: Guo Fenyang 郭奮揚. "Yibusheng de mingju *Nuola* zai Zhongguo" 易卜生的名劇《娜拉》在中國 (Ibsen's famous play *A Doll's House* in China), *Zhongguo qingnianbao* 中國青年報 (China youth daily), 25 July 1956, p. 3.)

When the wars between China and Japan and between Nationalists and Communists were over, *A Doll's House* began to serve another purpose in contemporary China. The recognition of the PRC by Norway in the early 1950s gave rise to increasing contacts between the two countries. The performance of *A Doll's House* was treated as a gesture of China's friendly attitude towards Norway. In 1956, to commemorate the fiftieth anniversary of Ibsen's death, a new production of *A Doll's House* took place in Beijing. The Zhongguo qingnian yishu xueyuan (China youth arts academy), a sponsor of the production, invited Ibsen specialists from Norway to participate in their performance. The production team included Wu Xue, president of the Academy, as the director and Ji Shuping, Yu Chun, Jiang Zhulin, Bai Ling and Du Peng as the cast, playing respectively Nora, Helmer, Krogstad, Mrs. Linde, and Dr. Rank. Before rehearsals began, Wu Xue made a special trip to Norway in order to collect more information about Ibsen and to see how his plays were staged in Norway.

A Doll's House was staged on 28 July 1956. Cao Juren describes it as a production with "a perfect cast and acting." Wu Xue, the director, comments that "the play had a different but higher mission in socialist society," and it was treated "as medicine eliminating corrupt bourgeois morals" and "as a song praising new life." Cao Juren reports from his own experience that the audience's response was different from that in 1935 when the play was staged in Shanghai. He accounts for the difference by the changes in society. Supposedly liberated from all social bondage, both men and women in socialist China, according to Cao, were free human beings and therefore no longer identified themselves with Nora. They looked at the play as a satire of the bourgeois social system rather than as an appeal for them to rebel. An interesting example of the audience's response to the play in Beijing has been recorded by Wu Xue, who overheard the conversation of a couple after the performance:

WIFE: You have to reflect upon yourself!

HUSBAND: What do I have to reflect?

WIFE: What to reflect? Nothing is more clear. I feel that you are like Helmer!

HUSBAND: Nonsense. In our society, there is no Helmer.

WIFE: It's not nonsense. I have reason to say that. What I am referring to is that your mind is full of the ideas and attitudes Helmer has towards women.

Whether or not one agrees that in China in the 1950s women's status had substantially been elevated, one cannot deny that in the example Wu Xue cites, the wife no longer had to leave home but could request the husband to change his attitudes. What the stage production represented to the Chinese audience was a totally new experience. It is also interesting to note that this was the first formal production of *A Doll's House* in socialist China.

Ghosts (1881)

8.21

Guoli Beiping yishu xueyuan 國立北平藝術學院 (National Peking academy of arts), Beijing, 1929. Director Xiong Foxi 熊佛西. (Source: Xiong Foxi 熊佛西, "Lun *Qungui*" 論《群鬼》 (On *Ghosts*), *Tianjin yishibao* 天津益世報, 24 December 1929. Reprint. In *Foxi lunju* 佛西論劇 (Foxi on drama), pp. 123–133. Shanghai: Xinyue shudian 新月書店, 1931.)

In the 1920s, all the performances of Ibsen were more or less of an amateur nature. As Xiong Foxi, a renowned playwright and director, said in 1929: "Although now we have some Chinese dramatists who have been influenced by Ibsen, his plays have never been professionally presented on the Chinese stage; therefore most people still do not have an opportunity to see his plays." On December 25, 1929, the National Peking Academy of Arts, under the leadership of Xiong Foxi, formally presented *Ghosts* to the Chinese public, an initial endeavour to present an Ibsen play beyond the limited circles of students and intellectuals. According to Xiong Foxi's comments, the performance was successful in terms of its stage technique. Even though this was a commercial performance, the cast was composed of student actors, all up to professional standard.

For this performance, the director Xiong Foxi wrote an essay, "Lun *Qungui*" (On *Ghosts*), which was meant to promote the play before it was performed. The article was published on December 24, 1929. Xiong thinks that Ibsen uses "ghosts" as a metaphor for those people opposing Nora, as well as for corrupt ideas and false morals. Although Mrs. Alving has fulfilled her duties as a good wife and mother, she ruins her life. For fear that the hypocritical and corrupt power will spread, Ibsen proposes a "thorough clearance and thus brings out the problem of heredity in *Ghosts*. By the heredity of syphilis Ibsen implies that social corruption and hypocrisy can also pass to the next generation." Xiong's interpretation of the play, particularly on the point of heredity, is illuminating and it gives the audience a sense of how to approach the play. The focus of the analysis is placed not on the tragedy of heredity, but on the miseries of a woman living under the shadows of various kinds of "ghosts." Xiong further on discusses the artistic aspect of *Ghosts* and considers the play a pioneer in modern tragedy.

An Enemy of the People (1882)

8.22

Nankai zhongxue 南開中學 (Nankai middle school), Tianjin, 1927. Director: Zhang Pengchun 張彭春. (Source: Tian Benxiang 田本相, *Cao Yu zhuan* 曹禺傳 (A biography of Cao Yu), pp. 80–86. Beijing: Shiyue wenyi chubanshe 十月文藝出版社, 1988.)

The year 1927 saw a performance of Ibsen's *An Enemy of the People* in Tianjin. As the northern part of China at that time was still under the reign of the warlords and was more conservative than the south, the performance of *An Enemy of the People* by Nankai Middle School was mistakenly considered by the district army commander, Qu Yupu, as a burlesque attack upon him. After much trouble, the students at Nankai Middle School finally had to alter the title of the play to *The Brave Doctor*. In this play, the Chinese dramatist Cao Yu, who was then a seventeen-year-old school boy, played the part of Dr. Stockmann's daughter.

8.23

Zhongyang shiyan huajuyuan 中央實驗話劇院 (Central experimental theatre), Beijing, 1996. (Source: Wang Ning 王寧, "Yibusheng de *Renmin gongdi* zai Zhongguo" 易卜生的《人民公敵》在中國 (Ibsen's *An Enemy of the People* in China). In *Bijiao wenxue yu dangdai wenhua piping* 比較文學與當代文化批評 (Comparative literature and contemporary cultural criticism), pp. 360–372. Beijing: Renmin wenxue chubanshe 人民文學出版社, 2000.)

This was a new attempt in adapting Ibsen's *An Enemy of the People* for the Chinese audience in the 1990s. In the performance, many changes had been made to the plot and the characters, so that the distance between the original and the audience's reception can be minimized. The focus of the adaptation was also placed on the theme of anti-corruption in China.

Hedda Gabler (1890)

8.24

Xianggang huajutuan 香港話劇團 (Hong Kong Repertory Theatre), 1983. Director: Yang Shipeng 楊世彭 (Daniel S. P. Yang). (Sources: Chan Hoicheong, ed. *Celebrating 20 Years: The Hong Kong Repertroy Theatre 20th Anniversary Souvenir Book*. Hong Kong: The Provisional Urban Council of Hong Kong, 1997, p. 90; "Yang Shipeng" 楊世彭, *Xianggang huajutuan jiuba/jiujiu juji taopiao jihua* 香港話劇團九八/九九劇季套票計劃 (Hong Kong Repertory Theatre ticket plan for the 1998/1999 season). Hong Kong: Linshi shizhengju 臨時市政局, 1998, p. 3.)

The script is based on Gao Tian'en's (Kao Tien-en) 1970 translation. The performance, which ran on 2–10 July 1983, was done in a realistic style. The most fascinating aspect of this production lay in its treatment of the suicide scene, in which the death of Hedda Gabler was made one of the most dramatic moments.

Appendices

Appendix I
A Chronology of Ibsen's Plays

1850	*Catiline*
	The Warrior's Barrow
1851	*Norma*
1853	*St. John's Eve*
1855	*Lady Inger of Ostraat*
1856	*The Feast at Solhaug*
1857	*Olaf Liljekrans*
1858	*The Vikings in Helgeland*
1862	*Love's Comedy*
1863	*The Pretenders*
1866	*Brand*
1867	*Peer Gynt*
1869	*The League of Youth*
1873	*Emperor and Galilean*
1877	*The Pillars of Society*
1879	*A Doll's House*
1881	*Ghosts*
1882	*An Enemy of the People*
1884	*The Wild Duck*
1886	*Rosmersholm*
1888	*The Lady from the Sea*
1890	*Hedda Gabler*
1892	*The Master Builder*
1894	*Little Eyolf*
1896	*John Gabriel Borkman*
1899	*When We Dead Awaken*

Appendix II
A Chronology of Chinese Translations and Adaptations of Ibsen's Plays

1918 *A Doll's House*. Chen Xia 陳嘏, trans. *Kuilei jiating* 傀儡家庭 (see 7.14).

A Doll's House. Luo Jialun 羅家倫 and Hu Shi 胡適, trans. *Nuola* 娜拉 (see 7.16).

An Enemy of the People. Tao Lügong 陶履恭, trans. *Guomin zhi di* 國民之敵 (see 7.28).

Little Eyolf. Wu Ruonan 吳弱男, trans. *Xiao Aiyoufu* 小愛友夫 (see 7.47).

1919 *Ghosts*. Pan Jiaxun 潘家洵, trans. *Qungui* 群鬼 (see 7.24).

1920 *The Lady from the Sea*. Yang Xichu 楊熙初, trans. *Haishang furen* 海上夫人 (see 7.37).

The Pillars of Society. Zhou Shoujuan 周瘦鵑, trans. *Shehui zhushi* 社會柱石 (see 7.12).

1921 *Ghosts*. Lin Shu 林紓 and Mao Wenzhong 毛文鐘, trans. and adapts. *Meinie* 梅孽 (see 7.23).

1922 *The Master Builder*. Wu Qirui 巫啟瑞, trans. *Jianzhushi* 建築師 (see 7.45).

1923 *The League of Youth*. Wu Qirui 巫啟瑞, trans. *Shaonian tongmeng* 少年同盟 (see 7.06).

1924 *The Wild Duck*. Yang Jingci 楊敬慈, trans. *Yeya* 野鴨 (see 7.32).

1925 *A Doll's House*. Ouyang Yüqian 歐陽予倩, trans. and adapt. *Kuilei zhi jiating* 傀儡之家庭 (see 7.17).

1926 *A Doll's House*. Pan Jiaxun 潘家洵, trans. *Nuola* 娜拉 (see 7.18).

An Enemy of the People. Pan Jiaxun 潘家洵, trans. *Guomin gongdi* 國民公敵 (see 7.27).

The League of Youth. Pan Jiaxun 潘家洵, trans. *Shaoniandang* 少年黨 (see 7.05).

The Master Builder. Pan Jiaxun 潘家洵, trans. *Dajiang* 大匠 (see 7.42).

1927 *Rosmersholm*. Liu Boliang 劉伯量, trans. *Luoshimazhuang* 羅士馬莊 (see 7.33).

1928 *Hedda Gabler*. Pan Jiaxun 潘家洵, trans. *Haide Jiabolei* 海得加勃勒 (see 7.39).

1929 *When We Dead Awaken*. Pan Jiaxun 潘家洵, trans. *Women siren zaixing shi* 我們死人再醒時 (see 7.51).

The Wild Duck. Xü Gudi 徐鵠荻, trans. *Yeya* 野鴨 (see 7.31).

1930 *Ghosts*. Fang Letian 方樂天, annot. *Gui* 鬼 (see 7.22).

1937 *A Doll's House*. Shen Peiqiu 沈佩秋, trans. *Nuola* 娜拉 (see 7.19).

1938 *The Pillars of Society*. Sun Xu 孫煦, trans. *Shehui dongliang* 社會棟樑 (see 7.11).

The Wild Duck. Sun Xu 孫煦, trans. *Yeya* 野鴨 (see 7.30).

1939 *Hedda Gabler*. Sun Xu 孫煦, trans. *Haidan* 海妲 (see 7.40).

1940 *John Gabriel Borkman*. Shi Ling 石靈 (Sun Shiling 孫石靈) , trans. and adapt. *Bao Zhiyuan* 鮑志遠 (see 7.50).

1941 *Lady Inger of Ostraat*. Shi Ling 石靈 (Sun Shiling 孫石靈), trans. *Yingge'er furen* 鷹革爾夫人 (see 7.02).

1945 *Hedda Gabler*. Wu Lümei 鄔侶梅, trans. *Heda furen zhuan* 赫達夫人傳 (see 7.41).

1947 *A Doll's House*. Zhai Yiwo 翟一我, trans. *Kuilei jiating* 傀儡家庭 (see 7.21).

1948 *A Doll's House*. Shen Zifu 沈子復, trans. *Wan'ou furen* 玩偶夫人 (see 7.20).

Ghosts. Shen Zifu 沈子復, trans. *Gui* 鬼 (see 7.25).

John Gabriel Borkman. Shen Zifu 沈子復, trans. *Bukeman* 卜克曼 (see 7.49).

The Lady from the Sea. Shen Zifu 沈子復, trans. *Haifu* 海婦 (The lady from the sea) (see 7.36).

The Master Builder. Shen Zifu 沈子復, trans. *Jianzhushi* 建築師 (see 7.44).

1959 *The Pillars of Society*. Pan Jiaxun 潘家洵, trans. *Shehui zhushi* 社會柱石 (see 7.10).

1960 *A Doll's House*. Liu Jinmei 柳津美, adapt. and trans. *Kuilei jiating* 傀儡家庭 (see 7.15).

1969 *A Doll's House*. Cao Kaiyuan 曹開元, trans. *Kuilei jiating* 傀儡家庭 (see 7.13).

1970 *Ghosts*. Yan Yingyou 嚴影悠, trans. *Qungui* 羣鬼 (see 7.26).

Hedda Gabler. Gao Tian'en 高天恩. *Haida Gaibole* 海達・蓋伯樂 (see 7.38).

1981 *Peer Gynt*. Xiao Qian 蕭乾, trans. *Pei'er Jinte* 培爾・金特 (see 7.03).

1995 *Emperor and Galilean*. Huang Yushi 黃雨石, trans. *Wangdi yu Jialiliren* 皇帝與加利利人 (see 7.07).

John Gabriel Borkman. Pan Jiaxun 潘家洵, trans. *Ruohan Gaibolü'er Bokeman* 約翰・蓋勃呂爾・博克曼 (see 7.48).

The Lady from the Sea. Pan Jiaxun 潘家洵, trans. *Haishang furen* 海上夫人 (see 7.35).

Lady Inger of Ostraat. Pan Jiaxun 潘家洵, trans., *Esiteluote de Yingge furen* 厄斯特羅特的英格夫人 (see 7.01).

The League of Youth. Pan Jiaxun 潘家洵, trans. *Qingnian tongmeng* 青年同盟 (see 7.04).

Little Eyolf. Pan Jiaxun 潘家洵, trans. *Xiao Aiyoufu* 小愛友夫 (see 7.46).

The Master Builder. Pan Jiaxun 潘家洵, trans. *Jianzhushi* 建築師 (see 7.43).

The Pillars of Society. Pan Jiaxun 潘家洵, trans. *Shehui zhizhu* 社會支柱 (see 7.09).

Rosmersholm. Pan Jiaxun 潘家洵, trans. *Luosimozhuang* 羅斯莫莊 (see 7.34).

When We Dead Awaken. Pan Jiaxun 潘家洵, trans. *Zamen siren xinglai de shihou* 咱們死人醒來的時候 (see 7.52).

The Wild Duck. Pan Jiaxun 潘家洵, trans. *Yeya* 野鴨 (see 7.29).

1997 *Emperor and Galilean*. Lin Xianghua 林驤華, trans. *Wangdi yu Jialiliren* 皇帝與加利利人 (see 7.08).

Appendix III
A Chronology of Chinese Stage Productions of Ibsen's Plays

1914 *A Doll's House*. Shanghai chunyang she 上海春陽社 (Shanghai spring willow society), Shanghai (see 8.12).

1923 *A Doll's House*. Beijing nügaoshi 北京女高師 (Peking normal college for women), Beijing (see 8.03).

1924 *A Doll's House*. Ershiliu jushe 26 劇社 (26 drama society), Beijing (see 8.04).

1927 *An Enemy of the People*. Nankai zhongxue 南開中學 (Nankai middle school), Tianjin (see 8.22).

1928 *A Doll's House*. Nankai zhongxue 南開中學 (Nankai middle school), Tianjin (see 8.09).

1929 *Ghosts*. Guoli Beiping yishu xueyuan 國立北平藝術學院 (National Peking academy of arts), Beijing (see 8.21).

1934 *A Doll's House*. Shanghai yeyu juren xiehui 上海業餘劇人協會 (Shanghai amateur actors association), Shanghai (see 8.14).

A Doll's House. Molun zhongxue 莫倫中學 (Molun school), Shanghai (see 8.08)

1935 *A Doll's House*. Guanghua jushe 光華劇社 (Bright China drama society), Shanghai (see 8.05).

A Doll's House. Jinan minjiaoguan 濟南民教館 (Jinan people's education house), Jinan (see 8.06).

A Doll's House. Mofeng she 磨風社 (Windmill society), Nanjing (see 8.07).

A Doll's House. Shanghai yeyu shiyan jutuan 上海業餘實驗劇團 (Shanghai amateur experimental drama troupe), Shanghai (see 8.15).

A Doll's House. Shanghai zhirenyong jushe 上海智仁勇劇社 (Shanghai wisdom-benevolence-bravery drama society), Shanghai (see 8.16).

1939 *A Doll's House*. Qingnianhui 青年會 (YMCA), Shanghai (see 8.11).

1941 *A Doll's House*. Peidu jushe 陪都劇社 (Chongqing drama society), Chengdu (see 8.10)

1948 *A Doll's House*. Peidu jushe 陪都劇社 (Chongqing drama society), Chongqing (see 8.10)

1956 *A Doll's House*. Zhongguo qingnian yishu xueyuan 中國青年藝術學院 (China youth arts academy), Beijing (see 8.20).

1962 *A Doll's House*. Shanghai xiju xueyuan 上海戲劇學院 (Shanghai theatre academy), Shanghai (see 8.13).

1983 *Hedda Gabler*. Xianggang huajutuan 香港話劇團 (Hong Kong Repertory Theatre), Hong Kong (see 8.24).

Peer Gynt. Zhongyang xiju xueyuan 中央戲劇學院 (Central Academy of Drama), Beijing (see 8.02).

1985 *A Doll's House*. Xianggang qingnian jutuan 香港青年劇團 (Hong Kong Youth Theatre Company), Hong Kong (see 8.18).

1990 *Peer Gynt*. Xianggang huajutuan 香港話劇團 (Hong Kong Repertory Theatre), Hong Kong (see 8.01).

1996 *A Doll's House*. Siding jushe 思定劇社 (Augustin drama group), Hong Kong (see 8.17).

An Enemy of the People. Zhongyang shiyan huajuyuan 中央實驗話劇院 (Central experimental theatre), Beijing (see 8.23).

1997 *A Doll's House*. Xianggang yingshi jutuan 香港影視劇團 (Hong Kong Movie and TV Theatrical Company), Hong Kong (see 8.19).

Indexes

Author/Translator Index

Title Index

Title Index by Year

Subject Index